Worceste
Within Living Memory

Compiled by the Worcestershire Federation of Women's Institutes from notes sent by Institutes in the County

Published jointly by
Countryside Books, Newbury
and the WFWI, Worcester

First Published 1995

COUNTRYSIDE BOOKS
3 Catherine Road
Newbury, Berkshire

ISBN 1 85306 372 X

The cover photograph shows the village of Broadway
in the 1930s

Designed by Mon Mohan
Produced through MRM Associates Ltd., Reading
Typeset by Paragon Typesetters, Queensferry, Clwyd
Printed by Woolnough Bookbinding Ltd., Irthlingborough

Contents

STOURBRIDGE
KIDDERMINSTER
STOURPORT
REDDITCH
TENBURY WELLS
WORCESTER
MALVERN
HILLS
EVESHAM
BREDON
UPTON ON SEVERN
WORCESTERSHIRE

Foreword

Worcestershire is a county with a long recorded history – notably of the battle of Evesham in the 13th century and the battle of Worcester in the 17th century. Its industries include Worcester sauce, Worcester china and the gloving industry to name just a few. From the Worcestershire County Cricket Ground, across the river Severn, there is an imposing view of Worcester Cathedral which houses the tombs of King John and Arthur, Prince of Wales (brother to Henry VIII) and celebrated in 1995 the 900th anniversary of St Wulstan, a former Bishop of Worcester, a Saxon bishop who survived to serve under the Normans.

It has been a great joy, as County Chairman, to be privileged to read of its more recent history in excerpts of *Within Living Memory*. To read of a time of great community spirit, a time when pleasures were made and not bought, a time of cycling and walking without fear of being molested, a time when even hardships were accepted. Members throughout the county have enjoyed getting together, reliving their memories – some young enough to enjoy just listening to them, but all of them reaching their pot of gold at the end of the rainbow.

Freda Davies
County Chairman

Acknowledgements

I would like to express my thanks to Anne Harker, of Queenhill WI, for the lovely map and illustrations, to Anne Quiney for her help with typing, to Brenda and Greta in the office and Frank and Vivienne at home who patiently answered queries, and, lastly, to the Institute members who sent in such a wealth of fascinating material. I hope they will all find something of interest in this book.

Eileen Chapman
Co-ordinator

TOWN & COUNTRY LIFE

SOME TOWNS AND VILLAGES REMEMBERED

Horse-drawn fire engines, animals driven on foot to market, buying home-made ice cream from a 'shop' in someone's front room are just some of the memories we have of times not so long since past, when life seemed a little calmer and not so rushed as it is today. These are just some recollections of life in a few of our towns and villages a few decades ago.

MEMORIES OF BISHAMPTON

'Grandfather was the local blacksmith and, as we lived in the centre of the village next to the public house, there was often a lot going on when I was small. We quite often had gypsy horses and caravans by our back door. As well as shoeing he did other metal work such as putting the hoops round the cartwheels after the wheelwright had made them, for we had a wheelwright and carpenter in the village too. The smell of burning hoof and wood was frequent. It could be a busy time if the local hunt was meeting at the pub next door and we would sometimes watch the hounds from a bedroom window for quite a distance.

One of the local farmers had cows and, after they had been milked in the morning, he cooled it, bottled it, put on cardboard lids and delivered it all in one day. We had half pints as well as quart and pint bottles. Some people enjoyed making table mats and bags out of the cardboard rings after covering them with raffia or wool.

The small local post office with its telephone switchboard was a place I loved to visit and I remember wanting to run a post office when I grew up so that I could have a long-handled rubber stamp to bang onto a pad and then onto people's books. The village shop, before it moved into a small hut, had been one room in a lady's house and two of the great smells were those of liquorice skipping ropes hanging from a nail and the sickly sweet lemon crystals which were supposed to be for making lemonade but were great in a pointed paper bag so that you could lick your finger, dip it in and then suck the sharp crystals.

We used to have weekly visits from Ward's van, from which many people bought everything from soap to paraffin or pegs and lots of things in the hardware line. It seemed very clever to me that everything stayed on the shelves, and you could tell when the van arrived by the mixture of smells in the air.

The smells of childhood are very strong with one of the main ones being that of bread when it was fresh delivered on the van from two villages away, and a treat was to choose a cake on Saturdays. The baker would make an interesting shaped loaf for Harvest Festival in church. This was a very special time when everyone who wanted to helped to decorate the church with fruit, vegetables, flowers and sheaves of corn. We could choose a window to "do" and, being a big church, there always seemed to be enough windows to go round. The final thing to decorate was the font which had all the left-over vegetables piled on top with the corn and michaelmas daisies around the base.

We had a midwife in the village who delivered most of us and later, when we were at school, also served as the school nurse.

Later, as a teenager, things started to change. We moved next to the church, a grocery van from Evesham started to deliver groceries that were cheaper than the shop and carried wrapped bread, all the houses got electricity and bathrooms and we gradually became "modernised" but the sense of freedom I felt as a child I still cherish now. Looking back I realise how lucky I was.'

BELBROUGHTON SHOPS

'In the 1930s and 1940s the village boasted no less than 22 shops, selling a wide variety of goods, along with the services of a dressmaker, a tailor, a hairdresser, a saddle and harness maker and even a coffin maker!

Each morning came the inviting smell of home-baked bread from Handley's bakery and their specialities of iced buns and lemon buns were available. Tuesdays and Fridays real crusty loaves could be delivered to your door.

You could not ask for the wrong thing in Miss Moore's drapery shop in Church Road. She had two windows and changed the displays every two weeks. Inside the walls were lined with rows of wooden drawers containing a wonderful assortment of haberdashery. The floor was plain wooden boards, no linoleum or carpets here, and the long, wooden counter was fitted with a brass yard measure. Miss Moore stocked everything the boys and girls at school would need, blouses, shirts, trousers, caps and ties. Flannelette was 1s 11d per yard, check gingham 1s 11¾d per yard and you could buy knicker elastic, suspenders, buttons and tape. Directoire knickers could be had in all shades from saxe blue to marzipan green and, of course, there were more conservative items such as interlock vests in pure white!

Mrs Burford's shop at the other end of the High Street had a grocery department on one side and drapery on the other. Here you could browse through knitting patterns and choose your wool from hanks in all colours of the rainbow. Should you not be able to afford all your wool at once, it was put away for you and you could collect it an ounce at a time. There was a lovely choice of baby clothes, ladies' aprons, underwear, cardigans and jumpers and, if it wasn't in stock, it could always be ordered. At Christmas time the drapery shop window would be decorated with stocking fillers, tree decorations, soft toys and a Christmas tree with twinkling lights. Children coming home from school would stand, nose pressed against the window, deciding what they wanted for Christmas.

Next door was Mr Harris' shoe shop. He not only sold shoes but repaired them. Should you decide to buy a new pair, however, you had to be careful for sometimes the left shoe might be a lighter shade than the right – the reason being that it had been displayed in the window while the right shoe had remained in its box on the shelf, but, as you were told by Mr Harris: "A little bit of polish will soon even them out."

The bicycle shop, across the way, not only stocked bicycle tyres but also recharged wireless accumulators at ninepence a time – as most people had this type of wireless in the 1940s it was a useful service. They were also happy to mind a pram or pushchair while you took your child to town on a bus.

The two largest grocery shops were Weaver & Guest's and Wilson's. Both offered real old-fashioned customer service. There were chairs to sit on while you waited and local village news was discussed by customers and staff. They were busy places on Friday mornings when orders were handed in. These would be delivered by Friday afternoon by a boy on a delivery cycle. Tea, sugar, sultanas and rice were all weighed out and made into neat paper packages with end flaps tucked in – an art in itself. Weaver & Guests's shop had large, round cheeses, wrapped in thick muslin, standing in the window and these were used as stools to stand on when cleaning the windows. Biscuits were sold loose and you could choose from a variety of tins in front of the counter. When the bottom was reached the remaining broken biscuits were sold cheaply. They also had a grain department and always kept a large, white cat, which was put to prowl this area at night to catch mice, but in the daytime the white cat was allowed to sleep in the shop window among the cheeses. They also sold pipe tobacco – twist – in a large, coiled, thick ring. Men coming home from work would call in to buy an ounce. A piece

A quiet street at Barnt Green in the early 1900s.

would be cut off and weighed on the little brass scale kept on the counter for this sole purpose. The men would keep it in a tin to smoke in their clay pipes.

The village post office not only dealt with the Royal Mail but had its own franking service. It even opened on Sundays for the sale of stamps. It also sold daily papers and patent medicines such as Carter's Little Liver Pills, raspberry vinegar and Indian Brandee. In fact our village shops sold everything you could wish to buy.

The village had five inns and all were well patronised. Each one sold beer from a different brewery so most villagers stuck to one pub – but, during the war, if their "local" had no beer they would all rush round to the one that did have, whether it was their favourite or not! Each inn had a bowling green with their own team and there was great rivalry between the five teams.

In the early 1900s the Queen's Hotel had the distinction of having its own mortuary at the back of the inn. Not for those who got "dead drunk" but as horses and traps came down the hill at speed and tried to turn the sharp corner there were fatal accidents and victims were carried there until the inquest.'

POPULAR BARNT GREEN

'There have been many changes in the 81 years since, as a very young child, I came to live in Barnt Green village. Its importance then lay with the railway; there was a good and reliable service to Birmingham, to Redditch and stations and junctions beyond. There was also a large siding to service the goods trains, including the movement of cattle from the cattle market and the many farms in this district.

One of our childish excitements, before the use of large trucks for moving the animals to the local market, was the escape of cows, hotly pursued by a drover, through the village street.

There were about 50 houses in the village, instead of the built-up area it is now. The shops were adequate for the area – three butchers, a post office, two grocers, two haberdashers, a tailor's shop (ladies and gentlemen), a shoe shop and what is now known as a DIY shop.

At one time, all the shop owners lived "over the shop", and as they were supporters of the local churches, the WI, the cricket club and sports club and the working men's club, they were well known in the district.

Barnt Green, because of its proximity to Birmingham, was popular with Brummies on Bank Holidays, the most favoured being the first Monday in August. In the 1920s the Lickey Hills and woods were given to the City of Birmingham by the Cadbury Trust, and families poured into the district from early morning, the cost being sixpence return on the railway. Thousands of people flooded the woods and hills and the village was innundated with trippers bringing their food in paper carriers (no shops open) heading for the "Victoria", the local pub, where father could have his beer, and mother too, and the children could play in the large garden and bowling green. No children allowed inside of course!

By the evening thousands of people had to be persuaded to board the trains, whilst the local constabulary, consisting of a sergeant and a constable, was augmented by a dozen men, to help the revellers through the village and on to the trains.'

GROWING UP IN REDDITCH

'Redditch, in those pre-overspill days, was a very different place. We had two main shopping streets, Evesham Street and Alcester Street, with more shops on "The Prom" – now Church Green West. We had a very good variety of shops. For groceries I remember Liptons, Home & Colonial, Masons, also the Co-op, which sold just about everything else as well. There must have been at least six butchers, several locally owned, and several greengrocers.

When I was small I remember a shop called "The Penny Bazaar" and there was a bran tub in the corner where, for the sum of one penny, children could dip their hand in and come up with a small wrapped mystery gift. I think the other items in the shop cost more. As a keen dressmaker I look back with nostalgia to the half dozen shops I can remember selling dress materials. We had a department store – Hollingtons – and several shops of every type. In fact, compared with today, we were spoiled for choice!

They stayed open fairly late, too, I remember. Woolworths – which really was a threepenny and sixpenny store then – was always the last to close on Saturday nights at about 8 pm.

There were still horse-drawn vehicles about. I think the railway waggons were among the last to use big carthorses for collecting and delivering the goods which were transported by rail. There were four horses to the big waggons and sometimes the weight proved too much for them as they came down Unicorn Hill to the station yard, and they would gallop down, quite out of control, scattering pedestrians and cyclists. There was a fatal accident to a young crippled man caused this way.

We had four cinemas: the Danilo, the Gaumont, the Palace – which doubled as a theatre – and the Select. The programme usually ran from Monday to Wednesday, then changed for Thursday to Saturday (no Sunday films). So it was possible to go every night of the week and still not see them all. Most people went at least twice a week. Sometimes a very special film was on for a whole week, and often the prices increased then too, but usually the top price was one shilling and ninepence.

Buses ran between Redditch and Birmingham and also outlying villages, but not round the streets of Redditch, only straight through the centre, as part of the route. By putting up your hand it was possible to stop them anywhere.

Buses also ran to Bromsgrove, Evesham and Stratford on Avon, and it was possible to go by train to Studley, Alcester and Evesham, as well as Birmingham. Goods trains were frequent, and coal, grain, herds of cattle and flocks of sheep were all transported this way. Farm workers went down to the station and drove the animals through the town and out to the farm they were destined for.'

CHURCH GREEN EAST, REDDITCH

'Reflecting on my life at Church Green East before 1960, I'm reminded that it was a self-contained community. At that time it was an interesting area in which to live as most of us lived "over the shop", including the bank manager at the imposing Lloyds Bank. Neighbourliness was inevitable.

Within this small area all our needs were catered for by the variety of shops and offices. Freshly-baked bread from Webbs, newspapers and sweets from Miss Davis at the newsagent's, hair-dos at Tudor House, household goods and ironmongery from Foulkes the builders' merchants, legal advice at Beech House, and even the animals were not overlooked as there was Gold, the vet's. There was still a quaintness about some of the shops, such as Harry Harbons, with just a few musical instruments and sheet music on a stand in the window, and especially Mr Styler's with its black iron spiral staircase, general drapery and old-fashioned clothes, including flannelette shirts, vests, long-johns and directoire knickers. Anything you asked for, he had it in stock and always found it easily and quickly even though everything was in brown boxes on the shelves.

Whenever I see a rosette I recall Mr Tomlin, the butcher, who always had some hanging in his shop from his prize-winning cattle. He would tell me of his visits to Henley market and how he did his own slaughtering. His beef had a special flavour. That's something I miss. If my daughter was with me in the shop she would often be given a sausage. You don't get that at supermarkets! Personal service was of the essence.

My favourite shop, though, was the Redditch Indicator one, linked to the other buildings by Smallwood Arch. Its exterior, with small windows, was painted black and white, giving it an "olde worlde" appearance. Inside was like an Aladdin's cave, full of interesting gifts and beautiful cards, particularly at Christmas time.

Although at No 18 we had a backyard and small lawn with flower border where we held Jane's summer birthday parties, we always thought of the church grounds opposite to us as "our" garden. Each spring we would wait with anticipation for what we called the Umbrella Tree to blossom with its mass of white blooms. The tree is still there.

In those days I didn't own a car. That meant daily walks with my baby had to be round the town. For example, crossing Birdcage Walk with its drinking fountain, to go to Church Green West and the post office and library in Church Road. A delight in the summer was to sit round the fountain near the bandstand with the water lapping and the children playing happily.

Before the recent pedestrianisation, Church Green East was a main road for all the buses and cars from Birmingham but we weren't aware of too much noise. Of course, there were fewer cars then.

As well as a feeling of "belonging", another bonus for living at Church Green East was that we could watch the spectacle of the annual carnival from the window seat in our upstairs lounge and only had a few yards to walk to see the many weddings at St Stephen's. A favourite Saturday pastime.

To some people the sound of bells can be a nuisance but to my husband and me they were a joy, particularly on New Year's Eve as they rang in the New Year and we would drink a toast to the future.'

MALVERN LINK

'Milk was delivered to the door, twice a day, usually morning and afternoon. The milkman would come in his horse-drawn float and bring a can of milk to the door into which he dipped a pint measure and the milk was then poured into a jug. This was kept in the coolest place in the house, which might be on a marble slab, or the jug was stood in a bowl of cold water, as very few households had a refrigerator.

Someone else who made a delivery, but on a Friday night only, was the fish and chip man, who carried his goods in a large basket covered with a white cloth.

At the grocer's shop, biscuits weren't in packets but were weighed out from a tin, during which quite a few were broken and many was the time I called on my way to school for a "pennyworth of broken biscuits" to eat at playtime, hoping there would be some creams or wafers among them.

Close to my home was a draper's shop which also had a workroom, where dressmaking was done. Often I would go as a child for a "bundle of pieces" (odds and ends left after dresses were cut out) and then have a lovely time making things for my dolls.

An elderly man named Fred Adams didn't deliver evening papers, but walked round the streets tapping his white stick on the curb and shouting "*Evening Times*!"

As a child I attended St Matthias Sunday school and we had a book into which we stuck a stamp which depicted something from the Bible, for each time we attended. In the summer we had an outing which took the form of a journey on the train to Colwall, which was about five miles away. We had a short walk to a farm where we played games and then had our tea in a barn where we sat at trestle tables.

Between the wars there were always a lot of "gentlemen of the road" passing through Malvern, quite a number spending a night or two at the casual ward (or "Tramp Ward" as it was generally known) which was situated on the edge of the Link Common in Moorlands Road, next door to where my grandparents lived. Before the tramps left they had a certain amount of work to do, such as stone-breaking, and were then given a ticket which could be exchanged in certain shops for food or tobacco.

An ex-serviceman, who had no arms or legs, used to sit on the pavement at the top of Church Street, selling boxes of matches from a tray which hung round his neck. He also had a box in which the money was collected. Occasionally, some kind soul would stop and light a cigarette and put it in his mouth.

Two or three quarries on the Malvern Hills were being worked in the 1930s and 1940s and, when blasting was taking place, red flags were hoisted and traffic halted. I remember hearing the sound of blasting clearly at Malvern Link.

The building of the Morgan car has provided work in Malvern for craftsmen since 1909, when the first three-wheeler was made. Between 1930 and 1940 several of the men cycled to their work from Worcester, a round trip of about 14 miles. Today very little has changed in the way the cars are made, most of the work still being done by hand, but now four-wheelers have taken the place of three.

A hop farm in Malvern Link provided work for several people all the year round, but in September each year considerably more people were required for hop picking. The grown ups picked the hops into cribs (wooden frames about seven feet by three feet with hessian sewn on to form containers) and I, like many other children, picked them into an opened umbrella which was stuck in the ground. The hops were measured with a basket called a bushel, which contained eight gallons and four or five bushels had to be filled to earn one shilling. 1988 marked the end of an era, as after that date no hops were grown on that particular farm.

On the occasions of the Jubilee of King George V in 1935 and the Coronation of Queen Elizabeth in 1953, a torchlight procession wended its way up the Worcestershire Beacon led by various youth organisations such as the Guides and Scouts, and a very impressive sight it was when watched from such places as the Link Common, looking like a giant illuminated snake. When the summit was reached a hugh bonfire was lit and everyone joined in community singing.

For more years than I care to remember, entertainment at St Ann's Well was provided by "Blind George" who played his harmonium almost daily. Once a month he went to Madresfield Court and played at the dances held for the staff.

The Winter Gardens and Priory Park were popular leisure places, with dancing to Billy Gammon and his Orchestra being one of the items enjoyed in the former. In the latter the children had small boats on the pool, while the open-air swimming baths were enjoyed by all ages.

Fun fairs and circuses which were held on the Link Common were well patronised and in those bygone days worth attending both for their size and quality.

Malvern Festival was a highlight for young and old, and on the first night of a popular play quite a crowd would gather round to see the theatre-goers arriving with top-fashion dresses – long evening ones in beautiful colours and jewels sparkling, and the gentlemen looking immaculate in evening dress.

A familiar sight, before there was a ban on picking wild flowers, was that of cyclists, many of them riding tandems, going at weekends towards Worcester with bunches of wild daffodils tied to their machines. These had been picked at Dymock or Eastnor.

Speaking of cycles reminds me of Mr Walford who kept a cycle repair shop in Malvern Link and who used to celebrate his birthday each year by riding his penny-farthing round the streets. I have been told that in 1893 he rode it up to the top of the Worcestershire Beacon and down again.

There was always a good train service between Malvern and Worcester. The local train, which called at five halts on the way – Newland, Bransford, Rushwick, Boughton and Henwick – only had one or two coaches, brown in colour, and was known as "The Coffee Pot". The return fare after 4 pm was sixpence. Outside Foregate Street station, in Worcester, one could board a tram for journeys to Barbourne in one direction and Sidbury in the other.

My father, who was a railway employee, said that when horse-drawn carriages were used as transport, people travelling by train went to Great Malvern station, their heavy luggage having been taken off the train at Malvern Link to save the horses such a steep climb.

During my childhood in the 1920s there were very few cars on the road, and one of my favourite pastimes was sitting outside our house, which was on the main Worcester Road to Malvern and writing down the registration numbers of all the cars that passed. Monday was market day in Worcester and the cattle that were bought by the butchers in Malvern Link walked the distance of about seven miles. No cattle trucks in those days. We had to make sure the garden gate was closed on Monday afternoons, otherwise a cow might wander up the path.

My husband walked from Newland to Madresfield school, about two miles, and he often tells how he and his friends bowled their hoops along the road, no footpaths for most of the way, and usually the only vehicles they saw were two horse-drawn milk floats.

In the early part of the century one could reach the top of the Worcestershire Beacon by riding on a donkey owned by a lady named Mrs Betteridge.

In the 1940s a lady used to travel around Malvern in a horse and trap, surrounded by two or three bags of wood shavings which she had collected from the local saw mills to put down in the stable. The only part of her that was visible was her little black hat. On very cold

Stopping at the horse trough in Broadway in the 1930s. The cart was on its way to the cider mill at Cheltenham Road.

nights her horse shared a room in the house with her, each keeping the other warm.'

STOURPORT ON SEVERN

'In the early 1930s Stourport on Severn was a small town and had a population of just under 6,000. Life was more leisurely in those days, when I remember the shops in the High Street and the activity on the river. Stourport then consisted of one long central street which started at the lower end from the river – this part was Bridge Street and further up it was High Street and continued into Lombard Street. It was quite a self-contained little town with a high class dress and haberdashery shop, gentlemen's outfitters, shoe shop, four public houses and a cinema called The Haven. St Michael's church, a lovely old building, sadly had to be demolished and replaced by a more modern one in 1980. Tan Lane school is the only one I can recall and this is still going strong. The power station was a very imposing building with its seven chimneys which were quite a landmark as you approached the town.

There were the usual shops for those days: grocers, greengrocers, fishmongers and butchers. The grocer's shop at that time was run by the Butler brothers, two bachelors, who were always immaculately dressed in snow white shirts, sleeves rolled up to their elbows, white aprons tied round the middle with a frill over the front. The shop was also immaculate as everything was scrubbed clean, the counter top spotless. All the goods were in bulk, so had to be weighed while you waited and put in little blue bags. A large square of butter on the counter was patted into shape.

Further up was the butcher's. Sides of beef hung in the window, only the best beef there and Mr Tunkiss, the butcher, prided himself on buying the best at the cattle auctions held at Kidderminster market. The cattle and sheep would then be herded by drovers from Kidderminster to Stourport High Street where they would be slaughtered behind the shop. There would be a lot of competition to be the one to buy the champion beast. The then Prime Minister, Stanley Baldwin, purchased his meat from there and on occasions would be seen arriving in his motor car, which caused some interest.

The greengrocer's cum fish shop was open-fronted and that was scrubbed through every night including the pavement. The sweet shop, Lashford's, was of particular interest because he made his own ice cream. As there were no refrigerators in those days, block ice was delivered every day. The ingredients were put into a container and a thin layer of the mixture was released onto a drum of ice as a handle was turned and, as it froze, was collected into a bucket.

The coalman came round with a big black shire horse pulling a dray. He wore the usual leather covering for his head and back and had leather straps round the knees of his trousers. He was kept busy calling at most of the houses. Stourport had its characters in those days and two come to mind; one had a donkey and flat-based cart and he would take fish round to the outskirts of town. The other always wore a brown smock and trilby hat, and rode a very old bike on which he had two milk churns on the handlebars. This he would ride with much difficulty with his knees stuck out either side of the churns. The milkman, though, was better equipped with pony and trap and a large churn complete with tap. He would dispense the milk using pint or half pint measures.

In those days if a funeral went along the High Street, everyone would stop to pay their respects and men would doff their hats. The hearse, an elaborately decorated carriage, was drawn by four beautifully turned out black horses.

The river Severn was a centre of attraction and oil tankers and large boats would come into the basin carrying, amongst other goods, timber and coal. There were pleasure boats for trips up the river where Mr Lashford could sell his ice cream. The railway station was the other side of the town and, on Bank Holidays, hundreds of trippers could be seen converging on the town. It was a very popular holiday resort for people from Birmingham.

Today it is sad to remember all these places and things that have disappeared. No more barges or tankers come up the river, the power station completely demolished and replaced with a housing estate. The station no longer exists and life is at such a pace now we haven't time to stop and marvel at the "characters" that make life so interesting. That's progress!'

STOURPORT FIRE BRIGADE

'In the early 1920s the Stourport fire engine was horse-drawn. Two horses were pastured between the Bridge Inn and the river and were in the care of a local character who was a part-time fireman, who worked at a stables in Bridge Street. When the fire alarm sounded, he would race down Bridge Street to catch the horses, with two bridles over one shoulder and carrying a bowl of oats. A few minutes later, with a horse on either side, he would pound along York Street and Lion Hill on his way to the fire station. Once there the engine could soon be on its way to the scene of the fire.'

RUBERY

'I was born 70 years ago in an old cottage-type house, the last of four children. My father lived in that house from the age of 18 months. When his mother died, giving birth to twins, an older sister brought up four children, but my father came to live with a widowed aunt and he lived there until he died.

My childhood was very happy, a big garden, a quarter of an acre, to play in, and an old coachhouse with a loft to go into when it rained. I can still smell the apples which we stored in the loft.

I went to St Chad's school, which was the only one until Waseley was built. At about eight I went to Miss Gill's – what was then called a dame school. Just a semi-detached house with one class for the small children downstairs and one class upstairs. Two teachers, Miss Gill herself and a Miss Bancroft. It was a very good school.

My memories of Rubery are of a small village and the people who lived there. Just above our house lived an elderly woman who used to sit in the front garden wearing a man's cap and smoking a small, white clay pipe. A little further up was the sweet shop where you could get four things for a penny and home-made ice cream, soft and yellow like custard, delicious, and only a ha'penny for a small one.

The grocery shop of Bennet's was equally as appetising, with ham boiled by Mrs Bennet, and biscuits displayed in their tins. They had one of the few cars in the area, and they took me to Banbury once or twice. I was a queen, sitting in the back of this big upright car.

I can remember going to the pop factory to collect the marbles which they put in the bottles and roaming barefoot through fields which are now covered with houses. We lived next door to a butcher's and, in a field adjoining his house, he used to put manure. One Sunday, in my best dress, shantung with smocking, I fell in. I don't remember being punished. I think my mother thought I certainly would not do it again.

There was a forge at the top of Rubery, and a brickworks near Waseley Hills. These have long gone, as has the marl hole where boys used to swim, one or two with fatal results.

On Bromsgrove Fair day what seemed like hundreds of ponies clip-clopped past the house. Some days walkers in races came by and girls in marching bands, what excitement. The longed-for day once a year was a big flower show, held in the grounds of the Monument which stands on the top of the Lickey Hills, a memorial to Lord Plymouth.

The Lickey Hills and Rednal are very entwined with Rubery. In the summer hundreds of people came to the hills from Birmingham and queued, tired but happy, for the open-topped trams which they ran at holiday times.

The hills in winter are a good memory. My brother, the next one to me in age, was eight years older. No doubt I drove him mad trailing after him, but we used to go sledging. My father made a large sledge which could hold about three or four. We came right off the top of the Beacon and also came down the winding road with very steep bends. I suppose I would be about six or seven years old.'

REDNAL AND THE LICKEYS

'Our earliest memories of childhood revolved around life on the Lickey Hills. Most Brummies would say they knew Rednal and "the Lickeys", but did they? Most of them (and it would seem at times as if the whole of Birmingham was on the move) would only make the pilgrimage by the number 70 tram on Bank Holidays and sunny weekends, when the terminus at Rednal would become a seething mass of people and trams! The visitors would disperse to explore Beacon Hill, Rednal Hill, Bilberry Hill (so called because of the bilberries to be found there and which we gathered as children) and the nearby Rose Gardens. Walks in the woods were a real pleasure, particularly in the springtime, when there was a carpet of bluebells. Also on Bank Holidays a fair would visit Rednal on the corner of Leach Green Lane. This was always popular and we would wander round the sideshows and go on the various rides, including the roundabout and the dodgems! Now the site is a housing estate.

About a mile from Rednal was the then Austin Motor Company, birthplace of the famous Austin Seven. During the war the company made various army vehicles and was also involved in aircraft production. We remember how well the Austin Motor Company was camouflaged to avoid enemy air attack and in fact they did not suffer a great deal of damage. Barrage balloons were situated in the park opposite, part of which was given over to wheat crops during the war. Also in Cofton Park were air raid shelters for the local population and I well remember a visit on one occasion! We often saw the POWs who were working on local farms.

The Lickey area itself at the top of Rose Hill had a church built in 1856 with the infants school opposite. The old school was replaced in 1954 with a new one built on land near Lickey Square. The parish hall was subscribed for by local residents and was opened in 1937. There were four shops, one being the post office which changed hands frequently, whereas the other three remained unchanged throughout the war. During the war years one shop obtained a wine and spirit licence: this then became our "outdoor". Prior to that our requirements were obtained from either Rednal or Barnt Green.

One of the characters of The Lickey was George Timings who owned the garage and filling station. During the war he changed the name of the garage to Hokey Garage to fool the Germans! One side of the workshop was devoted to charging accumulators for wirelesses. On a Saturday afternoon we would be sent to the garage with one accumulator and sixpence and would receive in return the one which had been on charge during the week.

In Monument Lane there were two tearooms next door to each other which were converted garages. During the war Mr Thurlby made his own version of ice cream using powdered milk. This was very popular with the local lads after playing cricket on the Beacon!

In the late 1940s the 1st Lickey Guide Company was formed by Miss Mary Bowers who lived with her parents in a large house in Monument Lane. This had extensive grounds and many happy hours were spent by those of us in the Guide Company pursuing all sorts of activities.

Prior to war being declared The Lickey had its own football team known as "The Lickey Swifts", which sadly was not revived after the war. Also before the war an annual flower show was held and this too was not revived. The Lickey Flower Show, complete with jazz bands and decorated floats, was a highlight of the year. One float vividly remembered depicted a little old lady sat behind a lattice window of a mock cottage which had red roses climbing up green painted trellis. One regrets that cameras were then not so common to capture the colourful occasion.

The winter of 1946/47 was a memorable one, with snow which lasted for nearly three months and caused drifts of over ten feet in some places, so much so that a tunnel was dug for people to walk through. The summer of 1947 was glorious and the gardens had obviously benefited from the winter snow.

For as long as could be remembered the Lickey woods were surrounded by substantial fencing, with access only at certain gateways. This made obtaining leaf mould for Dad's garden difficult as the park keeper had only a few entrances to cover! Today there is no fencing to give protection to the trees.

One remembers well the smell in the pine woods when they were being felled for pit props as part of the war effort. A searchlight post adjacent to the woods illuminated the night skies when searching for German aircraft, much to the horror of our parents who were meticulous about blackout precautions.

The Lickey escaped unscathed from the war. Two or three bombs were jettisoned from aircraft returning from raids on Coventry and Birmingham. During the war potato picking was preferred to staying at school during the autumn half-term!'

WICHENFORD

'When I was a child my father was the village baker and my mother kept the shop, selling "everything from a pin to a steam roller", or so she said. Mother's first customer every day was a man who came in for half an ounce of twist at five o'clock in the morning. Father made and baked the bread and delivered around our village and the neighbouring ones in a large van. The shop was closed in about 1935

Palmer's Bakery at Wichenford in 1930.

owing to Mother's illness and never opened again, but my brother is still the village baker today.

In our part of the village there were only six cottages, four council bungalows, a wooden bungalow up the lane by Myrtle Cottage, a large house on the corner (Malvern View), and two farms (Bush Farm and Woodhouse Farm). The school was just round the corner and the church, Memorial Hall, and vicarage were a bit further down Venn Lane.

Mr Dyson was the village blacksmith and wheelwright; he and his wife looked after the church and churchyard for many years. Sunday school was held on Sunday mornings in the church and taken by the vicar's wife. The vicar amused us as children as he used to sing quite loudly when he rode his bicycle.

The school had two lady teachers, one for the infants (Miss Allcott) and one for the older children (Mrs Tombs). Children went to the village school up to eleven years of age when they had to attend either Martley or Hallow school. The infants teacher rode a bicycle too and if it was wet she always carried her umbrella aloft, we often wondered how she managed this without falling off.

Most of the villagers had a well and a pump for drinking water and large water butts to catch rainwater for washing clothes and bathing. If there was no rain for weeks we had to use pump water instead, but this was hard water and so soap wouldn't lather in it. Everyone kept poultry and most people kept a pig too which helped to feed the family. The gardens were all cultivated, mostly with vegetables, fruit bushes and fruit trees; there were of course no freezers and so the women all made jam and pickles, and bottled fruit. Everyone tried to be self-sufficient as one couldn't go to town very often. There was only one bus a week but the driver was very obliging and would do some shopping while in town. I well remember him bringing my mother a breadbasketful of crockery from Pratley's in Pump Street.

Every year there was a fête in the hall meadow with lots of stalls and sideshows, with teas in the hall. There were cricket and football teams; the cricket team played in the hall meadow and the football team at Mallender's meadow. Both were always well attended. The men's club met in the hall twice a week, and once a year they had an annual dinner. My father cooked the joints of meat in the oven and Mrs Tyler and helpers cooked the vegetables on the open fires in the hall. At Christmas the schoolchildren put on a concert in the hall which we all enjoyed very much; very often it was a case of standing room only. There was also a Christmas party in the hall for all the children who each received a present off the tree.

As cars were very few and far between, we children played up and down the roads with hoops, marbles and hopscotch. We also wandered through the fields and meadows, picking blackberries and wildflowers. One evening I remember seeing the aurora borealis (Northern Lights); the whole sky was lit up a brilliant red colour and everyone came out to look as at first they all thought it was a large fire.

When the war broke out we all had to do our bit, either as fire-fighters, air raid wardens, or in the Home Guard, and quite a lot of people used to meet in the hall to make things for the war effort, such as camouflage nets. We had two very bad winters during the war, which made life very hard indeed; the snow was so deep that only tractors could get through. We awoke one morning to find everything coated with thick ice and all day long we could hear the elm trees which made an avenue to the church crashing down under the weight of it. There were very few left afterwards.

First aid classes were held in the hall and quite a lot of people attended. As we did not have street lights the blackout really made things difficult in the countryside, as we were used to being guided by house lights or lanterns that we carried. All the arms were taken off the signposts; one man thought this was so that low-flying enemy planes wouldn't know where they were.

After the war, in 1953, a small housing estate, named Queen's Estate because of the Coronation, was built opposite the bakery and then in the 1960s mains water and sewerage were laid on to the other houses as well.'

COOKLEY

'There has been an ironworks next to the canal at Cookley over most of the last 300 years. Here the first tin plate ever produced in the country was made. Some of the walls in the village were built with cinder bricks made with molten ash from the factory. Many people from the village were employed here, the other source of employment being at Lea Castle where the Squire, Mr Brown-Westhead, lived. Young girls went into service and the men worked in the gardens and other outdoor works.

The Squire was very generous to the church and his daughter gave land to the village for the parish hall to be built in 1933. The annual flower show at Lea Castle was a very important event, with most of the villagers attending. Apart from the flowers and vegetables on display, there were always races for the children with prizes given by the Squire.

Many people remember the homes in the village when they were lit by oil lamps and cooking was done on the open range. Toilets were in the garden, with some lucky families having "two holers" and all of them with newspaper cut into squares hanging on a nail.

Water came from a pump or the well, often shared by several families. Washing was done in the brewhouse over the yard, the copper was also lit to provide hot water for the weekly bath night, youngest first then the rest of the family in order.

Many families kept their own pig and poultry and also grew their own vegetables. A big event was the pig killing, which took place in the garden and absolutely every part of the pig was used.

The village had its own bakery, butcher and cobbler and was one of the first villages to have its own Co-op. Milk was delivered by Mr Mannington from churns on his horse and cart and, once a week, Mr Wilkins delivered fresh fish in the same way. On Fridays another man would come round with a basket of fish and chips, already wrapped. Twopence for fish and a penny for chips.

Coal was brought by canal barge to Mr Cox, the coal merchant, and he would deliver it around the village by horse and cart. There was also the village police station and the village "bobby" was known by everyone.

The vicar was a very important and respected member of the community, as were the midwife and the village layer out. At funerals the body was always taken to church on a bier by foot, with everyone standing in respect and the men and boys always doffing their caps.

The only transport in the village, at the beginning of this century, was a public brake, which went from Cookley to Kidderminster and back, on Thursdays and Saturdays. Then came the covered waggon, a type of lorry with long benches and a cover over the top. Mr Davis from Cookley Garage bought the first charabanc, a big step forward in luxurious travel, although it was often crowded to the door with passengers.

The doctor from Kinver held a surgery in Cookley on Tuesdays and Thursdays, but there was a walk to Kinver of about two miles each way to get prescriptions, or to see the doctor at any other time. A baby clinic was also held in Kinver.

Children attended the village school from the age of five to 14, boys and girls always having separate playgrounds. The dinner-time break was two hours long, as most of the children had to walk home for their midday meal. The 3Rs were strictly taught and times-tables, poems and the catechism were learnt by heart by chanting them aloud. The children walked to Wolverley school for woodwork and cookery classes and the oldest children went to Kidderminster public baths in Mill Street for swimming lessons.

Children's games were skipping, iron hoops, top and whip, skimming cigarette cards, marbles and in the evening, many children joined in a game of Tally Ho! through the fields around the village.

After the First World War, Remembrance Day was always held on the 11th November and after the two minute silence, the Roll of Honour was read out by a schoolboy whose father had died in the war.

The village always had a cricket and football team, both based at the Eagle and Spur, and Cookley Tennis Club is the oldest in Worcestershire. There was also a bowling green at the Eagle and Spur and at this pub, like several others, they brewed their own beer. In the wall outside, you can still see the marks of the rings where customers tied up their horses.

Both the church and the chapel had their own glee clubs and a concert party, who always entertained at the Easter Tea. Every Friday night a dance was held, first a sixpenny hop at the parish room and then, from 1934, the parish hall, often going on until one o'clock as the next day was Saturday.

In the early 1930s there was great excitement on the day an aeroplane flew very, very low over the top end of the village. A lot of people followed it on foot and it landed at Axborough. The plane was made from balsa wood with a silvery material stretched over the frame. The pilot tried to take off the next day but crashed and many pieces of the plane could be seen in different houses for a long time after.

During the Second World War, WI members worked hard making jam and marmalade and bottling all kinds of fruit. They also had a Comforts Fund where members would knit balaclavas, gloves and socks, make up food parcels and write letters to the men in the forces.

The Cookley Players were formed and concerts were put on to raise money to send the soldiers special parcels for birthdays and at Christmas. At two shillings and sixpence a ticket, it took a while to raise £100. When the American army hospital opened at Wolverley Camp, the soldiers would come to the dances and concerts and several married girls from the village and some settled here when the war was over.

The first development in the village was Westhead Road, just before the war, when the castle and grounds were sold. After the war came the development of the council estate at Lionfields, which up to then had been open fields.'

HANLEY SWAN

'On St Valentine's Day, 1935, I came to Hanley Swan village to work for the Church of England Children's Society, helping a married couple look after 24 boys aged six to 14. It was supposed to be a light job as I was recovering from a bout of rheumatic fever. How anyone could call looking after 24 boys a light job I'll never know. I was supposed to stay a year and then move on.

Hanley Swan was a lovely village, it had everything, a church, pub and lovely village green and pond with swans, ducks and moorhens. Some of the older lads sang in St Gabriel's choir. There was a choirmaster called Mr Main-Price, always referred to by any boy as Mr Main-Spring. There were several big houses on the outskirts of the village. There was Catterall occupied by four sisters and a brother, all single, named Boyle. Then there was Albion Lodge with four sisters called the Miss Willans, and the Grange with four or five sisters called Shackleford. All these houses employed four or five local girls to help in the house, a gardener and handyman to drive the car, except for the Miss Boyles who had a chauffeur to drive their car.

There were two schools, St Mary's and St Gabriel's. Girls stayed from five to 14 unless they got a scholarship to Tewkesbury High for Girls, or Hanley Castle Grammar School for Boys. Hanley Castle also had boarders. At twelve years of age, boys went to Upton on Severn for carpentry lessons.

There was a working men's club in the village and younger people had a social club, which was run by Mrs Nellie Creese, whose husband was verger of St Mary's church. It was held in a sort of hall attached to the vicarage. We had dances there and played darts or cards with Mr Frank Jarrett supplying the music. I was taken there by one of the local bachelors, who later became my husband. In 1937 we were married and moved into a four-bedroomed cottage with six acres of land. There was a single storey building attached to the cottage which, we were told, had been a butcher's shop.

During the war, when Frank Jarrett was called up, Geoff Ball, also a local band leader, did sterling work going around local dances, carrying his instruments on a bicycle.

There was a row of houses called Glanford in the village. There was no water laid on, everyone had a pump in the garden. Although there was a mains sewer, everyone had to take a bucket of water for flushing. Except for one, all the Glanford houses had electricity. The exception was occupied by two elderly ladies who were terrified of electricity.

There was a Methodist chapel down Gilberts End. It was demolished before we moved into Southview and two council houses and two bungalows built there. Opposite us was another smallholding, in which lived a Miss Reynolds and her brother, Walter. She ran a shop in one of her front rooms but would never open the door, so one would have to go around to the back door to enter the shop through the kitchen where Walter was always seated on a settle in front of the fire. Miss Reynolds was noted for her hats. She wore a woollen shawl over her head and two or three felt hats, one on top of the other, which she took off one by one as the weather got progressively warmer, but I never saw her without the shawl. A number of people had these front room shops which sold a few basics, such as tea, sugar, chocolate and boiled sweets.

There were plenty of buses in those days. The Bristol Blue ran four or five buses a day from Gloucester to Malvern and from Malvern to Cheltenham via Hanley Castle. Also there was a Mr Woodward who ran a bus twice a week from Guarlford to Upton on Severn. The trick was not to pay him as one got out but say "I'll pay on the way back" and he'd always wait for you.

Then came the war and soldiers moved into the village, mostly searchlight battalions. The Home Guard was formed and they took over Hanley Swan post office, which was housed in what had once been the village school, so Mr Ted Brown and family had to use their front room as shop and post office. I used to man the exchange three or four nights a week so the usual operators could have a rest.

Then came the Yanks – a lot of Nissen huts went up at Merebrook and Blackmore, which, we were told, were for American hospitals. When they opened lots of girls went and worked there and made us envious as they used to have grapefruit and ice cream which we could not have. When the Yanks departed, German POWs occupied the camps and the loveliest thing I've ever heard was at Christmas Midnight Mass when some POWs stood in the aisle and sang *Silent Night* in German. Then the war was over.

Bill Drinkwater announced he'd bought Lombard Tree Farm on the Welland road. Before Bill moved there he decided to have the well cleared so he commissioned someone to do it. The man went down into the well and was overcome by the fumes, but Bill went down and rescued him. For this he received the BEM. There was a presentation on the village green. Snow on the ground, and the band could not blow their trumpets, but everyone turned up to honour him.'

SCENES FROM KIDDERMINSTER

'In Brinton Park, Kidderminster, crowds of people, bands, flags and entertainments were in full swing. Suddenly the crowds parted to form a wide avenue, which made way for a man dressed in shorts, wide-brimmed hat and coloured neck-tie, carrying a pole. He was followed by a host of boys similarly dressed. They proceeded to light fires without matches and erect tents with the use of their poles. The man was, of course, Baden Powell, with the Worcestershire branch of the organisation for boys he had created, and this was before 1918.

There were 20 shire horses belonging to the Bantocks Brothers, hauliers, whose stables were in Marlborough Street. Their main

Floods brought chaos to Upton on Severn in 1916, this rescue boat being taken across Fish Meadow.

business was hauling carpets up to the railway station. Station Hill was paved with sets which enabled the horses to get a better grip. Two horses and a waggon would collect rolls of Wilton, Brussels and Chenille carpet. When the load arrived at the bottom of Station Hill, four waiting shires would be hitched up, making a team of six horses to haul the load up the hill to the railway station. The Bantocks allowed no switches or whips to be used, so each horse had its own haulier to encourage its efforts.

Before 1914, the main means of getting around was by horse-drawn vehicle, cycle or Shanks's pony. But, when the men returned from the First World War, many had learned to drive motor vehicles. So some enterprising young men bought lorries from the army, put in benches and started to bring factory workers in from the outlying villages. The Dunkly Brothers did Cookley and Wolverley district; Wadeley Brothers did Bromsgrove; the Owen Brothers did Witley; and Whittles did Highley.

Then, one day, into town came a Birmingham firm with grey buses fitted with proper seats. This led to the local lads taking off their jackets, rolling up their sleeves and having a punch-up! Man to man, with bare fists. The outcome of this was that Midland Red stepped in with good financial offers to the locals and the buses had come to town.

"The Bull" was a loud hooter. Every Saturday at one o'clock it sounded for five minutes so that everyone could check their clocks. This was before Big Ben was broadcast and "Tim" was not even born.

Another function of the Bull was as a fire alarm. Kidderminster only had a part-time fire brigade, so the Bull summoned them to their duty. Thirty seconds blast, 30 seconds silence followed by another 30 seconds blast signalled a country fire. A one minute blast meant a town fire and a two minute blast meant a serious factory fire. The firemen would drop everything, the two drivers going to collect the horses from a field at the bottom of Green Street and the rest to the fire engine, which was kept in the police yard next to the town hall. They proceeded to light their fire-engine fire to get up steam for the water pump. By the time the horses were hitched a crowd would have assembled to give a cheer as the engine dashed out of the yard. This was in 1904, a far cry from today.'

THE ROYAL OAK, BROADWAS

'I first came to the Royal Oak as a visitor from London's East End in 1934, travelling by motorcycle. The contrast could hardly have been greater, from ships, docks and busy streets to what seemed a sea of tranquillity. The inn was run by "Ma" Hood and three of her daughters, Dolly, Edna and Chris. The charge was two guineas a week, full board. The meals were served in the clubroom which was only used for special events. There was electric light but no power, so breakfast was cooked over the fire of the blackleaded range in a large smoke-blackened frying pan and kept in the side oven. Water was brought in buckets from the pump outside, and heated on two primus stoves or the range. Water was taken to the bedrooms in large jugs, used with marble-topped washstands. One of the great charms of the place was the smell of frying bacon and eggs, combined with the smell of methylated spirit and paraffin, while from the bar came an aroma of beer and tobacco, built up over many years.

Breakfast over, the day's work began, sweeping out bar and taproom, fresh sawdust on the floor, wash and disinfect spittoons, polish table and brass, wash ash trays. Edna replenished stocks, checked the till, ordered new supplies. Ma presided over the kitchen preparing the midday meal, cutting thick sandwiches for the bar. Dolly and Chris rushed upstairs "doing" the bedrooms, emptying the slops, washing chamber pots, jugs and basins, making beds and doing their best to get rid of the grey fluff that accumulated under the beds. There was much flicking of dust out of windows.

Meanwhile a steady stream of "backdoor patrons" had to be dealt with before opening time, plus tradesmen and reps, as all groceries, household linen etc were delivered by van. Names such as Beards, Pratts, Home & Colonial and Maypole were familiar then.

Gypsies called often, trying to sell pegs or tell fortunes and begging clothes, but were usually given short shrift. Edna opened up at 10 am and presided over the bar. Dolly and Chris were busy feeding hens, geese and young pigs in the orchard at the rear, and pumping water to wash out the urinal and privy, which consisted of a seat with three holes, set over a very large hole, which had been dug many years before. You got the rich smell of the countryside there alright, but as it was next to the pigsty it blended well.

Vegetables were gathered from the kitchen garden – mint, thyme, parsley as required, eggs collected. The day's washing would be pegged out, coal scuttles filled, the clubroom prepared for dinner. Much of the outside work was done by "volunteers", grass and hedge cutting, tidying up at a pint of scrumpy per rod, pole or perch. A slow, steady trade was done in the bar, a few farmers or "gentlemen" passing along the A44, which was as quiet as the churchyard, more occupied by sheep or cattle than traffic.

The bar closed until four o'clock, then there was high tea to prepare for guests and the bar gradually came alive. The regular farmers took their accustomed seats for the evening card school, townees came from Worcester, farm workers crowded the taproom. It was all hands to the (beer) pump. Often there was noisy singing from the taproom and, occasionally, one adventuresome soul would invade the bar, only to be firmly dealt with by Ma.

Ten o'clock brought closing time. Towels were put up, "drink up" ordered. Outside stood PC Lambert, ready to do his duty, which would warrant a pint or two in convivial company in the kitchen after all the riff-raff had gone. Every night, after the glasses had been washed, the kitchen table would be laid for supper – cold meat, pies, cheese, pickles and jugs of beer for the favoured few who "came through" at closing time. There was much hilarity and relating of scandal until quite a late hour. PC Lambert often organised night-time expeditions to collect glow-worms from the hedgerows. These expeditions, strangely, seemed to be arranged when pretty girls were in the company, and many were the giggles and oohs and aahs as glow-worms were put into jamjars.

In the autumn the hop pickers arrived, families from the Black Country, speaking a strange language which I, a Cockney, found hard to understand. They were mostly old regulars, welcomed back, the clubroom put to use to cater for the influx, including their children, which meant more work for Dolly and Chris.

Other events were shooting lunches, when the "guns" sat down to a full meal and the beaters were provided with hampers of sandwiches, cheese and pork pies. Quite a few regular guests were music-hall turns appearing at Worcester Theatre Royal, Angel Street. I remember particularly a ventriloquist and a conjuror who gave impromptu turns at supper in the kitchen.

In the course of the year, fruit was picked and bottled, walnuts from the orchard pickled, chutney made, chitterlings washed and cleaned and chitterling suppers arranged. In winter, musical evenings were enjoyed in the clubroom, Edna at the piano, Chris on violin, Dolly on mandolin, Mr Burns, the rector, on cello and the drums that Sam Hood used to play for anyone to use.

Sundays were quieter but, in summer, cyclists would call for tea – a pot of tea, a heap of bread and butter and a wedge of cake, for one shilling and sixpence. There were hunt meets, fishing contests, fêtes, WI, Mothers' Union, Young Wives and music classes in Worcester. A hard, seven day week for little more than their keep and a little pocket money, yet happy days with a contentment not often known today.

I obviously didn't learn this all at once – no, Chris and I fell in love on sight. Our eyes met as she served meals, but nothing was said or done. Patience was the order of those days! My visits continued, 130 miles each way by motorcycle, summer and winter, until, six years later in 1940, when I was already in the army, we married and embarked on 51 years of happy, family life.'

LOST DUDLEY

'For many hundreds of years Dudley was a detached part of Worcestershire, until the West Midlands Order Act was passed in 1965.

Mr J.W.R. Roe, a Dudley councillor, began a campaign to prevent Dudley being taken from Worcestershire and becoming part of Staffordshire.

"Oliver Cromwell destroyed in part our ancient castle," he wrote to the Prime Minister, the Rt Hon Harold Wilson, Ministers George Wigg and Richard Crossman, the Bishop of Worcester and others. "We still retain the scars, and the effect on the morale of our citizens, although serious, was nothing compared to what it will be if the present proposals are implemented."

He received massive support from organisations and residents in the town, and from as far away as New Zealand. It was pointed out that there would no longer be county cricket in Dudley and centuries-old links would be severed.

However, the campaign was unsuccessful, and the boundary change was implemented in 1966, as planned. The Church of

England, though, still retains its interest, as the Bishop of Worcester has as one of his assistants the Bishop of Dudley. The rest is history.'

FAR FOREST TELEPHONE

'There was a telephone line from Far Forest station to the post office in the village, and the local people first heard the news of the death of Edward VII from this office. The first telephone was two lines from Bewdley, known as X and Y lines. These were party lines, and a man came from Bewdley asking for subscribers. He had to get four for each line. You had to count the number of rings to see whether the call was for you. In those days, the 1920s, the rent was low and you had a number of free calls.'

THE TRAMP WHO STAYED

'In 1934 my parents married and went to live at Old Gaines Farm, Whitbourne, near Bromyard. It was common in those days for tramps to turn up at the farm and do a few days' work helping with the harvest, fruit picking etc. They would sleep in the most comfortable barn they could find, be fed by the farmer's wife, and after being paid would make their way to the next farm. Such a man was "Fred".

Fred was getting on in years but would turn up frequently. He was a pleasant, jovial old man and didn't mind what task he was set but his greatest pleasure was feeding calves, "my young things", he said.

By 1938 he was too old to travel. He had a horror of the workhouse so a barn was tidied up, a bed and stove installed and Fred moved in and became a permanent part of the farm. In 1941 my family and Fred moved to Wichenford. Here Fred made his home in the washhouse. Under the bed he placed numerous pairs of boots because he could never find a comfortable pair. Whenever he went to Worcester he always came back with a new pair!

The years passed until one afternoon my father found him in the calf shed where he had died feeding his "young things". On clearing out "Fred's house" Father found 20 pairs of hardly worn boots and £75 in a cocoa tin under his bed.'

TENBURY WELLS STORIES

'There's a true story about two neighbours whose gardens and orchards adjoined. George kept sheep in his orchard but he was none too fast in repairing his hedges and his sheep were always getting through into Bill's garden. They argued about this a lot, but one day Bill decided to repair the gap himself. He'd almost finished when suddenly a head broke through the gap he'd just repaired. Thinking it was a sheep that had managed to push through, he immediately took his stick and started to beat the "sheep" on the head, only to find that the "sheep" was his neighbour George who thought he'd play a trick on him – but ended up with a very sore head that eventually needed stitches in it.

One day my father had been to market to buy some pigs, and when he brought them home they needed to be kept away from the other animals. At the time the only place available was a barn, in which were two barrels of cider that were being kept for drinking at a later time. My brother came home from work on his bicycle and, as usual, went to put his bicycle away in the barn – but on opening the door was almost knocked over by the two pigs as they came staggering out and rolled over on the ground as drunk as lords. They had, it seemed, managed to knock the bung out of one of the barrels and then set about lapping up the cider.

Most people are familiar with the "call from the rent man" and many stories have been told of people dodging the rent man by fair means or foul.

However, in Tenbury Wells, much of the property, including farms, belonged to "Squire" Godson – who lived in a large house within its own grounds, with gardens and tennis courts and stables. After his death, the house and land was replaced by an estate of houses and bungalows called Greenhill Close and a footpath through it is called Godson's walk as it was the boundary wall of his property.

Unlike today, the collecting of rent had to be done in the correct manner. On rent day the house had to be tidied and the table covered with a clean white cloth on which the money was placed. Mr Godson or his agent would arrive at the house, and would come in carrying a bag for his money – and he always wore gloves to pick up the money. After taking his leave he would go on his way to collect from the next tenant, who would be expected to follow the same procedure.'

CHURCH AND CHAPEL

Sunday was a special day, set apart from the toil of the week, when many families attended church or chapel and most children went to Sunday school. The church or the chapel was at the heart of village life then. Sunday school outings are remembered with great affection, often the only outing during the year for local children.

SUNDAYS

'Sunday was a sombre day, folk at Fairfield often attending each of the three services in the church. Children were not allowed to play their usual games, and a walk in the afternoon was often the only treat.'

'Sunday was not a day we enjoyed. After breakfast, dressed in our Sunday clothes, we had to sing hymns and learn the collect before setting out for matins at 11 am. My father, being a churchwarden, wore a top hat, frock-coat and black trousers. In summer we wore muslin hats with tight elastic under the chin, muslin frocks and white kid button boots.

After the usual Sunday lunch of roast beef, we were allowed to play with our Sunday toys (our usual ones having been put away on Saturday night), or else we went for a walk around Heightington. After tea we either had a Bible lesson or else were read to, such books as the *Fairchild Family*, *Jessica's First Prayer* or *A Peep behind the Scenes*, most of which related to horribly pious children who died. When we were older we had to go to evensong, which was preferable.'

'Sunday school was obligatory and we went to church three times every Sunday. Sometimes we walked along the bank of the Severn to Hallow church and were put in the front pew where my father could see us while he was singing in the choir. We walked over the green (no swings or see-saws, they were chained up on Sundays) to my paternal grandmother's cottage. On our way, my father would make us repeat the text of the sermon. The first question from my grandmother was, "What was the text?" Dead silence and sheepish looks from us. "Ernest, your children will surely go to the devil!" We were made to eat caraway seed cake, the seeds sticking in our teeth.

To this day I can never remember the text of any sermon.'

'My grandmother was a fearsome woman who was deeply religious. When she came to stay we were not allowed to sing, laugh or play games on a Sunday. We were only allowed to read the Bible. I remember my father walking down the road at Broadway to intercept the paper lady one Sunday and popping the paper into the copper at the end of the garden. The idea was to bring it in after Grandmother had gone to bed. The only thing was, the copper was full of soapy water and the Sunday paper was ruined. Be sure your sins will find you out.'

'Sunday evening walks were commonplace in the 1920s and 1930s, especially in summer time when the family would go out for a walk after tea. A round trip of four miles was quite normal.'

'It was my job, as a child in about 1910, after I came home from Great Comberton church on Sunday, to sit on a stool near the fire and keep turning the Sunday joint, which hung on a hook in front of the fire. Some cottages did not have a range large enough to take a joint of meat, and those people would pay the local baker to use his ovens. There was a waiting list for the ovens at Christmas.'

HARVINGTON – CHURCH AND CHAPEL

'To the people whose memories are recorded here, the ancient church of St James was the focal point of village life and Sunday was a sacred day.

All services were very well attended and there was a large choir of men and boys, many of the latter having been energetically coaxed into it by the headmaster of the village school, he being also the church choirmaster. The boys' reward for Sunday's appearances in the choir was sixpence so that was an added incentive! The men did not get paid.

The rector was a most respected member of the community and known by all. He visited the school regularly and every Friday took the assembly as well as the scripture lessons. On Sundays, the children gathered at the school for religious instruction then, in time for the 11 am service, set off along the road walking two by two to the church to take part in the worship. When it was time for the sermon, however, they were allowed to go home. One lady remembered that, as a little girl, she was allowed to stay because she relied on a neighbour to see her home but she had to sit still and keep "very quiet".

There was Sunday school in church in the afternoon, with boys sitting on one side of the nave and girls on the other. If a baptism was taking place (and that was always in the afternoon) the children were allowed to watch by kneeling on the pews and looking over the backs. The last service of the day, evensong, usually meant another visit to church for children of about eleven or more.

Rectors' wives were usually actively involved in both church and village life and one of these ladies is remembered as a familiar sight riding around the village on a tricycle. If the going was steep or rough, any boys in the area were called upon to give her a push. The reward for this help (at least during the harvesting season) was an invitation to call at the rectory for an apple.

The staff of the church consisted of the rector, a people's warden, a vicar's warden, a sexton and a verger. The sexton was responsible for the bell-ringing and the digging of graves. The verger attended the Bishop if he ever visited but mainly he prepared the altar for services, changing the frontal drapes when necessary, performing general duties and being responsible for locking and unlocking the church.

The rectory was a very important place in the lives of the people. Many church functions and meetings were held in or around it, especially the annual church fête and parish teas. Here the women of the village came into their own. Indeed, they and their daughters were the backbone of the domestic side of church life. They were responsible for cleaning, arranging flowers, washing the linen, acting as Sunday school teachers and working energetically at the many festivities and functions.

There were many weddings, baptisms, and, of course, funerals all of which attracted "onlookers", everyone knowing each other and feeling involved. Confirmations (with the girls all in white with veils, and the boys wearing white shirts) were held in one or other of the local churches, depending on which one the Bishop was visiting.

At festival times, when there were extra-large congregations, chairs were borrowed from the public house across the road to enable as many people as possible to sit in comfort. Sermons are remembered as having been at least half an hour long.

Harvest Festival was a great occasion, the village being situated among orchards and farms. After the special services on Harvest Sunday the produce was gathered together, loaded onto a dray, taken to market on the Monday for sale and the proceeds put into church funds.

The other two great festivals of the church year – Christmas and Easter – also hold special memories of lights and flowers and singing, though one parishioner also recalls the silence in the village on Good Fridays when "one could hear a pin drop".'

'I remember the chapel in the early 1930s when as a child of four or five I attended regularly three times every Sunday.

On Sunday morning there was a Bible Study session which was organised by the elders of the chapel, all men. They always wore suits and highly polished boots; we children were in our Sunday best, the girls wearing hats. We were expected to sit quietly; I remember having my knee held so that I could not swing my legs. During this session, from the time we started to attend day school, we were expected to take our turn in reading a verse from the chapter as it was passed round. We sat in a semi-circle because at that time we only had an open fire for heating so, of course, in the winter this was the best arrangement for seating.

In the afternoon the ladies of the church arrived to take the various Sunday school classes which we had to attend. These were a little more relaxed than the morning sessions.

The evening service was organised by our minister who attended once in three weeks. The other two weeks were arranged by lay preachers, many travelling several miles either walking or cycling, whatever the weather. The sermons always seemed long and tedious with very little meaning to the younger members of the congregation.

The Sunday school Anniversary held in midsummer was a great event in the chapel calendar. The choir and children worked on this every Sunday for about two months. Completely new hymns were learned and some of the children were chosen to sing solos while others performed duets. Readings and poems, many verses long, had to be learned by heart and we were expected to be word perfect, or woe betide us. On the big day the girls all had new dresses and hats or straw bonnets with flowers; the boys wore suits which seemed to have lots of buttons and button holes. We performed during the afternoon and again in the evening, each time for about one and a half hours. The chapel was always packed with parents, relatives and friends. Book prizes were presented to all who had attended during the year, according to the number of attendances. The collections taken during these services went towards paying for the summer outing for the children.

Summer outings were usually to Weston super Mare. This was a really exciting treat as it was often our only glimpse of the sea; there were no holidays in our day. We started very early, travelling in Mr Marsh's charabanc and the journey took four hours. We all did as we wished all day, meeting at four o'clock for tea before starting the journey back, by which time the sea was coming in.

On the way home the teenagers on the back seat made music with mouth organs, bazookas and combs and paper while the rest of us sang along. It was always a wonderful day to remember.

A Christmas party was held once a year for the children and there were games afterwards to which parents and members of the congregation were invited. The traditional games were spinning the plate, Oxford and Cambridge, nursery rhymes sung in groups etc – all very noisy and boisterous. On the way out of the chapel we were each given an orange and a bag of sweets.

Teas seemed to be held on every possible occasion – on the Monday following Harvest Festival for example. Tea cost us threepence, other children sixpence. The church was decked with fruit, flowers and vegetables for Harvest, the produce being brought in wheelbarrows by the men who grew them in their allotments. The large bunches of mixed vegetables hanging from the rafters always fascinated me as they would suddenly start to spin round, slowly at first but turning faster and faster as time passed. I expected them to come crashing down at any moment during the service.

Another event held in those days was a Tuesday evening meeting held during the winter months, particularly exciting because we often had a magic lantern show. These were mainly missionary based but of course they depicted people and places in far away lands which none of us every expected to visit. I well remember one lady speaker bringing costumes from India and dressing us children in rich saris so that the congregation could have a clearer picture of the country.

The preachers in those days were far more commanding than they are today. I remember them thumping the pulpit and shouting during the sermons. There was, however, a closeness amongst members which is not quite so obvious nowadays. Then many were market gardeners and they always helped one another to gather the crops in, going from one to another. Winter spraying, too, was another time when they rallied round to help each other. One always felt part of a family and if there were problems it was usually someone within the chapel one turned to.'

THE BELLS OF OFFENHAM

'I was not very old when I went into the choir at Offenham. Several of us went for a test at the vicarage where the Rev Coombes gave us a job of varnishing some chairs – we all passed for the choir. I was given the job of pumping the blower for the organ. Sometimes I would get sleepy and the organist would bring me to as the little lead weight had gone down and the organ started to make noises –

well, I did go to church three times on Sunday, 11 am, Sunday school in the afternoon and 6.30 pm evening service. The bellringers fascinated me, watching the ropes going up and down with red, white and blue sallies – little did I think that later as a church warden I would help to restart this as no bells had been rung for a number of years, nor that I would be ringing myself.

There are six bells in Offenham tower, the earliest dating from 1701. Number six is known as the tenor or the Death Bell, because it is tolled at funerals. This is an old custom which was appreciated more before the advent of telephones. On the death of a local man three strikes on the treble were made, after a pause the same on the second and so on to the tenor. With a woman it was two strikes (so listeners knew the sex). The age was given on the third. This was then followed by the tenor being raised and tolled for five minutes or so, then brought down. By this time people in the village and beyond would know the sex and age of the deceased and in all probability who it was.

In the reminiscences of Rev Canon Lawson, who was vicar of Offenham when the old church was pulled down and a new one built in 1861, I particularly like this passage:

"On the last Sunday (Sexagesima) in the old fabric the afternoon congregation was an overflowing one, and, after the last words of prayer and praise and blessing had been uttered, the people gathered up the worn bibles and prayer books which had lain there so long, and as they slowly departed the ringers began a buff peal (muffled). I shall never forget the sound or the sight. As the old church seemed to be knolling its own knell, and the echo of it, as it were, was mysteriously cast back upon us from the upper air, a few persons in small groups lingered mournfully about the churchyard, whilst all the way up the village street the cottagers stood at their doors, their faces shadowed by a solemn, tender pathos, like more who listen to a last farewell of a departing friend, endeared by old and precious associations to their fathers' memories and their own."

The bells are also rung on happier occasions. At weddings at Offenham church apart from ringing methods we also fire the bells. This is when the tenor bell leads but all the bells strike together, and this is only done at weddings.

Where there is a clock in the bell tower, as there is in Offenham tower, there is a "Hammer" which strikes the hour. Before ringing, this has to be pulled off "away" and this is done by way of a wire which runs down to the ringing chamber; if this was not done there would be a definite danger of cracking the bell, in our case the tenor – and that would be expensive.'

EMBARRASSING MOMENTS

'On two occasions prior to 1960 embarrassing situations have occurred at funeral services at the little church of St Mary, Doverdale. On the first of these a cousin of the deceased asked for a bugler from his Highland Regiment to play the Last Post. It was early in January and, to everyone's dismay, blood-curdling noises emerged from his bugle. On shaking out his instrument a biro pen fell out, placed there no doubt by a joker at Hogmanay.

Prompt action on the part of the rector averted disaster on the second occasion. A lady asked if the coffin of her deceased sister could lie in the church overnight. He explained that this was impossible as the service was to be preceded by a wedding. Lines of communication evidently got crossed as on arriving to take the wedding ceremony he found the coffin placed in the chancel. He and the verger hastily bowled the lady into the tool shed in a wheelbarrow, hid the wreaths in the font and covered it with an altar cloth, just in time.'

SENT EVERY SUNDAY

'My parents were not regular churchgoers, but my brother and I were sent to matins every Sunday morning. Our "upper class" friends from Kidderminster processed to church *en famille* – Father in top hat and tails, Mother in smart costume and plume-trimmed hat. They paid for their own marked pew; seats were not made "free" until the 1920s and even long after that, parishioners clung to their own chosen seats, interlopers receiving withering looks!

My brother was a boy chorister in the choir of the parish church. Choirboys received a small annual sum for their services plus sixpence extra for weddings and funerals. When my brother became a soloist for a couple of years, until his voice broke, he was paid threepence or sixpence for each solo performance.

Every Sunday afternoon we went to Sunday school in the large parish hall. We were overseen by a superintendent – a gentle little man with a beard who kept a draper's shop in the town. The pupils were divided into small groups, mostly taught by young women who delighted in using their authority, particularly over the young boys!

We had "treats" – tea parties twice a year and an annual charabanc outing to a field about 20 miles away, belonging to a country squire, where we picnicked and played games.

Every Whit Monday the combined Kidderminster Sunday schools organised a rally. Hundreds of children and their leaders assembled in the town centre and, led by the Boys' Brigade and other local bands, processed to Habberley Valley, about two miles away, where they had breakfast followed by sports and other jollifications for the rest of the day.'

BISHAMPTON CHURCH

'Bishampton church was a large church for the size of the parish, with an excellent peal of bells. Whilst most people love the sound of church bells, if we had a visiting team of bellringers ringing for up to eight hours the sound at such close proximity could be extremely wearing, whereas, because we did not have a team of ringers in the village, the sound of the small bell being rung by Mr Ansell was a light and welcoming call to church. Weddings of local people were often an occasion for some of the local men to ring for the bridal party, not always to any tune but a very joyous sound. Our vicar also bought a set of tubular bells to the church which I don't remember anyone ever playing but we children had great fun with when going into the church, which we often did as the doors were never locked in the daytime and the church was a cool, welcoming place in the summer.

Sunday school was an important part of growing up. The vicar's wife took this and two memories for me are of Mothering Sunday when we coloured in cards to take home for our mothers, followed by a walk in the lanes to pick violets with their sweet perfume, and of earning little proverb papers about the size of postage stamps for good work or attendance. The eldest boy and girl each year had a bible or prayer book bought with money left to the parish by a beneficiary and, when it was my turn, I was given the prayer book, because I was told by the vicar it would be more use as I went to church. However, because I had wanted a bible, he very kindly gave me one of his.

Because many of us did not have holidays at the seaside, the Sunday school outing was always looked forward to, even if the old coaches did sometimes have a habit of breaking down on the way to Porthcawl or some such far-off place. I can still feel the sand in my shoes as I sat in the coach on the way home and, on one occasion, the disappointment when, having found a starfish and put it very carefully in my bucket of sand to bring home, discovering next day that it had "disappeared". Whole families took part in the trip and one of my favourite photos is of my grandmother sitting in a deckchair drinking a glass of stout, the bottle by her feet with the label clearly readable.

Mr Wilkinson, the vicar, and his wife played a big part in our lives not just because of their roles but because of their personalities. Because we had very little public transport, he would always get shopping if he went to town, and I can still remember the sound of his car coming home as he drove a Morris Oxford. He told us stories of the pitch lake he saw during his time in Trinidad; he rescued the top of Abberton church spire when it was demolished by the Ministry of Defence (you could stand on top of it in his garden); obtained a large television so that all the village children could watch the coronation of the Queen, and was, generally speaking, the "friend next door" to us as much as he was the vicar.'

SUNDAY SCHOOL AT HEADLESS CROSS

'During the 1920s and 1930s I attended Headless Cross Methodist Sunday school in Redditch, from the age of two and a half years. We had services at 10.30 am and 2.30 pm. In the morning we assembled in the school hall and processed into the church at 10.45 am and joined in morning service until about 11.10 am when we went back into the hall for a hymn and then into classes for Bible storytime, finishing with prayers and our closing hymn.

Each year we had a Sunday school outing to places like the Lickey or Clent Hills, Evesham or Stratford upon Avon. As travel facilities improved we ventured to places like Weston super Mare, Porthcawl or Barry Island. In the summer we also had a sports day in a local field with games and races and squash and cakes.

The memorable time each year was our Sunday school Anniversary celebrations held on the first and second Sundays of May. We had a choir of about 150 children, teenagers and adults singing on a tiered stage in the church. All the ladies and children had new clothes, always with hats and gloves, and as they processed onto the platform it was like a mannequin parade. We sang anthems morning and evening on both Sundays and on the first Sunday afternoon the older children and adults performed a "Service of Song" and on the second Sunday afternoon the primary department and beginners sang and recited, and it was all most enjoyable.

We had our own Harvest Festival, the sale of the produce paying for our Christmas party with a tree and Father Christmas, who distributed presents for all. With sandwiches, cakes and jellies to eat and an apple, orange and chocolate and some sweets to take home, those really were the days!'

SUNDAY SCHOOL OUTINGS

'A lady who had lived all her life in Malvern pointed out to me where the old chapel, a corrugated iron building, used to stand. This was where all the local children attended regularly, looking clean and tidy. It paid to be a regular attender when the time of the summer outing arrived. The event caused much excitement and was eagerly looked forward to. On the appointed day off they would go in a charabanc, usually no further than the next village where a farmer would lend his field for a picnic, which was provided by worthy members of the chapel or a local benefactor. Races were held and there was much rivalry among the children to be the winner, although a piece of card bearing the word "First" was the best that the hero of the hour could hope for. Then, fun over, they would all pile back into the charabanc for the journey home, worn out.'

'Most children at Ashton under Hill in the 1940s went to Sunday school. We had one at the church and one at the chapel. There was a Sunday school Anniversary at the chapel every summer and most children took part by singing and reciting. There was a trip to Weston every summer as well, when three coaches of family and friends would leave the village at 7 am for a day out. We stopped at Bristol for a break on the Downs and fish and chips on the way back.'

'Father was "chapel brought up" so we attended the Methodist church at Wyre for Sunday school in the mornings, and always for the Whit Sunday Anniversary when we usually had something new to wear with a cream straw hat and new patent ankle-strap shoes. The Sunday school outing was perhaps to the Malvern Hills or to a pleasure garden at Bishop's Cleeve. The church Sunday school outing was generally to Fladbury rectory for tea and games.'

GETTING ABOUT

From horses to cars, our personal transport has changed so much over the years. Once we had to walk everywhere, then the bicycle gave us new freedom, and the first cars were seen on the roads and life changed forever. Buses were important to country dwellers too, and the local railway station was usually a hive of activity and an essential part of rural life.

FROM HORSES TO CARS

'In the 1920s, delivery vehicles were horse-drawn – the milkman with his two-gallon metal can and half pint and one pint "dippers" was a daily caller, as was the baker. The horse patiently waited and moved on to the next call unbidden, often knowing the round better than the roundsman, many of whom resisted the introduction of mechanised delivery vehicles in the early 1930s. Groceries were often delivered by hard-pressed boys on bicycles, which had large carriers on the front to hold the baskets of provisions.

It was a common sight to see young boys clinging to the back of coal-carts for a free ride – and to hear a passer-by warning the driver of his "hangers-on" by calling, "Whip behind"!

Handsome shire horses were used in Kidderminster to drag the heavy loads of carpets up the hill from the factories to the railway station. Often the horses slipped, sparks flying from the cobbles worn smooth by hooves and iron bound wheels . . . it was some job to get a ton or so of horse onto its feet again!

I worked for the Ministry of Road Transport during the Second World War and my enterprising boss started a canal haulage business carrying war requirements which had been brought up the Severn to the Stourport basin for delivery to munition works in the Black Country. One barge towing two or three butty boats was pulled by one or two horses. What a saving of fuel!

Into the 1930s more people owned cars – Herbert Austin pioneered the first 7hp car in 1921 and it became very popular in the locality.'

'The post office at Catshill used to be in Meadow Road and Hector Stokes, the postmaster, used to ride to Bromsgrove to collect the mail in a pony and trap. On the way back he would shout at the top of

Getting about by horse and trap at Yew Tree Hill, Droitwich Spa in the 1920s.

his voice at the bottom of Rocky Lane to tell the Bournheath people that their mail was ready. He also delivered letters, and the recipient would know what was on their postcards before they got them. "Your Auntie Elsie says it's very wet in Blackpool," he would call out while walking up the path, or, "Your sister's wrote, she's got a bad cold."'

'When my parents were married in 1906, they were driven from Hallow to Worcester in an open car preceded by a man with a red flag.'

'During the war my father brought a small two-seater car with a dicky seat at the back. My brother and I went out in it and we thought it was great, really exciting. Just to go in a car was so thrilling in those days. Of course, petrol was rationed then and my brother would say to me, "Don't smile. You mustn't go in a car for pleasure."

We used to cycle to Worcester to go to the pictures. We left our bikes at Elizabeth House, propped up against the wall. There were stacks of bikes there.'

'Shelsley Walsh is famous for its Hill Climb, started in 1905 by Mr Taylor of the Court House and a member of the Midland Automobile Club. At first it was just a test to get up the hill.'

THOUGHT NOTHING OF WALKING

'We thought nothing of walking from Rubery to Bromsgrove if we wanted to go the the market for something special. I did live at the top of Rubery, and as it is a mile from top to bottom of Rubery village that made it a little nearer. Many of us walked to Longbridge to work, saving the penny fare on the trams.'

CRAMMED IN TIGHTLY

'A Worcestershire woman I overheard on the train between Malvern and Ledbury was recalling how in her youth, whenever there was to be some social gathering in the neighbourhood, one of the farm workers would take them in his truck, cramming everyone in tightly until no one could move. This may have been to their advantage at times because the truck was open to the sky. Off they would go in all weathers, and she remembered with a laugh being thrown about in the darkness on bleak, awful nights. Sometimes they arrived home stiff with cold and hardly able to move, with frost on their eyebrows and hair.'

OUR LOCAL BUSES

'Tenbury Wells is served by several bus companies, but the longest serving is Yarrantons, which is still a family business.

Even today it is not unusual for the driver to deliver messages for people on the route – but I remember at one time the driver would be a delivery person as well. Things such as vegetables or bread would be collected from one farm and the driver would stop off and deliver them to another house or farm on the way. They were even known to collect accumulators from a farm, take them into Tenbury to the shop to be charged and, when they were ready, the driver would collect and deliver the recharged accumulator back to its owner.

I can remember often having a rough ride home from Ludlow on a Friday night after going to the cinema, as the driver crammed in as many as he cold, then drove fast along the lanes as he wanted to get home to bed. It used to be quite a bumpy ride sitting on each other's laps because there were so many in the bus.'

'A bus service was started at West Malvern in about 1920, and a terminus was made at the bottom of a hill as it was felt the buses would not be capable of running up the fairly steep incline.'

'In the early 1930s motor cars were not so plentiful and the advent of the Marks Blue bus service was very welcome at Tibberton. It was run by a father and daughter from a garage in Red Hill, Worcester. After her father's death, Sylvia, who was quite a character, carried on the business and was exceptionally generous with service people on leave. Fares from Tibberton to the Cornmarket, Worcester, were ninepence return. Later this increased to one shilling. People appreciated this homely bus service and organised a social evening and presentation in August 1967 at the Bridge Inn, Tibberton, upon Sylvia's retirement.'

'There was a regular bus service between Stourbridge and Bromsgrove, the return fare fivepence halfpenny. Workers from Fairfield for the Austin car factory were collected in a black van, called the Black Maria.'

'Bus services were few and far between in Wythall in the 1950s. Most days you could meet young mothers with prams going to the Grimes Hill station to catch the steam train. They had to travel in the guard's van with the babies still in their prams, and it was the easiest way to get to the shops at Shirley or Birmingham.

In 1956 there were still no proper roads or pavements, so residents cut across fields to catch the bus on the main road. Everyone had to wear wellingtons because of the mud, so they changed into their shoes for going to work in and left their wellingtons under the hedge. In bad weather there was a long line of wellies waiting for their owners' return and they never got stolen.'

SEVEN DAY WONDER

'In the early 1930s a light aircraft landed in a field near the village, a rare enough occurrence for anywhere at that time but especially for Wichenford. Most of the inhabitants came to see it and to talk to the pilot, who arranged for some of the bigger boys to sit in the cockpit while he set off to get petrol to continue his journey.

On his return he was able to take off, getting a local man to hold down the tail while he revved up the engine to full speed. He flew off into the sky, a seven hour experience which became a seven days wonder!'

BY WATER

'Until the Second World War there was a ferry across the river Severn between Pixham and Callow End. There was a small boat for people and a long, flat-bottomed barge for animals and cars. It was moved across the river by means of a submerged chain. Charges in 1930 were twopence for foot passengers, threepence for a bicycle and a shilling for a motor.'

'In the 1920s and 1930s Upton was a busy market town. Markets were held on Wednesday, when farm animals and produce were brought for sale. Sometimes furniture and property were also sold. The town crier used to stand on the Cross and announce what time the sale would commence, ringing his bell three times.

The river Severn was used constantly for business. My grandfather was a hay and coal merchant. He owned two canal boats which carried hay from Upton to Cannock where it was unloaded at the colliery, and a load of coal would be brought back to Upton and stacked in Bridgehouse Yard.

My father, William Biddle, used to drive the *Sarah Jane* boat and my uncle, Percy Biddle, was in charge of the *Shamrock* boat which, at times, worked the Gloucester canal.

The old bridge was a pillar bridge with a wooden swing front which was opened in high water to allow the tugs laden with timber to pass through. Schoolchildren enjoyed seeing the bridge opened because it meant they were late for school.

The swing bridge at Upton on Severn open for river traffic.

Fishing was a big industry. Elvers were caught in the spring and salmon were netted here. Several families of fishermen lived in cottages on the west bank called Fishermen's Row.'

A RAILWAY VILLAGE

'Honeybourne was essentially a railway village. Until its closure by the Beeching axe, Honeybourne station was a busy junction through which trains passed to and from Birmingham, Stratford, Cheltenham, Worcester and Oxford and London. Up to 200 people were employed at the station and most of them lived in the village. One evocative memory that people have of Honeybourne in the heyday of the railway is of midnight on New Year's Eve when all the steam engines in the station would sound their whistles to greet New Year.

A major day for the station was the day of the annual Honeybourne Lamb Sale when 20,000 sheep would be moved, and boys from the village would be driving sheep from the sale yard to the station until late at night. This lasted until 1949 when road transport began to take over. Fresh produce from the Vale of Evesham was also moved by rail and it was not unusual to see up to 50 trucks of fruit and vegetables in the station on their way to Wales or Covent Garden. Often a train load of produce going to Wales would be made up of trucks all labelled for separate towns.

Besides two refreshment rooms for passengers the station also had a workers' canteen which was a dining car drawn up in a siding. At first the meals for the canteen were brought from Worcester but later they were cooked on site. One lady who worked in the canteen met her husband while he was working in the booking office. When they left for their honeymoon, by train of course, it was to the sound of detonators which their friends had placed on the track.

There are many memories of Honeybourne station during the war. It was in an area which contained a large number of military bases, particularly airfields, and so was busy with service personnel travelling to and fro. A lady who was working in the refreshment room at the time also remembered a trainload of evacuee children passing through on a very hot summer day and a churn full of lemonade being made for them.

Because of Honeybourne's relationship with the railway, village people travelled everywhere by train, and, in fact, there were no buses to Honeybourne until shortly before the station closed. Those who worked for the railway of course would receive privilege tickets and a number of free passes per year. Children went to school by train, ladies went shopping by train and people went on outings by train. The Friday shopping train to Evesham was particularly popular. One gentleman remembered the pre-war Saturday night special which took people for a night out in Worcester. Sometimes the return journey could be a bit lively and, if it got too rowdy, the train would be terminated at Evesham, leaving Honeybourne folk to find their own way home.

Before car ownership became common personal transport was by bicycle, and a sight that was common then was a toddler being carried in a child seat on Mother's bicycle. People went to whist drives and dances by bicycle, and families went on bicycle rides together with younger children either in a seat behind Mum or on a saddle on Dad's crossbar.'

A LEADING ROLE

'The railway has played a leading role in the formation of Barnt Green village, which is beside the main line from Exeter to the North with the *Devonian* passing through once a day.

The Cofton Tunnel was opened up to extend the line from two tracks to four. The soil from this project was dumped beside the railway line in Hewell Road on the site of the old cattle market, which enabled sidings to be laid for the delivery of coal and the unloading of animals. The new cattle market was resited in Rocky Lane, now renamed Hewell Lane, and has since been closed to make way for maisonettes.

In the early part of the war these sidings were used to house the ambulance trains and it was during this period that George VI and the now Queen Mother, with their two daughters, would visit. The royal train would often stay overnight in the sidings, nicknamed "The Royal Sidings", adjacent to Barnt Green station. Although it was never known when the Royal Family was coming to Barnt Green the "jungle telegraph" started working and people gathered in Hewell Road, and even on one occasion the children came out of school to see them pass by in their car on their way to the station. On one or two occasions as the royal train left Barnt Green station the King and Queen were seen to wave from the windows.'

HOUSE & HOME

THE WAY WE LIVED THEN

So much has changed in the way we live and in our homes, particularly with the coming of modern heating and lighting. It is tempting to see the past as rosier than it was, and to forget the constant work needed to keep old cottages clean and warm, but perhaps we all at times yearn for the softness of lamplight and the unhurried pace of the past.

UNDER THE PROTECTION OF THE SQUIRE

'I was born on 6th September 1893 at Queenhill, the first child of Henry and Harriet Roberts. Eleven more children followed me into this world to be brought up in a small cottage, the boys occupying one bedroom and the girls another, and our childhood was happy. My mother died and Father took as his second wife, Mary Payne, who was a cook for Squire Dowdeswell at Pull Court. Mary's father owned a public house called the Barley House on the Ripple side of the river. We used to gather oziers to make baskets.

Father was a hard worker and it didn't do him any harm for he lived to the good age of 83. He worked for the Squire on the estate, cider making, grafting apples, fencing, wood cutting and doing all kinds of odd jobs. He worked from six in the morning until six at night and brought home 14 shillings a week. The Squire was a good man and he only charged £4 a year for rent and rates. When I look back I realise that, despite our background, we lived rather a privileged life in some respects, as so much of it revolved round "the big house". The Dowdeswells had bought up much of the property around Queenhill and had enclosed the whole within a ring fence. They employed a lot of the villagers from Bushley and Queenhill and were very good to their workers. The Squire visited all the people in their cottages and he was known and loved by us all.

He modernised all the cottages and farmhouses. Bushley church was rebuilt by Berens Dowdeswell and the family built new roads and a bridge across the brook. The Ham at Tewkesbury belonged to them and the old Squire owned the toll house by the Mythe Bridge. He paid off the dues and, because they were relieved of tolls, the parishioners presented him with a gold watch. They also built the Pavilion at Moss Green as a holiday home. They would load their coach with luggage and drive off down the track to Bushley and holiday on their own doorstep. Afterwards they threw it open for use by the community and we had lots of dances and social occasions there.

The Dowdeswells did so much to raise the standard of living for the workers. They started a clothing club, a Sunday school and a dame school at Queenhill and took a great interest in every person around. Mind you, they were strict and if a girl got herself into trouble and had a baby out of wedlock, the family were turned out.

Well, you couldn't keep a family on 14 shillings a week now, but my parents did and we lived well. People didn't expect as much in those days and we learned early how to make ends meet. We always had two pigs in the cot and nothing was wasted. When a pig was killed my parents cured the bacon and the neighbours shared it. They did the same for us. Father always had a thick slice of bacon with egg and bread to go to work on and we children loved home-rendered lard spread on thick slices of bread.

We had a few hens scratching about and the boys caught rabbits; rabbit pie and rabbit stew was tasty, but people don't bother with that now. A sheep's head made a tasty meal. Father always had lots of vegetables in the garden and the boys used to go round with clappers to scare the birds off the land. Milk from the farm cost three-halfpence but one could get a can full of skimmed milk for a halfpenny. Most of us made our own bread. Mothers bought baking flour by the sack from Healings in Tewkesbury and it came out on a horse and cart. The Drum and Monkey was then a bakery, owned by the Foort family, and we used to go there for a can of barm for baking.

Most clothing was hand-made although Mother did eventually manage to buy a sewing machine. Farrs, in Upton, sold materials and haberdashery. Mother bought brown calico, which washed white, for three-halfpence a yard to make underwear and brown twill for sheeting. Sheets worn out in the middle were turned sides to middle for more life. Aprons were made from sacking for outdoor work. My aunt always had nice clothes as her mistress, Mrs Ballard, passed on unwanted clothing. Some things were eventually unpicked, turned and made up again into clothing for us.

We always wore boots but at Putts in Old Street one could get a pair of shoes made for two shillings. There were no wellingtons. Working men wore twine wound round under the knee to keep trouser legs out of the mud, whilst the gaffers wore leather gaiters.

No clothing was ever thrown away without salvaging reusable pieces. We made rag rugs from the thicker pieces and real dust traps they were. Mother would save tea leaves to lay the dust before sweeping. We knew an old lady who actually whitened the lines between flagstones to keep the witches out!

But life wasn't all work. We went to church in those days, dressed in our best dresses and met up with all our friends. The farmers and landowner had their own seats. All the children learned their catechism. If everyone knew and tried to keep the commandments there would be less trouble in the world. Marriages lasted then because once a girl got married she was content to look after her man and raise his children and your man looked after his family. He was the breadwinner.

There was always some relaxation. Fairs came out to Longdon, with roundabouts. Better off ladies organised social events and fêtes. Men would enter vegetables; women knitting, sewing, darning, etc. If a girl was in service she had to get her mistress's permission to put work in. The women had the Mothers' Union in Longdon, the men cricket and bands. There were choral concerts and the children entered musical competitions at Madresfield. We celebrated Oak Apple Day, Empire Day, St George's Day and May Day. We were more patriotic than now. On May Day children from the three parishes met up at Pull Court and the boys elected a queen for the day. A king was also chosen, together with two maids of honour. Then we went down to Moss Green, headed by the Bushley band, where we spent the day dancing round the maypole, singing and making merry. There was a Scout troop for the boys.

Harvest Homes at Pull Court were huge affairs. Besides the local gentry two members from every cottage would be invited, something like 600 sitting down to dinner. There were amusements all day in the grounds. Christmas was another lovely occasion when we were invited to Pull Court to share in the Squire's festivities. They always had a lovely tree, magic lanterns and games, and we were given presents. We were treated like one big family by the Squire.

Yes, they were magic days . . . gone forever.'

BORN ON WAKE DAY

'I was born on 12th July 1926, the same day a Wake was going on in Chaddesley Corbett village: after that year the name was changed to "fête". I was born in a little cottage on the top of Lodgeford Hill and was the seventh child of nine. My father was a builder and he was only allowed to work on dry days, which meant there wasn't much money. Our living was very primitive: we had a black fire grate where my mother did the cooking and she also put irons close to the fire to get hot when she did the ironing. Clothes had to be aired around the fire.

There was a little room with a fire under a boiler and this was where my mother did the washing. She would pound the washing with a wooden pronged instrument called a dolly, in a tub of hot soapy water to get the clothes clean. It then went through an old fashioned mangle which had huge rollers and heavy weights on the bottom. We also washed ourselves in this room. There were no taps or hot water but outside there was a pump from where we got spring water – we used this for drinking and washing. During the winter there was no electricity but we had a paraffin lamp in the living room which wasn't a very bright light but we would play cards or board games. I remember someone gave us a radio, we all thought that was marvellous. We took candles to bed and stone bottles filled with hot water. Fortunately there was never an accident. I suppose it was drilled into us not to play with fire.

The children would sleep three in a bed and we had very few toys. I don't remember any of us having birthday cards when it was our birthday, we had clothes.

We had a large garden with chickens and pigs and lots of fruit trees. During the summer Mother made lots of pies and jam. We all had jobs to do, the girls helped with the cooking and housework, the boys collected wood for the fire and chopped it up and also ran errands.

We started school when we were four years old and we would go to Sunday school every Sunday. It was a two mile walk, there were no buses to take us. My sisters and I wore long boots – we hated them but Mother said they were sensible and kept our legs warm and dry. If we wore holes in the bottom of our shoes my father would repair them.'

GRANDMOTHER'S COTTAGE

'I can remember waking up for school on a cold winter's morning after sleeping in my grandmother's big bed in her cottage in Pedmore. There was a fireplace in the bedroom and a picture of Jesus, *Light of the World,* over the bed. I went down the creaking stairs to the cold kitchen to wash in cold water in the belfast sink. We were lucky if it had not frozen over. There was no hot water. The loo was at least inside the cottage at the far end of the kitchen and this was also often frozen up. It had a large wooden seat and newspaper cut in squares on a nail. The old copper was still in the kitchen. My mother would get up very early on washing day to light it. It had to be done on that day even if it was raining.

Coming home from school I remember sitting thawing out by the fire burning brightly in the old blackleaded grate, toasting bread on

A typical cottage at Himbleton in the 1920s.

a fork and it always tasted so much better then. I can still see the brasses, one of Queen Victoria, and the copper hooks hanging over the fire. There were heavy curtains in this room which pulled across the whole room to keep out the draughts. My sister and I would put on our little entertainments for my grandmother and we would pretend those curtains were a stage.

I can still see that cottage so clearly. Now there is a block of flats built over it. I hope that they can feel all the love that was once there and in the garden where we used to pick plums, pinch the sweet pods of the peas, climb the apple trees and feed the chickens.'

HOLLYDENE COTTAGE

'The earliest Honeybourne to live in the cottage at Stoke Prior was John Honeybourne, born 25th September 1835, and great-grandfather to the present owners. Hollydene Cottage is a semi-detached cottage fronting onto a country lane; it has an extensive garden and old orchard. The flower garden and vegetable garden are edged with original box hedges. The orchard had fruit trees and bee hives. A pigsty was situated between garden and orchard.

The cottage is approached from the lane by a short garden path to the front door which still bears a very old door knocker.

A passage from the front door leads straight to the back of the cottage. The kitchen is a small room with a fireplace which has replaced the old blackleaded grate with small side oven and trivet for the kettle; the high mantelshelf, where the front was always enhanced with a pelmet with a knotted fringe, is gone. The tea caddy with caddy spoon, various ornaments and two hand-made wooden money boxes all lived on the shelf.

In front of the fire was the fender with fire irons, all of which required cleaning. The floor was quarry tiles with a rug, and the room contained a corner cupboard and large dining table which could seat ten people, plus four wooden chairs with rexine covered seats. The table was protected with a gold coloured chenille tablecloth. A built-in cupboard beside the fireplace provided a dry storage space for preserves and jams.

On the opposite side of the passage is the parlour. A wooden floor with carpet here, two easy chairs and a sofa upholstered in red patterned plush, with four straight-backed chairs. A small round table with aspidistra under the window and a small sideboard completed the furnishings. A small iron grate with tiled surround provided the only source of heat. A cat's whisker/crystal set provided the "modern" entertainment. The back kitchen was the working room for the household, with a bread oven in one corner and a copper for boiling clothes, heating bath water and boiling Christmas puddings in the opposite corner. A long brick sink with a blue brick front edge was for washing clothes, dishes, etc. A scrubbed-top table and a free-standing iron cooking stove, a "Dover" stove, were all here.

Monday was always washday. The copper was filled with water, the fire lit and, when burning well, backed up with slack. Clothes were washed in a dolly tub using dolly pegs, boiled in the copper, rinsed in a bath in the sink, and whitened with a squeeze of the blue bag (always left in a baby's sock in a King Edward VII enamel coronation mug). Main items were starched with Colman's starch, while Robin starch used for men's stiff collars. Washing was put through a mangle with heavy wooden rollers. This lived outside in the yard. Everything was pegged out on a line outside to dry. Pegs were bought from gypsies who made and sold them.

When dry, the washing was brought in, using a large wicker clothes basket, to be folded and starched items dampened and rolled prior to ironing. Ironing was usually done next day. Flat irons were heated in front of the fire on a grid. The kitchen table top was prepared, a fitted board placed on top, then a folded blanket and an old sheet. A brass iron stand was ready for the flat iron. An iron holder was necessary to hold the handle of the flat iron. When ironed the linen was folded and placed on a wooden clothes horse to "air" then put away in drawers.

There were three bedrooms, each having a bed with spring mattress. On top of this was a feather bed, the usual sheets and blankets topped with an eiderdown. They had a dressing table with crocheted cheval set, a wardrobe with mirror, and a wash-stand with a marble top. This held a large jug and basin with matching soap dish and toothbrush container, a carafe of water and glass. In a cupboard underneath were two chamber pots. A towel rail was attached at either end of the washstand.

Male members of the family always shaved using a cut-throat razor. These were dried after use and kept in a drawer, the strop left hanging in the kitchen.

Each bedroom had a fireplace, used only in cases of illness. Beds were warmed in winter using stone hot water bottles, or a shelf out of the oven wrapped in a blanket.

A blanket chest was left upstairs, as well as the old Singer treadle sewing machine which was left on the landing with a chest of drawers. Mother did her sewing here.

The stairs had stair carpet up the middle, kept in place with brass rods, cleaned weekly. Each morning chamber pots were emptied into a slop pail, the contents diluted with water and given to the

ECKINGTON

within a few minutes walk of the Midland Railway Station.

TO BE SOLD BY AUCTION, BY

E. G. RIGHTON & SON

At The Bell Inn, Eckington,

ON FRIDAY, MAY 12TH, 1922

at 5 for 6 o'clock in the Afternoon, subject to Conditions incorporating the Common Form Conditions of the Birmingham Law Society.

FREEHOLD PROPERTIES

LOT 1.

Comprising A Pair of Picturesque

COTTAGES

Brick, Timber and Thatch, with the large and productive Gardens and out-buildings thereto situate in the Manor Road, Eckington, and known as **LOWER [illegible]**. The Let to Mr. James Glover, as half-yearly Tenant, at £14 per annum rent. [illegible] property contains three living rooms and four bedrooms. There is a brick and tiled wash-house, W.C., three piggeries, wood and iron erection of covered passage, packing room and coal house.

LOT 2.

A

PASTURE ORCHARD

Planted with Plum and Apple Trees, and being No. 185 on the Ordnance Survey Map. Situate adjoining Lot 1, containing

2R. 18P.

or thereabouts, and having a frontage of about 96 ft. to the Manor Road, let to Mr. James Glover as yearly tenant at £6 per annum rent.

LOT 3.

ALL THOSE

THREE COTTAGES

Brick, Timber and Thatch, with the gardens and out-buildings thereto situate in Bunn Street, Eckington, let to Mrs. Banton, Mrs. Taylor and Miss Cull, as quarterly tenants, at £6 each per annum rent, Landlord paying rates.

LOT 4.

A VALUABLE PIECE OF

Market Garden Land

No. 146 on the Ordnance Survey Map. Situate in Peason Road, Eckington, and containing

3A. 2R. 11P.

or thereabouts, let to Messrs. W. Russell, W. Nicholls, J. Quarrell, L. Russell, A. G. and F. G. Berwick and J. Glover, as yearly tenants, at a total annual rental of £17 11s., landlord paying rates.

To View, apply to the Tenants, and for further particulars, to the Auctioneers at Evesham, Alcester and Pershore, or to

ALFRED & W. H. GREEN, SOLICITORS, 109, COLMORE ROW, BIRMINGHAM.

W. Fearnside, Printer, Pershore.

Sale of property at Eckington in 1922. The cottage rented by Miss Cull was sold for £366.

kidney beans!

A large walk-in pantry provided storage space for bread, pickles and sauces and for china.

Drinking water came from a pump in the yard, which was supplied from a well. The pump had to be thawed out before use in frosty weather.

An earth closet outside provided the sanitary arrangements. The closet had two seats, one low down for children, the other raised up. Toilet paper was not available, so orange paper was saved to use. When the supply finished newspaper squares were cut up, a packing needle pushed through the corner and string pulled through. This was hung up for use.

The closet was limed, the contents emptied once a year and used as garden fertiliser.'

THE EMPTY COTTAGE

'In 1949 my fiancé, Dennis, and I were planning to get married but deciding where to live was a problem. Few vacant properties were available in our price range and although we had placed our name forward for a building licence this was unlikely to mature for several years.

Dennis, however, had previously had a girlfriend, whose father was a farmer at Frankley, whom we visited from time to time during our courtship. At her suggestion we, with somewhat mixed feelings, approached the farmer to see if he would allow us to rent an empty cottage on the farm. I felt rather worried about the whole matter for I had never lived in the country and the state of the cottage was appalling. It was extremely damp and smelly, was three miles off a bus route, needed complete decoration, had no electricity, only pump water which was unsuitable for drinking and no main drainage.

The result of our visit to the farmer was that he gave sanction for us to rent the cottage, at the princely sum of ten shillings per week.

The next move was to get our parents' approval, whereupon they made a joint visit with us to have a viewing. My mother, in particular, was horrified and felt that she would rather give us a sum of money than allow us to live in such a place! However, my future mother in law who had great confidence in her dear son felt that he could make the place habitable.

Work began in April 1949 and the first job was to empty a room off the kitchen which had been used for all household rubbish and ashes from the fire. "Old Tom" who had lived in the cottage with his wife and children was classed as lazy and it was too much to

expect him to place anything in a dustbin if, in fact, they had one.
Another joy to behold was the outside loo which consisted of two holes in a wooden seat and to gain access meant crossing an outside yard. No doubt this was too much for "Old Tom" who had other ideas and places in mind. One of our first purchases was an Elsan chemical toilet, also a galvanised dustbin for the sum of ten shillings and sixpence.

Before we could commence work we needed to have electricity installed. This was organised and work completed for the sum of £25, being the cost of wiring the cottage, plus an outside light which we would need to cross the muddy farmyard.

The cottage was built in the mid 19th century and had previously been the main farmhouse. The living room had very fine oak beams and an inglenook fireplace, but the floor left much to be desired as the once red quarry tiles had been worn away to wafer thinness and ideas of putting down a carpet had to be shelved. Dennis began to think about the matter and decided to take up the tiles and relay the floor in concrete. As the room was quite large is needed a lot of muscle to mix and lay concrete over the area. Finally, a nice level floor was laid and covered with roofing felt as this was before waterproof membranes were commonly used.

Then began the task of redecoration which involved great areas of replastering. The plaster which had been used in the past was very powdery and contained horse hair and at times it seemed that it would have been easier to have replastered the whole room.

There was no damp course and the whole place was extremely damp, and apart from a two-bar electric fire the only heat was from the coal fire in the living room. We used to arrive there at about 6.30 pm to light the fire but it was usually a couple of hours before the place got warm. Being very bold we decided to paper the room, which was difficult because the walls weren't flat and the ceiling was uneven. The doors were painted in medium oak and followed with a second coat of scrumble which was put on with a brush or comb to get the grain. Unfortunately on one occasion Dennis's mother had the grain going across the wood instead of down which, in our opinion, was a serious error!

Water was a problem as this was from the outside pump, although Dennis thought it was good for me to pump to develop my muscles! Drinking water had to be fetched from the farmhouse where we also obtained milk which, incidentally, had not been pasturised. In later years it was a good idea to fetch the milk to get out of the washing up and to give the fire a chance to get going. We worked through the winter of 1949/50 to complete the decorations which consisted of painting the kitchen, distempering the hall, stairs and two bedrooms, also whitewashing the dairy. We had to travel five miles by motorcycle to get to the cottage from our homes and were often too cold to begin work straight away. But it all seemed worthwhile when carpets were laid, curtains were hung and furniture put in place.'

A RAMBLING OLD PLACE

'My childhood home was a rambling old place, with no conveniences whatever, modern or otherwise. It had two long brick-floored passages on the ground floor, and the equivalent in dark landings up. The latter were reached by a steep winding stair, leading to what I now understand to be a gallery landing. Around this were lots of bannisters, which I hated if ever I had to dust them.

The scullery had as much floor space as the whole of many a modern house. It had a baking oven, which was very rarely used, a copper and a kitchen range. The latter was very old and never used for cooking, but I have had many a bath in front of its fire. Opposite this range stood a long high table. On this stood an earthenware crock, in which the bread was kept, and the knife board. (Knives had to be cleaned after each meal.) Before I was able to do it myself, it was on this table that I was seated to have socks and shoes put on. There was a mangle, with large wooden rollers, and a shallow sink, with a tiled tram, which was of course the draining board.

The only water supply was from a pump in the yard. On washdays the water had to be pumped and carried to the copper, and then a fire lighted under it. The washing was done in zinc baths, one for washing, one for swilling, another for blueing and one for starching. Apart from the washing, the drying, especially in wintertime, must have been a nightmare. Just imagine five double sheets of linen or heavy cotton "twill", as well as the general wash for a household of seven adults and two children, to get dry on a pouring wet day!

The kitchen was, no doubt about it, "the heart of the house". The floor was of square red brick tiles, covered only by a pegged rug in front of the range. This range appeared to me to be massive. It had two square hobs, with an oven under each. In front stood a fender and fire-irons, all enclosed by a sturdy guard. Parts of all these had to be blackleaded, but parts of them all were steel, not stainless let it be noted, and these parts had to be cleaned with emery paper or bath-brick. I always remember that range as bright and gleaming, with a kettle singing on each hob, but it must have meant hours of hard work to keep it so.

Incidentally, when this chimney needed sweeping, the drill was as follows. Cut a nice large holly bush from the garden. Attach a rope to each end, and a brick to one of the ropes. Someone then climbed to the roof and let the brick down the chimney. The bush was then pulled down by the rope, and then up again by the other rope, and the process repeated as necessary. All the other chimneys were treated in the more orthodox manner, but there was one which, after the brushes had been up, needed someone to climb up and shovel the soot from a cavity where the soot would be trapped.

Lighting for the whole house was by paraffin lamp or candles, and heating was by coal fire or paraffin stove. It was lovely to go to bed in the winter by flickering firelight, but now I spare a thought to whoever carried the coal upstairs, and the ashes down.

High up on one wall of the kitchen was a row of bells, on circular springs, which could be set jangling by pulling bell ropes in the bedrooms, or working a kind of lever by the firesides of the downstair rooms. These were all disconnected after the day when I found that by running from room to room and activating them, I could make a glorious noise!

Beds, how these have changed. Bedsteads were usually iron-framed with a lattice of metal pieces, woven from top to bottom and side to side of the frame. On top of these went the mattress, sometimes of straw, or, for the more affluent, horsehair. On top of this went the bed, usually made of feathers, but sometimes of "flock". Both mattress and bed had removable cotton covers, and covering the mattress edges and falling to the floor were valances. The bed was completed with a bolster and pillows, each in covers, sheets, blankets and a bed cover. Mum and Dad had an eiderdown, but they were not very common at that time.

They also had a "box spring" on their bed. As far as I remember this was a wooden frame which stood on the iron bedframe. Over this was stretched a metal "blanket" consisting of interlocking springs. This could be tightened somehow with a key, but just how I never knew, but what I remember so well was what a wonderful trampoline that bed made. What a pity that the low ceiling rather cramped my style!

Bed-making was a complicated proceeding. Before going down to breakfast, the bed had to be opened, ie the bedclothes stripped back, one by one and the bed left to air. Later in the morning, whoever went to "do upstairs" took with them a slop pail, a slop cloth, large jug of water, and probably a mop. This of course because bed-making included emptying the water that had been used for washing, and also emptying and washing the chamber pots. Slop pails had lids with a slope towards the centre where there was a hole, protected by a raised knob which enabled liquid to be poured in without lifting the lid.

To make the bed, the bedclothes having already been stripped right off, the bed itself was well shaken up and then turned over, unless it was Friday or Sunday, when turning was omitted. The reason for this I can only guess, Friday was always a very busy day, and no unnecessary work was done on Sundays.

At bedtime you made a "trough" in the feathers in which to lie, and after being tucked up were snug and warm until morning. Not at all healthy or hygienic by today's standards, but oh so comfortable. Of course the regular airing, shaking and turning helped.

In these days of indoor sanitation, it is difficult to appreciate the primitive conditions that prevailed, and therefore the great need of the chamber pots to which I have referred. Most people had to rely on a privy midden, which was a hole in the ground, with a seat over containing one, two or even three holes. This was all contained within a building of some sort, and for obvious reasons situated as far from the house as possible. Torches with batteries had not yet arrived, a lantern was not always available and candles easily blew out, so after dark the chamber pot was almost a necessity.

In 1928 we moved to a much smaller house, where we had running water, gas for cooking and an indoor bath. By comparison luxury and far less real hard work, but also not the abundance of happy memories.'

CARPET SQUARES

'We lived in an old farmhouse, which did not get electricity until 1947. We made do with paraffin lamps, candles and log fires. Wall to wall carpets were not in vogue and living rooms usually had a carpet square with a linoleum surround and, most probably, a hand-made rug beside the fire. The main bedroom would be the same, but secondary bedrooms often had only boards or lino, with rugs placed at strategic places. Staircases were carpeted with 18 inch wide carpet held in place by brass rods (which had to be cleaned every week). In the late 1940s, the new carpet was three feet wide. It still left a bit of tread each side to be dusted – but at least the brass rods had given way to bakelite clips.'

IT KEPT UP THE PLASTER

'Most houses at Hanley Swan and Hanley Castle were rented. They were very small and sometimes in shaky condition. Pretty wallpaper was liked, and flower borders. As one man said: "Wallpaper was liked because it often kept up the plaster." '

PICKINS

'In cold weather Droitwich people warmed their beds with pickins. These were very solid lumps of deposit chipped off the brine pans (a strong brine stream flows beneath Droitwich and the brine was heated in large pans to make salt).

Pickins came in all shapes and sizes. They were kept all day in the bottom of the oven. At bedtime, wrapped in an old flannel garment, they made excellent bedwarmers.'

ROUND THE MANTEL

'Great Aunt Kate lived in a little house in Hewell Road, Redditch. The kitchen cum living room had a quarry tiled floor, with a rag rug at the hearth. There was a black grate and round the mantel there was a chenille pelmet with bobbles.

Occasionally we went into the parlour. It had lace curtains and a blind at the window that was always halfway down. The sofa and chairs were of horsehair and very uncomfortable. Over the fireplace was a picture, *The Monarch of the Glen*. By one wall stood a harmonium. This room had linoleum (oil cloth) on the floor.'

ONE UP, ONE DOWN

'Born in 1923 at Lower Moor, my first recollection of home is of a one up, one down thatched cottage, where I shared my parents' bedroom, along with my younger brother. The room had a dividing screen. I remember waiting for Father Christmas to come and fill my pillowcase and eventually realising that it was my own father creeping up the stairs.

In about 1930, my father approached the landlord about occupying the adjoining cottage, also one up and one down, as the elderly lady was moving. This was slightly larger than ours and my father made a doorway through both upstairs and downstairs.

Mother cooked on an oil stove before the cottages were linked, then she used a blackleaded grate in an inglenook. I remember looking up the chimney and seeing the stars shining.'

COAL AND SLACK

'Mr Edwards had a small coal business at Kempsey from his riverside depot. Barges came upriver with coal from the Forest of Dean, or downstream from the Black Country. It was sold to the villagers at sixpence a hundredweight.'

SPRING-CLEANING

'Spring-cleaning was an exhausting time which went on for a week. Curtains were taken down and washed, together with blankets and covers. Carpets were spread with tea leaves before being brushed to lay the dust. The chimneys would be swept, another day of upheaval. The paintwork and walls would all have to be washed down. And there was no mains water and no electricity to help with it all.'

COAL AND ELECTRICITY

'In 1949, the first few houses in Rock village were electrified. Total electrification came the following year. This included the church, as the wiring and equipment was purchased using £197, the balance left from the wartime WI Fruit Preservation Centre Fund. Local farms had to guarantee a payment of £80 for their first year, whatever their consumption, before electricity was connected. This gamble proved worthwhile once electric farming equipment had been purchased.

The urgent need for coal to power the post-war electrical generating industry led the National Coal Board to investigate an open-cast mine in Rock in 1950.

The proposed mine stretched from the Field House, Rock, to Abberley, and led to a campaign of great ferocity. Local people enlisted the help of their newly-elected MP, Gerald Nabarro, who cut his parliamentary teeth on "Rock Open Cast". The storm raged for six months until the NCB changed their course, and set up an experiment into the underground gasification of coal. They enlisted the help of the Ministry of Supply and the Cementation Company, and, at 24 hours' notice, moved onto a field at Rockmoor. The experiment: to see whether it was possible to burn coal underground, extract the gas and leave the land undisturbed supported by the residual coke. It took two and a half years and employed 80 local people. Although technically possible, the experiment proved impracticable and the NCB left Rock to concentrate on developing deep-mining.

So, by 1960, we had electric lighting and could cook using electricity, solid fuel and oil. We had piped water and our own sewage plant, which made our lives much less strenuous. However, we never have managed a piped gas supply to this day!'

TIME CONSUMING

'Lighting in most homes in Hagley in 1940 was by electricity supplied by the Shropshire, Worcestershire & Staffordshire Electric Power Company, but there were still a number who had gas lighting and a handful of cottages with paraffin lamps. The gas lighting was quite good as long as the mantles remained in one piece, and oil lamps were also acceptable but the daily cleaning of the glass, the trimming of the wicks and the filling of the reservoirs with paraffin was a time-consuming chore.'

WATER AND WASHDAY

Every drop of water was precious when it had to be drawn from the well or carried from the stream. Of course, no mains water meant no indoor sanitation, and we were all familiar with the little house at the bottom of the garden. Washday was perhaps the hardest day of the week for the housewife, who faced toil from morning to night washing, blueing, starching, mangling and ironing.

OUTHOUSES

'I recall that we had three outhouses, as did most houses in our area of Worcester. First, our slab, a low brick-built building near to and opposite the back door, and with a concrete surface on which we kept anything likely to be needed in the kitchen or scullery. It was also a useful place for shoe cleaning, for drying sticks and placing small buckets of coal, logs and, surprisingly, used tea leaves. These were mixed with slack and used to revive a sluggish fire. They nearly always did.

Our second outhouse was the coal house. It was very large and obviously intended to store a ton or more of large lumps for winter use. Fine, but someone had to break them up and store them to avoid any dislodged coal that fell which was a danger to anyone getting coal at any time. I recall the awful roar of coal falling there, it was frightening.

So to my third outhouse, our privy, built (and furnished?) about

1901. It had a tiled floor, a whitewashed ceiling and walls and an oak door with a six inch space above it. The furniture was a large plinth of crock about four feet high with an oak lid which, when lifted off, revealed an iron oval-shaped container, situated about seven feet below, with a drainpipe at each end, ie in and out, leading to the house drain under the paved yard outside.

When the container was over half-full, it tipped itself, thus releasing its contents into the house drain by overbalancing and clanging loudly, twice. We often heard it when within the house, where it sounded like a church bell tuning up. It wasn't, of course, but there *was* a church nearby, so could it be an interesting possibility? Mother's glance at us showed that it wasn't!'

TINY COTTAGES

'The people of Fairfield, before the war, mostly dwelt in tiny cottages, comprising scullery, living room with stairs leading out of it, and up to two bedrooms, one of which was on the landing and often was used by the children. An earth closet was down the garden, and water was obtained from wells, though sometimes there was a pump outside and some lucky ones had a cold tap indoors. A nailshop or glass house usually adjoined the cottage.

The kitchen contained an earthenware sink, and a big copper or boiler, enclosed in a brick surround and with a fire underneath, that was used for heating the water for washing and baths, and for cooking pig potatoes (and Christmas puddings!). The family bathed in a large tin bath in front of the fire.'

NEXT TO THE WASHHOUSE

'My home in the 1920s and 1930s was a cottage in Broadway village street, one of a row of three. There was no gas, electricity or water laid on. The toilet was shared between the three cottages. It was at the end of the garden and was a long, box-like arrangement with three holes, one small one for a child and two larger ones for the adults! Next to it was the washhouse and this contained an old stone sink with a tap, and a copper for boiling the washing. This too was shared by the three cottages.

All our cooking was done on an open fire with an oven each side. Hooks hung down from the chimney to hold the kettle. As the fire was started first thing in the morning it meant that the house was always warm in winter, although a little hot in summer – and the kettle was always boiling.'

BUILT ON THE BROOK

'Our homes in Childswickham were very primitive compared with those of today. Houses were built on or near the brook so as to have easy access to water. Piped water came to the village in about 1930.'

AN ELABORATE AFFAIR

'At Bentley House the "loo" was a large, elaborate affair at the end of the garden. There was a mass of snowdrops round it in February. Once, when my cousin Maud was staying, it was just getting dark and she had to pay a visit. She was soon back. She had seen the black dog walk through the closed iron gates dragging its chain! It was our resident ghost. We had an adult with us when we paid a visit after dark from then on.

Our loo at Upper Bentley Farm was at the bottom of the garden. It was whitewashed once a year and had newspaper cut up and hung on a nail. Dad emptied it into pits in the garden. The contents of the "guzzunders" were diluted with water and used as a fertiliser. I hated going down the garden at night. I would have a candle and cup my hand round it. Most of the time I would just get to the door and the candle would go out. I could hear the rats inside.

One night when I was cycling from a Webheath shilling hop, I heard voices and saw lights. It worried me a bit, but when I went past it was only the Lavender Cart, emptying the loos down Birchfield Road.'

PURE WATER

'As children at Blakedown we always drank water, with occasionally home-made lemonade and ginger pop in very hot weather. There were two springs of pure water, straight from the Clent Hills, in the village and I well remember collecting jugs of water from them to take home for drinking and washing hair.'

IVY COTTAGE

'When I was a child in the early years of the century at Great Comberton, the houses generally had no running water and the toilets were outside. We had a little hut in the garden with ivy growing over it, with a toilet which had to be emptied into a pit at the bottom of the garden. The family referred to it as "Ivy Cottage".'

A PROBLEM

'In 1938 my parents staked their all, and moved out of rented property into a seven acre smallholding near Droitwich which they managed to purchase for the princely sum of £1,000. Imagine the problems they must have previously experienced with having to go through my sister's bedroom to get to their own; and having to go down two steps to get into my little bedroom, which in turn led into another much larger room which was used as a general "storeroom"!

Our new home had only been built some 70 years previously and was of a more contemporary arrangement, being more or less square with a central hall and stairway, and four rooms up and four down – plus a small box room at the top of the stairs. Comparison with the homes of today must end there because although there were the four bedrooms and a box room upstairs, there was no bathroom; and downstairs there was a living/dining room and a pantry/dairy at the rear and the "sitting room" and the GPO telephone exchange room at the front! This was home to the exchange and public telephone for the whole village; and we were very pleased that Miss Bridgen (the niece of Major Sallis, the previous owner) was able to "live in" and carry on as operator, and would also instruct my mother who was to take over this task later on. During the war the exchange had to be manned for 24 hours a day, but that's another story!

Outside and adjacent to the rear door was the lean-to back kitchen which housed the coal-fired wash boiler, the Valor three-burner paraffin stove, and a big brown glazed earthenware sink; but it was without a water supply. All the food preparation, cooking and clothes washing were done in the back kitchen; and then on a Friday night, the tin bath had to be lifted down from the wall, filled with hot water from the wash boiler, and it then became the bathroom! After this facility had been used by all who wished to partake in the ritual, the water had to be ladled out into the aforementioned sink, from where it was simply piped away into a soak-away at the other end of the garden.

Just round the corner from the back kitchen stood the little toilet, and again this had no water supply and its contents had to be buried in a hole in the garden. This was later modernised with an Elsan chemical toilet, which sounds much better but was in fact only marginally so, and still had to be emptied.

The water supply was the ultimate problem because apart from the spasmodic rainwater collected from the roof in a tank across the backyard, the only other supply available was a hand pump situated through a gate and across a field, some 80 to 100 yards away from the house! All water required for cooking, drinking, washing and cleaning had to be conveyed down to the house from this pump, and in winter this often meant priming the pump with near-boiling water so that it could be thawed out and persuaded to work.

The telephone exchange went automatic towards the end of the war; the mains electric supply came early post-war, and this was followed by a mains water supply in the 1950s, and a sewerage system in the 1960s! Happy days? I certainly look back on them with very great pleasure indeed!'

REPLACING WELLS

'It was 1937 when water was first piped to Rock village, replacing 14 wells which had been of such dubious quality that four were condemned in 1935. However, we had to wait two years for a scheme to be completed at Chaddesley Corbett. This stopped the local boys' entrepreneurial talents, as every summer they wheeled a water butt around the village when the wells ran dry. This was not an easy task with our topography!'

SO QUIET

'It was much quieter then. I would lie in bed of a summer evening in the 1920s and there wouldn't be a sound but the murmuring of cattle and sheep. No sound of traffic until ten o'clock when you would hear the clip-clop of a horse's hooves, bringing the farmer home from the pub – the horse knew the way.

My childhood home at Earls Croome was a thatched 17th century farmhouse. The rooms were large, brick-floored below and uneven oak beams above. We were always losing pens, collar-studs and other small objects in the gaps between the boards. What a hoard will come to light one day! Lighting was by oil lamp, cooking on an oil range and water from an outside well (which terrified me) or by a pump. The house was very cold in winter. Housework took so much longer; half an hour to do the lamps, the same for bed-making. It was hard work shaking and pummelling feather beds. Beds were turned down at night; no one does that these days.

Washing day began at crack of dawn with the lighting of the copper (filled the night before). All the whites got washed first. Having been given a good rub with yellow soap, the sheets, pillowcases and tablecloths were all put in the copper to boil. When "cooked" they were fished out and put to drain over a little ladder placed across the copper. They were put through the wringer and then from one bath of cold water to a second bath where the water had been blued with Reckitt's Blue (a supposed relief for a wasp sting, incidentally). Tablecloths and pillowcases were starched. While the whites were flapping on the line, the soapy water wrung from them was used to wash the coloureds. Finally, socks, woollies and men's trousers found their way onto the line. If one managed to wash, dry and iron on the same day (a very rare occurrence) it was called a gypsy's washing day.

The big coal range had to be lit each morning. The youngest child, as soon as he or she was felt to be safe with a wood-chopper, was given the job of getting the sticks for the morning. We had plenty of wood which had to be chopped into sensible lengths and then put into the oven to dry thoroughly – very unhygienic. The oven was good for cooking rice puddings and overnight porridge.'

WASHDAY MEMORIES

'Washing the family's clothes and bedlinen was a major feat of endurance for most village housewives at Wolverley before, during and immediately after the Second World War.

From as early in the day as 6 am, when the copper was lit, everyone engaged in the cleaning process worked almost non-stop, until all items had been washed, mangled, dried and folded. If the day's weather had been favourable for drying, then it was possible that the ironing could be completed before nightfall.

Electric irons, washing machines and dryers were virtually non-existent at this time. The main appliances used were the copper, which provided all the hot water required in the operation, the dolly or puncher, used for punching the items to loosen grime, a mangle to wring out any superfluous water and a flat iron to smooth out any creases and press the dampened articles.

On the previous night, usually Sunday as Monday was the generally accepted washday of the week, exceptionally dirty garments were rubbed with a block of hard soap and put to soak. The most common soap powders used in the washing and boiling were either Rinso or Oxydol or Persil, while woollens and delicate fabrics were washed in Lux soap flakes.

Whites were invariably boiled and had to be rinsed in blued water; coloureds being rinsed in clear water. Both coloured and white cottons and linens were then starched before mangling and hanging out to dry.

The flat iron was heated by fitting it into a rack slipped onto the front bars of the kitchen grate. Care had to be taken that the fire glowed and was not smoking or the iron would become blackened and mark the cleaned materials, thus defeating the whole object of the washday procedure.'

FOOD AND DRINK

Our diet may have been more restricted in the past, but we ate well on home-made and home-produced food and drink. Most people kept chickens and a pig, and many remember home-made cider with nostalgia – though that was not the only potent drink to be found in our cottages!

TIGHT LITTLE COMMUNITIES

'During the 1940s and 1950s villages were tight little communities which were fairly self-sufficient. Long before the impersonal supermarket, most of what the housewife needed was brought to her doorstep. In North Littleton there were two bakehouses for fresh daily bread, milk was brought from the farm in a churn and ladled into jugs at the door. Twice weekly butchers made the rounds and the grocer called on Monday to take orders and delivered everything on Thursday. Newspapers, magazines and comics were delivered as regular as clockwork. The village had its own carpenter, painter and decorator, electrician and post office, which sold everything from a stamp to refilling accumulators for the radio. There was even an undertaker and a florist. Once a fortnight, a large van (Ward's of Evesham) came clattering round carrying ironmongery of every description; it dangled, it swung from every nook and cranny of this open-sided van, and there was always a smell of vinegar from the keg he carried and sold on draught. The fish and chips van was eagerly awaited every Friday afternoon.

There were two public houses in the village of which the landlord of one made his own cider.

Many other things were around just for the taking – watercress grew in abundance in the brook, mushrooms in the fields as big as dinner plates, wild horseradish, crab apples for jelly, blackberries, hazel nuts, and wine was made from cowslips, elderflowers and elderberry as well as parsnips, plums and various other things, and very potent stuff it was too!

Rationing was in force during the 1940s but there was always plenty of meat from the land, pheasant, partridge, rabbit and other game, and lots of countrymen had a gun licence. There was also the pig which many kept in the back garden to fatten and slaughter each year. From this animal nothing was wasted. Sides and hams were cured and hung for use throughout the year, faggots, lard with rosemary, dripping and brawn were all produced, the chitterlings, tail, ears and feet all made tasty eating and the scratchings, the bits left over after lard making, were everyone's favourite snack.

Fresh vegetables? Well, this was an intensive market gardening area so there was no shortage of these, the only difference from today being there was a season for all things and the taste was so mouthwateringly different from the bland "all year round" stuff in supermarkets today. Taste has been forfeited in the pursuit of the perfect shaped vegetable. Sweets were rationed too, but children improvised when Mum's toffee ran out with a stick of rhubarb dipped in sugar, as good as a sherbet dab any day, and corn would be chewed for ages like chewing gum.

Last but not least the fruit – oh, the fruit, tons and tons of it right through summer. Strawberries, raspberries, gooseberries and currants all had to be "got off" before the early plums were ready.

The road between Cleeve Prior and Littleton was a mass of billowing white blossom in spring, through sadly all the trees are gone now, then in summer the grounds around and about were filled with laughter and sometimes frayed tempers as families worked from dawn till dusk, stopping only for picnic lunches, reaping the harvest of fruit. The air was filled with the scent of it as each day piles and piles of chip baskets sat on roadside verges awaiting the haulage lorries which would transport them to the markets in Birmingham and Coventry. This ritual went on all through summer into early September until the last plum was picked.'

FAVOURITE FOOD

'At Bentley House there was an old bake oven in the wall of the brewhouse. Mum cooked her raised pork pies in it. It was quite a performance to get it hot. First you lit a bundle of twigs placed in the oven. When you thought the oven was hot enough, you brushed out the ash and put the pies in, and they cooked in a slow heat.

Mum had a paraffin stove she cooked on. It had two burners and an oven that fitted over them. She made lovely cakes on it and she used it for years. She thought paraffin was cheaper to use.

We had porridge oats for breakfast, and as a special treat on Sundays we had bacon and a large tin of tomatoes.

The favourite meal was stew and we had spotted dick or jam roly-poly for pudding or bread and jam or bread and butter. Never butter and jam together. We had chickens and sometimes an old one for a Sunday dinner. Most of the time we had rabbit stew. We would catch them Saturday afternoon. The skins were sold to the rag and bone man. Dad fattened two pigs, one paid for the other. We shared it with other members of the family. Mum made lovely faggots. The ham was hung up to be cured. The pig's bladder would be blown up so we could have a kick-about with it. Dad looked after the large garden. We had fruit trees as well. Mum said she didn't have to buy vegetables at any time of the year.'

IN THE FIELDS

'When the men of Hanley Castle ate fat bacon and bread in the fields, they always ate an onion to break down the fat. A shallot was often eaten with bread and cheese.'

'I took my father his breakfast at a farm before I went to school. This consisted of a cottage loaf, cut in half, with the middle scooped out and filled with fried eggs and bacon.'

AIRY KEEPING

'Our homes at Cutnall Green were draughty in the winter, but airy in the summer. We had no fridges but a marble slab in the pantry kept things cool, and this room on the east side of the house had perforated zinc in the window for a free flow of air. Bread was kept in a bread bin, and meat, cheese, butter and lard in a perforated metal box to keep the flies away.'

A GREAT HELP

'Every village had a grocer and baker; also a "rep" would come from some of the bigger stores and take orders for groceries which were delivered by van. We always kept a pig so there was plenty of bacon to eat, and lard to cook with was rendered down from the "leaf" which was the fat inside the pig. We also kept fowls so we had our own eggs.

My father had a very big garden at Clifton upon Teme and he grew all our vegetables. We had fruit trees – plums, damsons, apples and one pear tree. We also had raspberries, gooseberries, redcurrants and blackcurrants and this was all a great help, especially during the Great War (1914-1918) when food was scarce and several of us children were at school. On the front of the house, which faced south, we had an apricot tree. Dad trained it against the wall with short strips of material nailed to the mortar. There was beautiful blossom at flowering time and then lovely big fruit. Mum made delicious jam with them; we children had to crack the stones for the kernels which were put in with the fruit, making it very tasty.'

BUTTER TO MARKET

'My parents had a stall in Worcester Butter Market where they sold dressed poultry, rabbits, eggs and that delicious home-made, fresh butter. Market day was Saturday so Thursday was butter-making day.

The cream, separated from the week's milk and stored in the cool dairy, was put into a large end-over-end churn and the butter making began. Sometimes it took hours to churn the cream into butter, especially in hot weather. Mother knew by the sound when it had "turned" and the butter was quickly taken out and put on the cold slabs. It was patted into shape, weighed into exact half pounds, stamped with our butter mark and wrapped in greaseproof paper. On Saturday morning it was put into big market baskets and taken to market in the spring trap drawn by our spirited mare Topsy. The size of our weekly grocery parcel depended on the good or poor sale of the produce!'

KEEPING ANIMALS

'As a result of rationing in the 1940s, most people living in the country tried to eke out food by keeping a few hens and cultivating an allotment.

Some people at Hadzor and Oddingley even ran to keeping a pig in their back garden. The pig was quite an accommodating animal and seemed to thrive better in makeshift premises than in palatial piggeries. Give them a good roof over their heads and a warm bed to lie on and they responded accordingly. In fact some people got quite attached to their pigs and dreaded the time when the pig-killer had to be called in. But what a bonus when the salting was done and the hams were hung up for drying.

It was good to see a few Rhode Island Red hens scratching about the yards and they really didn't cost a lot to feed with a few handfuls of wheat thrown out twice a day.

When there was a glut of eggs they were put down in waterglass for the time when the hens moulted and stopped laying, and, of course, the cockerels were fattened up and eaten. In the spring the hens went broody and it was quite possible to sit them and get a few chicks.

Some people used to keep geese, but they needed more grass than hens, and plenty of water – a farmyard pool was just the job and you'd see geese and ducks swimming about and getting along together quite well. A goose will lay and start sitting in February and the goslings will come in 28 days. A goose was a great favourite for Michaelmas or Christmas and was a good return in cheap meat produced from natural foods and scraps which would otherwise be wasted.

If you liked more eggs you kept a few ducks – Khaki Campbell would lay even more eggs than the best hens. The eggs weren't so popular, though, as they were thought to taste strong.

Then, of course, in growing your own food you had to have a large garden or an allotment. You could have three rotations of fresh vegetables during the year, say, potatoes, cabbages, carrots, beetroot, turnips, onions, leeks, peas, lettuce and swedes.

Some very brave people kept bees. It was great if they lived near an orchard and farmers would be pleased to let you site your beehive near his field of beans or in his orchard. It was most exciting when the bees swarmed in trees and the beekeeper came dressed up in his big hat and veil. It was a specialised job preparing the honey but you'd buy the honeycombs, which were delicious.'

'People at Great Comberton often kept two pigs, one for themselves through the year and one to give away to local traders, with whom they had run up bills. This was their way of paying off their debts.'

KILLING THE PIG

'My Grandma at Upton upon Severn had a long, rambling garden where she kept a few hens and one pig. Once a year the butcher was alerted and duly arrived with two men. As a child of five or six, I was forbidden to go into the garden on this day, but, being curious, I crept in and hid behind some bushes, watching in horrified fascination the ceremony of killing the pig.

Squealing and kicking, the poor pig was seized and tied to a wooden bench, having been stunned (hopefully killed) by a blow on the head. Then a knife was stuck into his side and the blood drained into a bucket. Next, all his bristles were burnt off and he was brushed with a bass broom. Buckets of boiling water were poured over him and he was thoroughly scrubbed with a scrubbing brush. He was then taken away by the butcher to be cut up.

For the next week everyone in the family was kept busy. Every single part of the pig was utilised. Joints of pork were laid in salt, sides of bacon smoked and hung on hooks in the kitchen, brawn was made from the pig's head, and there were trotters, liver, kidneys, tongue, chitterlings, black pudding (using the blood), faggots, scratchings and a huge enamel bowl of lard obtained, spiked with sprigs of rosemary.

I was made to eat the brains on toast, which I hated, as "it was good for me". One pig could feed a family for a whole year.'

'We kept two pigs in the 1940s at Rubery, one for ourselves and one for the Ministry of Food, who then allowed a ration of meal for the animals. To supplement this, my husband used to take a bag to work at what was then the Austin Motor Company, and collect the leftovers from the men's lunch snacks. This was then boiled in my big jam kettle and the meal added. When the pig was killed and butchered, a small joint would be handed on to our near neighbours and perhaps a gift of vegetables from their garden would be given in return. Because times were hard and shortages the order of the day, we shared and helped one another.'

'A local man at Hill was always on call to kill pigs, when children would gather to watch the gruesome ceremony. Often the meat was shared with neighbours and there would be high living for a while.'

STRONG LIQUOR

'I remember strong beer being brewed at Eckington, as well as dandelion wine and hyssop tea. There is one tale of a lady from Chipping Campden who made peashell wine. One year she gave the local postman his usual drink on Christmas Eve when he delivered the post, but unknown to her it must have been a bottle which had been in the cupboard from the previous year and was very strong. He said goodbye, got on his bike and began his journey home. On the way he fell off the bike into a ditch, where his relatives found him, and he didn't wake up until Boxing Day.'

'Home brewing of wine was common and seasonal as cowslips, dandelions, elderflowers and vegetables ripened. On one memorable occasion at Kempsey, parsnip wine was offered to the choirboys when carol singing, instead of lemonade. The next house to receive this festive group had cause to complain to the vicar of unusually boisterous behaviour and saucy wording of the carols.'

PLUM-JERKUM

'My grandfather, a blacksmith, had a barrel which must have been eight feet high, and this was used for cider and for "plum-jerkum". For this, all the old windfalls – plums, apples and pears – were put into the open cask and left for days, the scum being skimmed off as it rose to the surface. It smelled dreadful. Eventually, the lovely soft, moist, sweet brown sugar was added and the concoction began to ferment. Sometimes, to hasten the procedure, my mother would put the red hot poker into the barrel's bunghole to warm the liquid up. Once she dropped the poker in the barrel and there it had to stay until the barrel was emptied.'

OUR OWN CIDER MILL

'My family (the Ingles family of Broadway) had our own cider mill at the Old Rickyard, Cheltenham Road, Broadway. Every autumn my father and grandfather were up to their necks in fruit, making cider for all around the area. I still have my father's account books, containing names of local farmers, market gardeners, etc, how many gallons they had made and how much they had to pay. In the 1930s the price was one penny per gallon for making it, then in the 1940s it went up to twopence. I well remember writing out Dad's bills for him, also delivering them on my bike, but all too often it was a long time before he got his money. I remember once, when the money was not forthcoming after some considerable time, Dad called at the house of the person in question. He pleaded poverty and a bad season with no money coming in, and so Dad, noticing a litter of puppies out in the backyard, took one of those instead of his cider-making money. When he came in our back kitchen door he said, "Here! Look what I've got in my pocket for you", and he took out this tiny little black scrap of a puppy. We called him Tinker.

The cider was made in the old traditional way, the fruit being pulped through a "scratter" which was activated by a very noisy and smelly old engine in the engine-shed; it sounded like an old train chugging along! The pulped fruit was then taken over to the press in buckets and laid on to cloths placed on the base of the press, the cloths were then folded at the corners envelope-wise, another one placed on top, spread with pulp, folded, and so on, until there was quite a large pile of cloths. A large flat board was placed on the top of the pile and then the handle was turned at the side of the press to bring down the large wooden top which was called the boss. Attached to this was a pole which was pushed forward by about three men and then pulled back on a ratchet kind of mechanism. This brought the press lower and lower and pressed the juice out from the pulped fruit, and it came flowing through the cloths and down into the trough round the bottom of the press and from there into a large half barrel. Then it was taken in buckets to fill very large barrels in the cider storeshed, or else into the customers' own barrels

Pressing the juice from the pulped fruit at the Ingles' cider mill, Broadway in the 1940s.

which they had brought with them on their horse and dray. It was all horses and drays in the 1920s and 1930s for transporting the bags of cider fruit to the mill and also for taking fruit and vegetables to the market.

After the juice had been extracted the press was raised and the cloths were emptied of the dry pulp onto a big heap up the field. This dry pulp was often spread on the land or sometimes fed to stock, here much care was needed that it was eaten straight away, as once it had started to ferment, which it would do after a few days, it quite often had a "staggering" effect on the chickens and pigs. There was an old enamel cup hanging on a nail at the side of the press, where the juice came down into the barrel, and from which we used to help ourselves to the fresh apple and pear juice. (The very thought of it is making my mouth water as I write this!) Dad always had a small barrel at home which he "doctored up" (to use his own words). To this he added sugar, sultanas, root ginger and all sorts of items. Some of the people hereabouts, my husband's grandfather was one, used to put in pieces of beef or bacon, also sometimes wheat or barley. This barrel was the one for special occasions and, believe me, it was *very* potent!'

A PECK OF DIRT

'I remember the horse and cart going round to collect the apples from the orchards at Queenhill. There were a lot more orchards then, of course. Mr Dowdeswell put a cider mill in the village for the locals to make their own cider. It was all pretty primitive. A lot of the old vats were open at the top, so things were bound to fall into them. We used to pick up the apples in the orchards, where the cows were, so they had cow muck and mud on them, and they went along with all the maggots and things in them. That's what made people so resilient. I remember going to Kempsey with my sister. We took an old pram and picked up the windfalls, beautiful apples – russets and all the old apples you can't get now – and we filled the pram with them and took them home. They were from fields with cows and were mucky. You eat a peck of dirt before you die.'

SHOPPING AND CALLERS TO THE DOOR

We shopped locally, and most villages had several shops which not only supplied our needs but were part of the community – 'characters' and all! Fresh food was brought to our door by tradesmen who became almost part of the family.

ONCE A WEEK

'As we lived four miles from Worcester, shopping was done only once a week. My Mum caught the bus (fivepence return) and, with only £2 to spend, she called at a shop in the Shambles and bought sugar in a blue bag, and flour, lard and butter patted with a pattern of roses on it. The bundle of groceries was wrapped in brown paper and tied with string, and a boy on a bicycle then took the parcel to the bus office to await my Mum. She had meanwhile bought a piece of beef for about three shillings and sixpence and also a pound of boiled sweets, which lasted me and my five brothers and sisters all the week, one for school and one for bedtime.'

THREE SHOPS

'Women had concertina purses with many pockets. One was for the rent, one for coal and one for bread, and the amount left, if any, governed one's shopping.

Hanley Swan had three food shops, two of them shacks. One in Gilberts End could supply almost anything during the war. The lady there wore three hats if it was cold and found the goods by candlelight. This was a good home for mice! The shop was well visited however. The butcher was at the end of the Swan Inn. I remember queuing for a packet of Smith's crisps every Friday at the Ewe and Lamb pub, for they were in short supply.'

SOLD FROM THE COTTAGE

'My parents lived in a cottage in Shaw Lane, Stoke Prior. My mother sold sweets, cigarettes and tobacco from the cottage, using the pantry as the shop. Sweets were stored in large glass jars weighed out on brass scales, put in a little paper bag and the top was twisted to close. The cigarettes included Woodbines and Park Drive. Tobacco was cut off a large piece, weighed and then the customer put it in a tin which he kept in his pocket. When required he would cut off a piece with his pocket knife, rub it between his hands until the right texture was achieved, then fill his pipe. This tobacco was called Black Jack.'

FORTUNATE VILLAGE

'Blakedown was fortunate as we had five shops and the post office, which also sold sweets, cigarettes and groceries. The butcher killed his beasts on the premises and you never heard a sound, except occasionally the bang of the humane killer. We had a newsagent's which sold sweets and cigarettes, a real grocer, another tiny mixed store in the front room of one of the cottages in Belbroughton Road, and a haberdashery whose owner was very scatterbrained and frequently left the shop to go on some errand, when we could go in and help ourselves, leaving the money on the counter! We also had a hairdresser.

Thursday was, and is, market day in Kidderminster and a great many people went by bus to shop. The bus service was good, regular, punctual and cheap. Many of the larger houses had a weekly grocery order with some larger town shops – Masons in Kidderminster for instance, or even shops in Birmingham. Shufflebottom's representative came to me at the Reddings once a week to take the order and advise about new lines, making suggestions to the housewife or the cook. Then the next day, the order would be delivered. Davenports and Cantrell and Cockrane provided bottled beer and lemonade from delivery lorries to your door once a week, although there were two pubs in the village and five altogether in the parish.'

'Virtually everything that you eat or drink could be bought in a wide range of shops in Hagley village. There were three butchers, one of whom still killed on the premises. Miss Clara Cutler ran a greengrocer's shop, her brother Ben had a garage next door and also ran the Station Inn.

There were several ladies' dress shops but Mrs Myra Crumpton ran the most diverse establishment including outfitters, drapers, hairdressers and a lending library.

The area between Chapel Street and Church Street not only housed the garage and a greengrocer's, but also the confectioner's run by the Misses Aston and Woolf, the post office for West Hagley managed by the Misses Gale, and Webbs the bakers. On the opposite side of the road was Greenwoods the chemist, supervised by Miss Raike, Moyles the grocer's and another confectioner's run by Mrs Freeman.

Alfred Strickley ran another grocer's in Station Road where cheese could be tasted before ordering, bacon was sliced to your liking and coffee was ground from your choice of beans and somehow was parcelled up with a series of deft movements from a single sheet of thick paper and no sellotape.

Other shops included Lee's the ironmonger, Bridges the tobacconist, Percy Carter the cobbler, Cartridges the fishmonger and Wyse's for boots and shoes.

In addition to the shops both Collins and Darby's bread was delivered, originally by horse-drawn vans, but by 1940 these had changed to motor vans.

Milk was delivered daily direct from several farms by horse-drawn floats, the milk being ladled from large cans into jugs and we all survived the hygiene, or the lack of it.'

ON A SPREE

'There were two village shops in Kington in the 1920s, one attached to the Red Hart public house and the other on the opposite side of the road. When people wanted to go on a spending spree they went into Worcester, travelling either by carrier's cart or cycling to Red Hill on the edge of the city and catching a bus into the centre. Some of their hard earned cash came from picking blackberries for one farthing a pound, and this was put towards buying the next winter's coat. The Midland Red bus service came to the village in 1935, which made life much easier.'

TROUSERS DOWN!

'In 1918, in Ombersley, there were three blacksmiths, a cooper,a shoemaker, an undertaker, a butcher and several grocer's, bakeries and clothing shops. Next door to the churchyard was a clothing shop known as "Tommy Rotten Cotton's", famous for his notice in the window which read: "Come early in the morning – trousers are coming down".'

THRIVING SHOPS

'In 1938, Mealcheapen Street, in the centre of Worcester, was full of thriving shops. Many families lived over their shop and we had three storeys above ours, the Excelsior Meat Co, next door to the Home and Colonial Stores. No one lived over the Home and Colonial as their rooms were used for storage. We had extensive premises at the back up to St Martin's churchyard. Here my father produced hand-raised pork pies and faggots (I can smell them now!), sausages, brawn and polonies. Every night my father would scrub down the wooden chopping blocks and sweep up all the sawdust from the floor, and each morning fresh sawdust would be put down to stop people slipping.

Only two shops remain exactly as they were: Durrants, who sell guns, fishing tackle and knives – a sportsman's shop; and the sweet shop that belonged to Mrs Lee, an ample white-haired lady who always wore an apron. There were other butchers, namely Marsh and Baxter, Melias and Price Bros, all on the opposite side to us. There were three public houses: the Shades, the Reindeer and the Corn Exchange (the only one left today). At Fletcher's the greengrocer, I was often given an apple, and at Keeys the grocer, and Home and Colonial, broken biscuits and nibbles of cheese.'

SHOPPING INTO THE 1920s

'At the grocer's in the local town there were counters on each side of the shop and chairs at intervals for the customers to sit on. On the grocery side just below the level of the counter there was a row of glass-topped biscuit tins and the biscuits were weighed out to suit your requirements.

I went with my mother and we sat on chairs while the assistant, usually a man in a white coat, wrote down our order. We took away nothing, or paid, as the order was brought round by the errand boys and the account sent at the end of the month.

At that counter tea, sugar, coffee and rice were all weighed out as you bought them: the sugar was put in blue paper and wrapped round with string. The coffee was ground for you in a large coffee grinder, and on the bacon counter on the other side bacon was sliced in the machine and butter was slapped and patted with butter pats into pounds and half-pounds.

If you paid cash, the money was put into a little container, plus the bill, and with a "ping" it shot along an overhead wire to the cash desk. A few minutes later the container arrived back with your change.

When I went with my mother to a department store we were met at the door by a shop-walker – a rather elderly gentleman, in a frock-coat and black striped trousers – who asked us which department we required. He then ushered us there, pulled forward two chairs and called for the assistants.

My mother wanted new gloves. A purple velvet cushion was produced on which she laid her hands, which were measured. From under layers of tissue paper kid gloves were produced: the assistant proceeded to stretch them with wooden glove stretchers and they were duly tried on. After this transaction was completed we were ushered by the shop-walker to the children's department. There I was measured. We looked at party frocks which would be suitable for me and my younger sister, also at muslin hats which we wore on Sundays. Nothing was tried on but a selection was put in a large box, covered in shiny American cloth and strapped down. These were to be sent "on appro" and were delivered the next day, when they were duly tried on in the peace of our own home. Some were selected and the rest returned when the horse-drawn van arrived to fetch them a few days later.

In one street there was a very good baker's shop. The smell of newly baked bread was delicious. They delivered their bread as soon as it was baked and standing outside the shop was the horse and van. This was completely open in the front where the driver sat and the rest had shelves all the way round; there was a large basket in which the loaves were put to deliver.

The procedure was that someone in the bakery threw a loaf to someone in the shop who then threw it up to the driver, who stacked it away. Cottage loaves, batch, tin, brown or white all went hurtling through the air and woe betide anyone who happened to be walking by when a loaf came flying out of the shop. None, of course, was either wrapped or sliced and no one questioned the cleanliness of the thrower's hands.

Everyone thought the bread was delicious, even though it had been driven around the town with rain, snow or dust blown into the open front.

Two large jars about three feet high with stoppers nearly a foot in length, one red and one blue, stood in nearly every chemist's shop window. On the counter in the shop was a little gas flame. Every purchase was meticulously wrapped in white paper, tied with fine pink string and sealed with sealing wax which was melted in the gas flame.

There was a small, rather dark, sweet shop we used to visit on our way home from school. The man who owned it had a squint and we very unkindly used to call him "Evil Eye". The shop was an Aladdin's cave of sweets. There were rows of jars containing acid drops, pear drops, raspberry drops, satin cushions, jelly babies, dolly mixtures and golden sticks of barley sugar and barley sugar fish, two a penny, and all the sweets a penny per ounce. On the counter were chocolate bird's nests for twopence containing little white marzipan eggs, sherbet, liquorice and little bars of chocolate for a penny. "Evil Eye" would plunge his rather grubby hand into the jars to weigh out the sweets, licking his fingers afterwards. Unhygienic as it was we never seemed to suffer any harm.

The milkman came twice a day. He had a wooden yoke on his shoulders and a pail hanging from each side. He dipped his pint or half pint measure into the pail and poured it into your jug, which was usually covered with a net with beads round it.'

CALLERS TO THE DOOR

'At Stoke Prior, milk was delivered daily from a local farm, by pony and float. The milk was measured straight from the churn into a milk can. Groceries were ordered in the shop by Mother on market day and were delivered wrapped in brown paper on Saturday night. The butcher also called on Saturday night.'

'Before the war the milkman at Broadway delivered in a churn on a horse-drawn float. The milkman would fill his bucket and then ladle it into your jug at the door. He had two measures, a pint and half pint. These would hang inside the bucket and a lid came down over the top. There was another milkman who came round with an afternoon delivery, and he carried two pails on a wooden shoulder yoke.'

The baker's delivery van from Bulfords Stores in 1938, still horse-drawn.

'There was a local baker at Wichenford during the First World War, otherwise food shops were seven miles away in Worcester. A grocer's traveller called once a fortnight for an order and the goods were delivered the following week. Large bars of salt were brought round occasionally on open drays. Milk was delivered by a farmer's son on his way to school. Gypsies called with their home-made pegs and pedlars with a variety of haberdashery and bootlaces. A man with a hurdy-gurdy and small monkey perched on top came from time to time. This caused excitement!'

'At Eckington we had men come round for rags and bones, and for rabbit skins. They gave goldfish for rags. The "elver man" came when elvers were caught down below Tewkesbury, at Apperley, on the Severn. Jimmy Watton, the scrap iron man, collected the unwanted iron and pots and pans from my father's heap of rejects (my father was the village blacksmith), and left us big blocks of rock salt for salting down the pig meat in November and December. With ice cream, Sabbatina's came from Cheltenham in a pony and cart, and the Eldorado and Stop Me and Buy One men also came, both on bicycles.'

'A very welcome caller at Norton and Lenchwick was the fortnightly

"Onwards" silver coloured van, bringing soap powders, toilet rolls, candles, kitchen and bathroom necessities, but most important of all, paraffin.'

AT THE BACK DOOR

'This was the 1930s method of "convenience shopping" with the motto "Families Waited on Daily" displayed outside most shops in Worcester. We were indeed waited on, at the back door, by various errand boys, with bicycles and notebooks for the housewife to write her order; more legible than that of the boy?

So, at 7 am, came the milkman by horse and cart, parked outside our gate – at least, unless the horse got fed up with a long wait and simply "walked on", chased by the milkman. Then came Emily, our daily help, full of gossip from town, mainly disasters or tragedies of course.

By 8.30 am the butcher's errand boy had arrived, to take an order and to return with the dinner for us, and for several other customers locally, by 9.30 am. Next, the baker's errand boy, with warm loaves, buns and a treacle tart or two, thus publicising our family dinner menu from the back door!

Ah, here comes the postman on the first of his *three* calls each day, but not always on time "because the trains were late". (Rather often, we thought.) The newspaper boy also had his problems with "late trains". Ha!

Now who is next? Oh! here is the laundryman, thus completing the daily business, and all at the back door by mid-morning. So now household work began – and so did some shouting and banging at the garden back gate. Of course, it's the dustmen – dogs barking, dustbins rattling and general disturbance of the neighbourhood. It was said that four men were needed on each journey to manage the lorry, the rubbish and, often, an angry householder or a lost dustbin.'

FROM THE CRADLE TO THE GRAVE

Far more likely in the past to be born, to suffer our illnesses and to die in our own homes, we also placed great reliance on home cures and remedies. In those pre Health Service days the doctor and nurse had to be paid for. Many people remember the terrible childhood diseases – scarlet fever, diphtheria, polio etc – which affected every town and village, and the equally terrible days in the isolation hospitals, where no allowance was made for childish fears.

HOME CURES

'When we had a cold coming on, Mum would cut out a brown paper waistcoat, cover it with goose grease and wrap us in it, give us a spoon of hen fat and send us to bed.

A large spoonful of brimstone and treacle was used for pimples, but you didn't light a match for an hour after you had it.'

'For bad colds, cider, brown sugar and ginger were put into a mug and a hot poker thrust in. When really hot, the "cure" was taken.'

'When we were children and had a cough, my mother would melt butter and sugar in a cup on top of the range. She used to say, "Drink it up and you'll find a butter drop at the bottom." We didn't need any encouragement because we loved it.

I suffered from nettle rash (urticaria) and my mother would boil nettles in water which I had to drink. It was disgusting.

The local teacher made a medicine for whooping cough. She steeped eggs in vinegar for several days until the shells dissolved. Then it was beaten up and bottled, and was very popular.'

'Boiled young stinging nettles for general internal and tummy problems. Warm camphorated oil for rubbing on chest and back when suffering a nasty cold and cough. For warts, wash the affected area with the dirty, smelly water kept by the side of the bellows in the blacksmith's forge, in which he had plunged his red hot rods of iron. For bee stings use the "blue bag", for wasp stings use vinegar.'

A real village wedding at Eckington in the 1940s. Weddings were great social occasions for the whole community.

'For chilblains, put your foot in the full "jerry", or rub snow over your feet, Chilblains were such a problem then.'

BEFORE THE NHS

'At the beginning of the century home treatment for the sick was provided by voluntary medical insurance with various Friendly Societies. This was made compulsory in 1911 by the first National Insurance Act instigated by Lloyd George. Under this Act, basic services were guaranteed to the insured working-man, but the system excluded his family. In some cases a large firm would provide their own doctor and treat the employee, his wife and children. Many local government authorities provided welfare centres, medical services and ambulances, but none was compelled to.

Services outside the town were poor. It cost about two shillings to visit the doctor and three shillings and sixpence if he came to see you. This doesn't sound much but a farm worker's wage was only 30 shillings a week. Doctors were often not paid, some didn't bother to send out bills.

The village where I lived, Cookley, had no resident doctor. On

Tuesday and Thursday evenings and on Saturday morning a doctor arrived from Kinver for two hours each time.

He would set up shop in a cottage in the centre of the village where the tenant would retire to the nether regions or upstairs. The parlour was his consulting room. The adjoining room was the waiting room. A variety of seats were placed all round the edge, ending in an ottoman box immediately outside his door. The first person to arrive sat on the box (for years that's where I thought the expression came from !). As they came in the patients occupied the succeeding chairs. When anyone went into the surgery everyone moved up until it was their turn to go onto the box!

Because it was first come, first served, everyone came very early. This only meant a longer wait, but whatever time you went, Leah was always there. She would move happily round the room, but when it was her turn to go in she would say, graciously, "Take my turn, dear, I'm in no hurry." She never did go in, she just started at the beginning again. It was her way of keeping up with the gossip and finding out what was wrong with everyone.

Now, you may wonder what happened if you were ill and it wasn't Tuesday or Thursday evening, or Saturday morning. The only phone was in the post office. If it was closed, the line was cut off, so to speak. Practically no one had a car, there was no bus service between Cookley and Kinver and nobody would fancy the long dark walk, especially if they were feeling rotten.

The answer was to send for the district nurse. She was a sort of "Sarah Gamp" figure. She advised on all things medical, dressed wounds, delivered babies and laid out the departed. She was undoubtedly the most valued member of the community. She wore a uniform dress covered by a navy gaberdine raincoat and a hat like an ATS cap, but without a peak. She rode a sit-up-and-beg bicycle with dress guards on the rear wheel and had a black gladstone bag strapped on the carrier. Any case which she considered beyond her capabilities was sent to Kidderminster infirmary. As she was a proud woman she rarely admitted defeat until you were almost at death's door. Sometimes all the infirmary could do was push you through it. Whenever it was known that the ambulance had been sent for, all the villagers turned out to see you off, because they never expected to see you again.'

'At Hanley Castle some villagers paid a weekly contribution towards treatment by the doctor, hospital nursing and medicine. An ambulance cost a shilling a mile. One lady had to pay 30 shillings for one trip to Worcester.'

'The doctor at Eckington visited twice a week and medicine cost three shillings and sixpence a bottle, with a further twopence if it had to be delivered by the postman. The local postman would shout, "Come and get your jollop!" A district nurse, Nurse Corbett, attended to medical problems for two shillings and sixpence a year.

The Lee–Midland Benefit Society ensured a very small payment if the member was ill and unable to work, but you had to stay at home and keep to the rules or the payment was forfeited.'

'Hospital treatment was available for most people only because hard work by caring people raised enough money to finance hospitals. In Norton a local lady collected monthly contributions from any household willing to pay into a scheme, and another called regularly to collect cash for the linen fund – all given freely. Annual fundraising events such as carnivals provided more cash. Even a stay in the ophthalmic hospital in Worcester for a difficult and sight-saving operation was possible because that hospital was partly financed by local business people. Patients just paid what they could afford.'

'Bentley and Tardebigge was a large area for Nurse Breen to cover, so a a fund was set up and whist drives etc held, and in the end an Austin Seven was bought for her.

The local doctor was Dr Daws from Feckenham, "Dr Peter" as he was called. He was a big hunting man and he would often visit his patients on the way to a meet, wearing his hunting pink.'

THE DISTRICT NURSE

'In recalling times past it is tempting to paint a rosy picture where everyone was happy, with long sunny summers, and winters with lamplit evenings with our parents, playing simple games, reading, doing jigsaws, enjoying roast potatoes put in the oven for our suppers.

There was great hardship and poverty after the Great War; through the 1920s and 1930s much unemployment, scrimping and saving to "make ends meet", wearing cast offs, thick black stockings, everything made to last. Old people had a great fear of becoming ill and being sent to the workhouse – a grim place, indeed, compared to the retirement homes of today. My mother (who had trained as a nurse) was the village midwife at Wichenford and therefore held in some esteem. No NHS in those days, no free doctor – people were loathe to send for the doctor, the fee being seven shillings and sixpence.

I remember the pregnant ladies coming to book their confinements with my mother (large families then); few went to hospital for births. Usually the husbands came for my mother, nearly always at night, when the baby was due. My brother and I had to make sure her cycle was OK – tyres pumped up etc – and off she would go, bag strapped to the back, usually on long country journeys, one of us going with her to be sent on messages (no phones in those days – only for the better off!).'

A HOSPITAL NO LONGER NEEDED

'The Forelands Hospital at Rock Hill, Bromsgrove, or "The Forelands" as it was affectionately known locally, was acquired in 1920 by the Royal Orthopaedic Hospital, Birmingham (then known as the Royal Cripples Hospital). The *Birmingham Mail* raised £15,000 towards its purchase. It was to form an extension to the Birmingham hospital in its care and treatment of children suffering mainly from bone tuberculosis and birth deformities. The numbers of beds increased over the years from 20 to 96.

Here the children were able to continue their treatment which, in those days, could be three years or longer. During their stay schooling was provided followed by opportunities to learn trades, eg, carpentry, shoe repairing, splint making, sewing and domestic work. Hobbies and other leisure activities were encouraged.

Boys from the Forelands Hospital who needed long term care for their disabilities.

Many of these children needed some form of sheltered occupation when they were able to commence work and quite a number were engaged to work at the Birmingham hospital.

Gradually, from 1950 onwards, the numbers of children requiring treatment decreased, due to improved housing, better pre- and post-natal care and the greatly improved facilities of the National Health Service. By 1967 so few children were being admitted that it was decided to admit adult patients in their place. The hospital finally closed in 1988 and is now a large housing estate.'

THE THREAT OF DISEASE

'When there was diphtheria in Evesham we were forbidden at school to drink Evesham water, so we had nothing to drink, unless we had a spare penny or two (which was doubtful) to buy a drink at the local tuck shops.

My little foster brother, aged twelve, died from polio, then a relatively unknown illness called "sleepy sickness", in September 1936. He was only ill for ten days, after swimming in the river Avon at Bredon, with his school. Two of his schoolmates also contracted this dreadful disease and one girl was paralysed until her death in the early 1950s. We were devastated when our little boy died.'

'When I caught diphtheria I was nursed at home in Bewdley instead of in the local isolation hospital. My grandmother volunteered to nurse me and we stayed in my bedroom for three weeks, neither of us leaving it the whole time. When the fever was over, a council employee came to fumigate the bedroom. Many of my little schoolmates died during this epidemic.'

SCARLET FEVER

'It was in the early autumn of 1940 that scarlet fever struck. I was seven years old, the youngest of four children, and was the third one to come out in the dreaded rash.

My eleven year old sister was hop picking but was unable to go on the second day as she was feeling rather poorly. It was discovered that she was "down with the fever"! She was whisked away to Newtown isolation hospital (Worcester) and had to miss the first few weeks of her first term at grammar school.

Next on the list was my nearly 18 year old brother and I followed a week or two later. My elder sister at 15 years old followed the rest of us, but had to go to Upton on Severn for her hospital isolation as everywhere else was full!

I was miserable and missing the others so much (suffering from early symptoms too, I expect) that my father brought me some toy soldiers I had seen in the newsagent's on the Ombersley road. They were to be my most valuable possessions for some time to come. It was very unusual at that time to have a present apart from Christmas and birthdays.

I can remember the ward at Newtown quite well. I was horrified to be put in a child's cot as beds were short. I remember our parents coming to visit, we waved from the windows while they had to stand several yards away with a lawn between them and the windows of the ward. It must have been dreadful for them to see us as we had never been away from home before. Our bedrooms at home were sealed up with sticky tape all round the doors and fumigated.'

'I was just five when I was taken into the fever hospital with what was later diagnosed as scarlet fever, although thought at first to be diphtheria after the death of a local child. I was jogged down the garden path on a stretcher, gazing up in fear at the sea of sympathetic faces as I was taken to the ambulance for the start of an unforgettable period of my life.

I was a child from a loving and sheltered upbringing and had never been away from home before. My parents visited regularly but were not allowed into the hospital, having to look at me and try to talk through the windows. I could not bear to look at them and see them go and hid my face and cried. How I must have upset *them*.

I was a misfit from the beginning, shyness setting me apart from more robust children, and intolerant staff. At the height of my fever I cried out in the night for a drink of water. No one came and I continued to cry out, "I want a drink of water". Eventually a very irate nurse appeared, in curlers and dressing gown, who berated me for disturbing her sleep.

Came the morning they wanted what I now know as a urine sample. No one had told me I must not relieve myself on rising – and I went. The anger of the nurse knew no bounds. I was left sitting on a potty, watching the fingers of the clock creep past ten before I could oblige.

Later, on being allowed in the grounds I followed five other girls and one boy. The latter found a bird's nest in the hedge and threw the eggs to the ground, where they smashed. A nurse coming upon the mess asked who had done it. With one accord they all turned and pointing to me, said "Her". In vain did I protest at the lie, and sobbing helplessly I was slapped across the face for punishment.

Even leaving was tinged with unhappiness. Thinking that my doll would comfort me, and despite protestations, my parents had sent in my "best" doll, and there she had to stay. I have no doubt that she was smashed and thrown out decades ago. As I look at my other precious china-headed dolls from childhood, I mourn her and am reminded of this dreadful period in an otherwise poor but happy life as a child.'

'I can still vividly recall suffering from scarlet fever at the age of four in 1943 when my family lived in Kidderminster.

After the family doctor had visited the house and diagnosed scarlet fever, I was aware of how serious this was as both my mother and father were in tears later that day when the ambulance arrived. With most of our neighbours solemnly looking on, I was stretchered into the ambulance and driven away, without my parents being allowed to accompany me, to Hayley Green isolation hospital near Halesowen.

I can remember nothing of the journey there, but can remember waking up in this strange place, all alone in the dark, and being very frightened as I was given awful liquorice medicine.

Most details of my treatment are hazy, but I can vividly remember, after having been warned severely by a nurse that my bed wouldn't be changed if I wet it again, lying there and deliberately doing so. Signs, I think, of a very disturbed four year old.

During the whole of the four weeks that I was a patient there, I can remember my parents only being able to visit me twice, and then they could only look at me from outside of the open window near my bed. My mother told me that the first time they visited she looked through the windows to try to find me and saw a poor little child with sores all round her mouth which were covered with gentian violet, and didn't immediately recognise her as me. Later, as my parents waited for the bus home outside the hospital grounds, all they could hear were my screams and sobs.

As I got better and was able to get around, I was allowed to choose slippers and a dressing gown from the stocks they had at the hospital, as anything of my own used there would have to be left at the hospital, because of the risk of spreading infection.

Eventually the joyful day came for my release and I was allowed to ride home in the front of the ambulance with the driver. When I finally got home, my parents were just being given instructions about not letting me kiss people or get too close for a while, when my two year old brother rushed in, flung his arms round me and squealed "Ga-ga's home!"'

'I contracted scarlet fever in 1946, aged 20, from the school where I had just begun teaching in Quinton. My family were immediately quarantined (a specially difficult time for my headmaster father).

I was despatched to Hayley Green hospital for a six weeks' stay. Visits were allowed about every ten to twelve days – only through an open window were we allowed to talk. My parents stood outside the window on a raised step and my bed was pushed within talking, but not touching, distance. Isolation was *very* strict. My room at home had a sheet soaked in disinfectant hung over the door, and fumigating tablets were burned in the room by the Public Health Authority. My mother forgot to remove my alarm clock (which had been to college with me) and it never went again. All my clothes and bedding had to be soaked in disinfectant, and pillows etc, after fumigation, left daily in the open air!

I was all this time in isolation. No one else in the family contracted the disease, fortunately, and, as far as I am aware, only two other cases from the area were reported. Several of my books were burned – things were very different in those days. "The Fever" as it was known often led to kidney and rheumatic problems. There were no antibiotics in those days. I seemed to suffer badly for a long time from severe throat problems and joint aches, and was off teaching for three months to recuperate.'

'When the only child of the butcher at Astwood Bank caught the fever in 1939, he was allowed to remain at home for his period of isolation and it was his father, because of his occupation, who had to move out. The father did in fact "visit" his son, by climbing up a ladder placed at the bedroom window.'

'At 16 I had scarlet fever. I was confined to my bedroom. My boyfriend climbed the ladder and kissed me through the glass! Father went through the house twice a day with Jeyes Fluid poured onto hot cinders on a shovel.'

MOST BABIES WERE BORN AT HOME

'Most babies were born at home at Hanley. We had a wonderful district nurse/midwife, Nurse Excell, who would visit before baby was due to see if you had everything prepared, and continued to visit after baby was born with advice. Only if there were complications was a doctor called. There was usually a good neighbour at hand to see to meals, and to the rest of the family.

Breastfeeding was encouraged, though a "National Dried Milk" was available for mothers unable to do so. Cod liver oil and orange juice was available at the baby clinic. This was held in a room at the local pub at one time, before the village hall was built. Babies were weighed and given injections and inoculations there. There were no disposable nappies.

In some cases, a village lady would take over the running of the household where there was a new baby while the mother was in bed, usually for 14 days. The prams were warm and comfortable coach-built carriages and babies were put outside to sleep after their 10 am feed whatever the weather. After their 2 pm feed, Mother would push them out, and they would watch the passing traffic, other houses and anyone Mother stopped to talk to.

Unless a baby was very small, they were fed at four-hourly intervals; 6 am, 10 am bath and feed, 2 pm, 6 pm wash and feed and 10 pm. Feeding in the night was discouraged.

Relatively few people had cars; certainly few women drove. If they needed a doctor, he would usually visit his patients at home.'

'When I was a baby, I was put to bed with a paraffin heater and lamp in the room. When my mother came to pick me up in the morning, she thought she had got a black baby as I was covered in soot!'

'After childbirth the mother was kept in bed for ten to 14 days. Babies were nearly always baptised at a private service in church, frequently on a Sunday afternoon. The custom of being "churched", giving thanks in church after a safe delivery, was prevalent and often it was considered unlucky for a mother to go anywhere until she had been churched.'

THE LAST JOURNEY

'At Heightington coffins were carried from the house to the church by four bearers, with four others walking behind so they could change over. However, they never changed places opposite a house, as that would have brought bad luck. All curtains were drawn in houses where deaths had occurred for up to four days. The coffin bearers had right of way across anyone's land. The church bell tolled seven times for a man, six for a woman and two for a child. The men all wore hard hats to the funeral but left them on the grass outside the church before going in.'

CHILDHOOD & SCHOOLDAYS

GROWING UP IN WORCESTERSHIRE

For most of us, it was a time of freedom to wander the countryside and to play safely in the streets, a time when perhaps families had few material possessions but found pleasure in simple things.

THE SQUIRE AND THE VICAR

'In the early 1900s a lot of Pebworth was under the Sheikel estate and Squire Sheikel would send a reprimand to any tenants of the thatched cottages if they were not kept tidy. A Miss Mabel Hemming collected the shilling a week rent once a fortnight and reported back to the Squire. The Squire's wife, Mary Sheikel, was an invalid and, once a year, the schoolchildren were invited to a tea party on the Manor House lawn when they played ball and sang to her, and she threw sweets, either from her bedroom window or sometimes she was wheeled outside. The last Squire, Bonar Sheikel, was shot in the leg by his brother in a shooting accident and couldn't walk. He got around in a basket-type bath chair and would pay the children a penny to push him up the steep hills in the village – and sometimes, after an argument over payment, they let him go again.'

'When my parents met children in the road (my father was vicar at Wichenford during the First World War) the girls always dropped a little curtsey and the boys pulled the peak of their caps or their forelock.'

A MALVERN CHILDHOOD

'I started at Madresfield village school as a child of five years old. The school had two classrooms, one for the infants, taught by Miss Taylor, and one for the older children up to 14, taught by Mrs Allen. There were between 30 and 35 children in the school, and as far as I remember there were only two five year olds when I started.

I remember sitting at my desk on my first day at school gazing at a painting of the crucifixion on the wall in front of me. Puzzled by the dreadful implications of the picture, I enquired what the man had done, only to be told, in hushed tones, that he was "Our Lord".

"Our Lord!" I repeated, rather perplexed. "He is with you always," came the less than comforting reply.

I was shocked and a little frightened by this information and wondered why I had been chosen to be companion to the poor, bleeding figure. "Even in bed at night," continued Miss Taylor, soothingly, "He never leaves you."

I found this news quite disconcerting and as a consequence slept on the edge of the bed for many years to allow him room to get in. I was even more mystified to find that at Christmas "Our Lord" became transformed into a baby lying in the hay. Oh, the strange and mysterious ways of adults!

I soon learnt from our religious instruction that God lived in heaven, and with "His All-Seeing Eyes" noted every misdeed on earth. The Devil also lurked around with his toasting fork, ready to prod the bottom of any miscreant. It was really a question of who got in first with the retribution, but I marvelled that most of the time neither of them was watching or listening.

One of my earliest memories at the school is a party at Madresfield Court to celebrate the Silver Jubilee of King George V and Queen Mary. I had no notion of what a Jubilee was, and, as the youngest member of the school, was quite flabbergasted to be lifted up onto a table to assist Earl Beauchamp to cut the special celebration cake. Two years later at the coronation of King George VI, I comprehended more fully what was going on. I had a white dress with red, white and blue trimmings, socks with turnovers in the national colours and hair ribbons to match. There was bunting festooned on trees, and parties at Newland and Madresfield. I helped plant an oak tree on Newland Common on 12th May 1937. We lived in Newland in a cottage, which is sadly no longer there.

There had been a village school in Newland once, but when I was young Madresfield school was the nearest, so I plodded down the lanes, unaccompanied, in all winds and weathers.

An uncle of mine had lived all his life in Newland, in a cottage opposite the Swan Inn. His father had worked for Earl Beauchamp on the estate, and had died as a result of an accident there. His widowed mother and seven children stayed on in the cottage and ran a sub post office to bring them some income. I remember him saying that when they all had scarlet fever, they were wrapped in red blankets, and laid out on the common like sausages cooking, waiting for transport by the "pestcart" to the isolation hospital. The hospital was in the country outside Malvern, so visiting was not easy. The children had to remain in hospital until all their skin had peeled.

People often remark that there were few cars about in the 1930s –

and I suppose this is true – but, at the weekend and on Bank Holidays, the Malvern Common played host to a large number of cars. People would drive out from Birmingham and its environs in their shining new possessions. In my memory, the cars were always black. The people would bring rugs to sit on, or if they had space in the back of the car, canvas seaside-type deckchairs. They had favourite places to sit, and Sunday after Sunday would find them in the same spot. One couple, whose spot was under a lime tree near to our home, brought a monkey with them, while another family were always accompanied by a large tabby cat, who would sit, with eyes like organ stops, surveying the scene.

There were a lot of tramps around in my childhood. I suppose they were en route between workhouses, but in the warmer weather would choose to sleep under the trees on the common rather than go to the casual ward of the workhouse. They would beg for food, money or clothing, but they posed no threat, and we children felt sorry for them as they reminded us of our grandfathers in reduced circumstances.

The gypsies in their brightly coloured waggons were a familiar part of life then. The women wore voluminous skirts, had their hair in coils round their ears, and sold pegs. They would put curses on anyone who didn't buy their goods so they were treated with awe. They parked their waggons on the wide grass verges where their horses would have sufficient grass to crop, and they would light fires. We were told they ate roasted hedgehogs, but whatever they were cooking always smelt good.

There was a permanent gypsy site in the field at the back of the convent in Malvern Link. They were the Gypsy Smith family. If anyone had a complaint which baffled the local doctor, Granny Gypsy Smith could be relied on to apply some well tried remedy of her own. She once told my Granny how to make a mixture from the root of a male fern to rid her young son of a roundworm. The old gypsy had given one look at the pale unhappy child, diagnosed roundworm, and proffered the remedy for it. According to my Granny it worked. The gypsies came into their own at hop picking and fair time. The Malvern Fair stretched all over the Malvern Link Common, which swarmed with fairground and Romany people. There was a large pond at the top of Cockshot Road which was used for the traction engines, and the animals. It is now filled in, but it was where the present, much reduced, fair stands when it visits Malvern.

When I was eight years old we moved to Poolbrook, where there were a great many more children to play with. It was not the custom to have friends to play in the house, or in the garden for that matter.

The garden was planted with vegetables, and trampling on the cabbages and sprouts was not allowed, so we played outside on the commons, fields and hills. The farmers, by and large, were a tolerant lot, and as long as we didn't do any damage we were allowed to play in the barns and jump on the haycarts. It was the era before stringent concerns over safety, but I can't remember anyone getting hurt.

In 1939 the evacuees poured into the town, and we assimilated the strange children, who spoke in unmusical accents and couldn't tell the difference between a crow and a skylark. They came to Great Malvern station on the 1st September 1939, all labelled and with gas masks slung across their backs. Some were frightened and confused, other confident and jokey. They were billeted with local people, and those who stayed soon fitted in comfortably with the rest of the children.

We received a penny a week pocket money, and the additional halfpenny for running jobs for old people in the village. At Christmas time carol singing boosted the funds. When the American troops came into the town, we filled bags with apples and plums, which we acquired from the trees of anyone who wasn't looking, and sold them for one penny a bag.

I think we had a freer childhood than today's youngsters. Our parents didn't concern themselves with our abduction, for who in their right mind would want to abduct *us*, and as long as we stayed together in a crowd other dangers were minimal.'

GIRL'S CLOTHING

'The modern mother would be appalled at the amount of clothing deemed necessary for the welfare of a small girl in the early years of the century.

First would come a thick woollen garment known as "combs" into which the child would thrust her icy limbs as fast as she could. This unlovely garment had long sleeves and legs and buttoned down the front.

Then came a liberty bodice, also buttoned, and from which dangled four suspenders in most inaccessible places, to which long black woollen stockings had to be attached. These were usually darned at the knees, as they bore the brunt of many tumbles.

All this being accomplished, the little girl put on her knickers – first a white cotton pair, then a more sturdy pair in navy blue with a pocket at the side for a handkerchief. It was not considered to be ladylike to be seen struggling to find a handkerchief. The knickers were more or less secured by elastic, which could give way, causing great embarrassment.

Then would come flannel petticoats, the number of which would decrease as the days grew warmer. For party wear they would be of broderie anglaise, and, if very dashing, there might be a lace frill.

A younger girl might have a jersey and a little kilted skirt. As she grew older, this would be replaced by the regulation gym slip and white cotton blouse. In winter she would need a warm woollen coat and gaiters, buttoned up the sides with much struggling and many tears and the aid of a button hook.

This poor child in her cocoon of clothes was then crowned with a hat, perhaps a woolly "tam" or, as she grew older, by a school felt hat or a straw boater. She was ready at last.

You lucky, lucky children of today.'

'Mother managed to save a few pennies weekly for the Overbury Boot and Shoe Club. Our vicar saved the money for us and provided his "interest", the aim being that once a year every child who saved could have a new pair of boots or shoes.'

BORN ON A FARM

'I was born on a farm at Charford, the youngest of six children, four brothers and a sister. After leaving school they stayed at home to work on the farm.

My father was a farmer as well as a haulage contractor and had 13 horses which worked hauling coal and other materials from the railway station. This included the bricks which were used to build Barnsley Hall. He also owned two traction engines and had the first motor lorry in Bromsgrove.

Besides these he owned a threshing machine, powered by a steam engine, which visited various farms in the district to thresh the corn.

We did tree felling, sawing wood into firewood logs and cider making, not only for ourselves but also for the local farmers who came from as far as Belbroughton. The cider press was run by a portable steam engine and was taken to some of the pubs who made a lot of cider of their own to sell. Sometimes it would take two or three days to make, the press being pulled by one horse and the engine by two.

We made a lot of cider for ourselves, about 10,000 gallons to sell to pubs, so there was plenty of work for us all to do. My sister helped my mother in the house, whilst I worked on the farm. One job was shovelling the fruit into the hopper to be ground up into a pulp, which we put into hairs (coconut mats) and built up into a ten, then it was pressed; the juice ran into a tub and was transferred into big barrels to ferment for six weeks before being bunged down to mature.

I helped with the milking, the cleaning out of the cowshed and the mixing of the cattle feed, which consisted of sliced mangolds (cut up in the pulper, which we turned by hand). This was spread on a bed of cut hay and straw along with some bran and ground maize, then all mixed together with a shovel.

We also owned a field about a mile away from Moat Mill Farm, up the Holloway, where Safeway is now, which was put up for hay. We used to take tea to the haymakers; the tea was carried in a two gallon milk bucket and we took a big butcher's basket filled with a large lump of cheese, some lettuce, spring onions, fruit cake and, of course, bread and butter.

I loved the horses and used to drive and ride the pony we had (although I never had a proper saddle). I would drive the horse-rake pulled by a pony to gather all the hay into rows after the waggons had been loaded.

When the grass began to grow again, I would go on horseback to take the cows back to the field after morning milking and fetch them back again in the afternoon for milking.

In addition we rented The Broom House, another farm nearer home, and took the cows over there until winter. Dad and I used to go over with the pony and float with buckets and churns to bring the milk back home. We milked them over there and turned them into the fields to graze. After getting the milk home in the morning, it was measured and I then took it to the bottling dairy on the Kidderminster road.

The mangold patch was always ploughed, rolled, planted, then harrowed on Good Friday; in the autumn the mangolds were pulled. The person doing this wore a bag apron, pulled the mangold from the ground, held it on their knee, trimmed off the roots and top and threw the mangolds onto a pile. This was covered with the leaves until the pile was carted off back to the rear of the cowshed where it was pulped.

Another job I had to do several times a year was to fetch the grains of barley from the brewery (which was at the back of the Dog and Pheasant) after it had been boiled and strained. Also from the Golden Lion, which was owned and run by the Bridgman family for years and was often referred to as "Bridgman's" rather than the "Golden Lion". We used to feed the grains to the cows and pigs.

In the dark evenings we used to make pegged rugs, cutting up lengths of cloth, about one inch by four inches, using a small hand tool, to be poked through a hessian bag that had been split open. You made a hole with the tool, poking it into the hessian and bringing it back up, then clipped the cloth and pulled that back through. I also did patchwork.

The seasons brought various games, some of which were played with a ball. I remember some we played such as whip and top, "Sheep, sheep come home", tip cat, marbles, hopscotch, hide and seek, tag, French cricket, running with a hoop and stick and also skipping.

We never had a holiday, but some Saturday afternoons one of my brothers would drive the bull-nosed Morris Tourer we had and take my mother, sister and myself out for a drive. Occasionally we would visit relations in Evesham.

Even though it was a big house, with twelve rooms, dairy and outer scullery, we had no indoor sanitation or flush toilet the whole of the time we were there, despite the fact that we didn't leave until 1957.

The toilet was up the yard away from the house; it was a square building with a red quarry floor and a long box-type seat with two holes in it. In the old days it was only emptied once a year and I remember one of my brothers telling me of a time he was there when it was due to be emptied, and a rat appeared to join him from the depths! At night you had to take a candle as there was no lighting, and very often on the way the wind would blow the candle out. Usually two of us females would go together and sit and chat and exchange our plans and opinions.'

RAILWAY CHILDREN

'We knew that the "light" engine went through Upton station at 7 am on its way to Malvern, but we did not get up until it came back again at 8 am with its complement of two carriages. It was impossible to sleep anyway, because outside on the platform were girls and boys chattering and laughing, waiting for the train to take them to schools in Tewkesbury.

Then it was a mad rush for five children to prepare for school and Father to be in the office for 9 am.

Washing arrangements were primitive, as there was no bathroom, but there was a basin and ewer in each of the three bedrooms. There was a bath situated, strangely, in the kitchen, but this was used only in the summer, as the wind howled in through windows and doors during bad weather. In any case, to heat water for the bath meant lighting the fire under the copper, which was a feat in itself. Better and easier to get the old tin bath out, heat the water from the outside butt in enormous saucepans and, one by one, bath in front of the enormous range.

We were lucky in having running tap water and an indoor lavatory. The water was pumped from a well into an enormous tank

Upton on Severn station was home to a family between the wars – a wonderful place to grow up.

in the kitchen, and was always cool and pure to drink. Which was strange, when you realised that the well was situated in the gentlemen's lavatory on the station.

Our station house was typical of all railway houses; well built, and with large airy rooms. When we were first there, in 1933, we only had oil lamps downstairs and candles to light our way upstairs, but later on gas was installed (downstairs only). The gas was so poor that the kettle had to be put on the stove the night before, so as to be ready for breakfast next morning. The enormous fireplace was used in winter only, and was far better for cooking and baking, and everything tasted much nicer.

I think Mondays were the worst days. Mummy was up early to light the copper for the weekly wash, and by the time we came home from school for lunch, the house would still be full of steam and the smell of washing. Mummy's fingers would be tied up with bits of rag where she had rubbed the skin away in her efforts to get the clothes clean. The meal was always the same – cold meat with bubble and squeak, but a lovely rice pudding afterwards.

Winter evenings were something to be remembered. An enormous fire singeing the knees, the soft light from the oil lamps, and the family together. Our games were mostly instructive, like spelling bees, history and geography. Or Daddy would read to us – always poetry, from Tennyson and Longfellow; *Hiawatha* being one of our favourite pieces. Then there would be singing, all of us joining in with tenor-descant in hymns and old Edwardian favourites.

The railway station was a busy place in the 1930s, as mechanised transport was slow in coming to Upton. Nearly everything came by rail and was then taken from the station by the farmers with horse and cart, or by Sam Crump on the station lorry. There were two freight trains per day, one of which was mainly coal. The coal-trucks were put in the sidings, or unloaded in huge mountains in the backyard, where the coal merchants, Messrs Biddle, Stallard and Moss would weigh and bag before loading it onto horse and dray to carry to their customers.

Apples, pears, plums and vegetables were brought to the station by farmers for transportation to Birmingham and Manchester markets. These had been picked into beautifully made willow hampers called either half pots or pots. Imported fruit, like oranges or bananas, would arrive, usually by passenger train in the guards-van, to be collected by "Pop" Deakin with his handcart, and there would be a daily delivery of wet fish which would be taken quickly to Mr Johnson who owned the fried and wet fish shop. Several times during the year, racing pigeons would come to Upton, to be freed by the porters to make their way back home.

Big agricultural machinery was offloaded into the goods-receiving shed, which was as big as a small church, and had a crane to lift the goods off the trucks and onto the lorry. Little did my father know what a busy life this crane led when the station was closed for the night, and a horde of small children used the crane for hoisting themselves round at high speed.

Cattle feed was kept in a large corrugated iron building next door, which was a favourite playground if it was wet. We tried to be careful, but cow-cake had a funny habit of breaking out of sacks when they were jumped on. We were caught, of course, and as there was only one means of entry, a thoroughly deserved clip on the ear was the fate of 20 girls and boys.

The porters' house nearby was a small square structure where the three porters could "brew-up" and have their lunch. There was always a fire going and a kettle on the boil. The porters were a jolly lot, and would occasionally push us about on the two-wheeled handcarts that were normally used for luggage and small parcels. A great treat for us would be to go with Sam Crump, the lorry driver, when he went round to the farmers delivering goods. This was a very leisurely job as the lorry, like Sam, was getting on in years and neither could progress very quickly. When the farm was reached, pleasantries and a glass of "home-brewed" were exchanged, so that the journey home was not only leisurely but erratic as well. What lovely days they were.

At the end of the platform was the signal-box, which was definitely a no-go area (unless you knew where the key was kept). There were two signalmen, their shifts being 6 am until 2 pm and 2 pm until 10 pm. The box was kept in pristine condition, the wooden floor being scrubbed once a week and then covered with sheets of cardboard, so that the white wood never saw the light of day. The brasswork shone and, to avoid fingermarks, the men used an oily rag called "waste" to pull the levers of the signals. (To be allowed to do this was a great treat.) As the building was half-glass, one side was given over to seedlings and tomato plants, all of which flourished in that hot-house atmosphere.

We had four gangers. These were men who were employed to look after the permanent way and whose area stretched from Ripple to Malvern Wells. They would traverse the rails by means of two sets of wheels, over which were placed strong wooden boards which fitted snugly into one another. They sat at the end of the board and pushed backwards with their legs, achieving quite a good speed. The gangers had a little hut at the end of the station, where, unbeknown to my father, they brewed cider (it tasted wonderful). In charge of the gangers was a man known as "Happy Jack", who helped us with bonfires on 5th November, and who never told Daddy when he caught us scrumping his apples. Nice man.

The station itself consisted of the booking office where Mr Rowe and his junior worked, the main waiting room which held a small weighing machine, the stationmaster's office, and the ladies' waiting room, which was never used. The booking office had desks of the old Dickensian type and high stools, all beautifully made, as was the huge desk in my father's office. The down platform side of the station was covered over with a wrought iron canopy fitted with glass, under which were seats and two chocolate vending machines. On the up platform was another building, rather like a large brick bus-shelter with a wooden seat all the way round.

Our house was attached to the main railway buildings and there was a connecting door, on which Mr Rowe used to knock three times if my father was wanted urgently.

Every fortnight Wednesday was market day which was very busy and exciting. Farmers would either walk the stock to market from the various farms, or transport them by horse and trap. The market was conveniently reached through the White Lion where a lot of business was conducted over a few glasses of ale. After the sales were finished, sheep and cows were walked to the station by their drovers, and put in the compound which stood in the middle of the front yard. From there they were put into cattle trucks and sent to their different destinations.

On Sundays in the fishing season before the war, special trains would come to Upton from Birmingham filled with keen anglers, to whom it was a treat to spend the day in the fresh air by the river. Whether they caught anything I don't know, but for us it was a great day, as the train drivers would allow us in their cabs, which we could not do with the regular drivers. We would try our hands at shovelling coal into the huge furnace, and would be lifted up to manipulate the levers and blow the whistle as the trains shunted backwards and forwards.

On normal Sundays we would wander down the lines on the actual rail itself, seeing how far we could go without falling off. Coming back we would stop to pick the wild strawberries which grew along the embankment among the moondaisies and violets.

The station was more busy than ever during the great flood of 1947. Upton was completely cut off by road, which was by then taking a lot of freight from the railway. All who worked out of Upton had to use the railway, and all goods coming into town likewise. Livestock, fish, vegetables and even coffins came to the station, the increase in trade being necessary if the railway was to survive. That year, though, seemed to mark the end of the busy time for Upton railway; after nationalisation in 1948 trade decreased, and the writing was on the wall.

Before nationalisation there were nine passenger and two freight trains per day, which afterwards went down to four passenger and two freight trains.

The station was finally closed in 1964, passenger services being withdrawn in 1961 and freight in 1964. Nothing now remains of the lovely Victorian buildings or the rails, only memories of a very happy childhood.'

CHILDHOOD

'The evocative scent of Drene shampoo; dressing up on a May morning in net curtains and hawthorn wreaths in your hair to be Queen of the May; and scrumping apples on the way to school. There was a code to scrumping. You only picked up what was on the ground, but oh, those Worcester Pearmains, Cox's Orange Pippins, Russets and even Victoria plums.

Going to a party and your mother putting your very straight hair into rag curlers and having a troubled sleep in consequence. Dressing up for Brownie Revels as gypsies, pirates or rainbow fairies and getting funny looks on the bus.

Spending your Saturday penny – the agony of deciding whether to have a halfpenny worth of banana toffee and a big gobstopper that changed colour every so often (you had to take it out to have a look) or four golly bars at a farthing each or red and black liquorice bootlaces. Does anyone remember the taste of red and yellow pear drops?

Going to Grandma's for your week's holiday in the country, sleeping in lavender-scented sheets, reading for the umpteenth time her copies of *Little Women, Good Wives* and *Jo's Boys*.

The smell of chalk and the sound of your teacher reading *Dr Doolittle* as a serial. Dressing up in white frocks, black patent shoes with ankle straps and a red, white and blue ribbon in your hair for Empire Day. It is a thing of the past now but we were proud to be British.

Haberdasher's shops, with money flying across the ceiling with a "ping" at the cash desk, tall bentwood chairs for your mother to sit on while buying buttons, tapes and trimmings and those awful beige lisle stockings and liberty bodices.

No tins of dog and cat food. Fourpennyworth of lights from the butcher for the dog, cooked in a special saucepan. Likewise, a cod's head from the fishmonger for puss. Potato peelings for the chickens, mixed with bran, and the smells that used to emanate from the kitchen!

Going to Woolworth's, threepenny and sixpenny stores in those days. Counters of biscuit tins with glass tops so that you could see your selections, and bags of broken biscuits to use for dolls' feasts. Coloured water for playing hospitals. Bottles of blue bag and cochineal water to dose teddies and dollies and smooth pebbles for pills. And the sound of the bicycle bell as the Walls' ice cream van went by.

Going to the pictures. Shirley Temple in *Susannah of the Mounties* and Tom Mix and Gene Autrey on Saturday afternoons.

And the war years. Gas masks and iron rations to the fore. The miles of pennies, miles of books, miles of keys etc the Guides collected for the war effort. And the shock of seeing lights shining from windows on VE Day, with no air raid warden fretting about the blackout. The war really was over.'

IDYLLIC

'The house I lived in from 1944 to 1948 at Peopleton was a cottage attached to two others with the only amenity being a cold tap outside on the wall which served all of the three families. The lavatory was some 25 yards down the garden adjacent to the pigsty and opposite the chickens and the hovel. My childhood was idyllic, playing outside in barns and in large buttercup and daisy-filled fields, scrumping in season for apples and anything else which took our fancy.

I went to a village school with about 20 pupils and by the time I was eight was told I could pass the eleven-plus, which I later did. We played with the Italian prisoners of war and also the Land Army girls who were billeted in Bowbrook House, where my mother worked for a short while. We never lacked for good food. The pig was killed up the garden and the skin was burnt on a fire. The chitterlings, both fat and thin, were cleaned under the tap and the liver was eaten fresh. It was always winter when this took place and then the flitches of bacon were hung up on the stairs wall after they had been salted.

My father always grew fresh vegetables and my mother cooked good, plain food on an oil stove or the black range in the front room. This range was set in a large walk-in fireplace, and I used to sit close to the fire and actually burn the front of my legs. In the winter, after going out to slide on the many ponds in the village, my mother used to get out the rack from the oven and wrap it in a small blanket for me to warm my feet. My reading was a little restricted because we only had oil lamps and a Tilley lamp, so I loved the radio.

I used to have to carry milk to the big house and I would swing it round and round in the can. If any came out I used to top it up at the water pump. In the summer we swam in the brook after wading through deep mud or stones, if we went paddling. The odd dead sheep would be reported floating, but, apart from that, the water was clear.

My life centred around the church where I went to Sunday school and sang in the choir with my father. The vicar taught us a lot and took us on educational outings, which we did not understand at the time, but now I see that he was very good to us.

We played team games in the road, also skipping, marbles, conkers, all in season.'

HOLIDAY TIME

Few people had a paid holiday from work, so holidays for the children often meant just a day out by the river perhaps, or a working holiday potato picking.

BAND OF HOPE OUTINGS

'The Band of Hope was a temperance society like a youth club. Over 60 boys and girls met fortnightly in the Methodist chapel at Pebworth. Juniors paid a halfpenny and those over twelve years a penny towards outings. Any denomination could go – the local publican's children went. We had talks on temperance to set a good example to us not to drink, as much drunkenness happened in villages up to the 1920s; each village had a cider press.

Once a year the local Band of Hope had an outing in the summer holidays, travelling by horse and dray and horse and trap. Once we were driven by Mrs Huckfield to Bidford on Avon (five miles away) for a river trip to Cleeve Prior on two steamers, returning to have tea by the riverside provided by the Bidford Band of Hope. The older teenagers would rock the boat and frighten the younger children, who would scream and shout. Sometimes the trip would be to Evesham or Stratford by river, the locks being scary when the boat rocked too much. The over-twelve year olds sometimes biked to Stratford. I was ten years old before I saw the sea. I went to Bournemouth by train, having walked to Honeybourne to catch the 5 am.'

BY THE RIVER

'When I was a child in the 1920s and 1930s, we used to spend weekends and holidays in a chalet by the river Severn near Bewdley. It was wonderful to get away from a noisy, built-up area to the beautiful countryside and clean air – there was much more smoke-pollution in those days.

My father and brother had made the chalet from a railway coach, which was easily adapted with a balcony along the front, onto which opened the sitting room (the luggage compartment), two double bedrooms (first class carriages), two single bedrooms (third class compartments) and a kitchen built at one end.

A sloping garden led down to the river where we used to swim. I doubt if my parents realised how strong the current was, for we could only swim downstream and climbed out further down, running back to repeat the swim.

In those days there were only three other chalets there, but I revisited it recently and found ours was still intact with over 50 companions!'

'When I was a child in the 1920s our annual holiday was a day by the river Teme. My family would be up early assembling all the picnic gear and fishing tackle, and we would then walk the four miles to Worcester from Kempsey, to catch the eight o'clock train from Foregate Street to Leigh, where we spent the day fishing. My Mum and I would light a fire and thread bacon and sausages onto a stick, which we would hold over the fire with bread underneath to catch the fat. Then, with the kettle boiling, we had a lovely meal, and finding some apples and plums in the hedgerow made it a perfect day. Later, we would journey home again by train, hoping to catch a ride on a horse-drawn dray back to Kempsey.'

THE POOL

'My father was a keen fisherman and, with a friend, rented the pool at the end of Silver Street from the farmer for Sunday fishing in the early 1930s.

In those days, working class people hadn't a car. We came from the now notorious district of Balsall Heath, hard working people with great friendliness and neighbourliness. The only way to get to this pool was the 35 bus from Station Street to the Maypole, then walk the rest of the way.

Carrying all our gear with us, we walked along the main road at Wythall. I remember a few houses along the road, and in Silver Street. One particular house on the Alcester road sold home-made ice cream and, as a special treat, we bought one.

On we marched, my parents and two older sisters, with our friends, we were ten in all. The first job when we arrived at the pool was to spread out the ground sheets, get the large crock jug from the basket and go off to the farm for milk, sometimes still warm from the cow, and the fresh butter for the bread brought from home. The two mothers competed each week for special goodies they had made.

The day was spent, the two men fishing, the two women gossiping about this and that, and we kids playing in the fields, walking the lanes, picking wild flowers, making daisy chains. Usually there was a bat and ball in the basket and a game of rounders was played.

We programmed our departure to catch the double decker Midland Red bus from Evesham, which stopped at the White Swan on the main road. Dad said we were too tired to walk back to the Maypole. Sometimes, if we were early, the men would go into the pub and bring out lemonade and a bag of crisps – Smith's, twopence, with the salt in blue paper. What a wonderful summer that was.'

WORKING HOLIDAYS

'A Malvern man told me how in his schooldays the holidays were eagerly looked foward to by schoolboys, though there were no thoughts then of going away. It was a chance to earn some money. An extra pair of hands was welcomed by farmers when the fruit was ripe, and there was work in the hopyards. The Three Counties Show brought plenty of work their way too. Those were great days out in the sun and fresh air, away from the schoolroom. Mind you, it was hard work!'

'Over 50 years ago at Wribbenhall, the long school holidays were taken in September when the annual trek to the hop fields began. For many this was the only holiday they could afford. A coach trip to the hop fields was a must, to see the band of hop pickers busily stripping the vines to fill a crib. This would be emptied by the bushel and the picker rewarded at so much a bushel of hops. A dewy morning was welcomed when the hops would weigh heavier. Children had a great time playing in the furrows of the hop vines, or scrumping apples in a nearby orchard. At the end of the day they would return to the farmer's barns to cook upon an open log fire and then retire to bed on palliasses made of straw. Not a very comfortable lifestyle but the wages paid would probably outfit the family for the coming winter, and also supply a few extra goodies for Christmas.'

'Our holidays were spent with relations who were farmers and market gardeners at the foot of Bredon Hill, and we had to help with pea and bean picking, radish and onion tying and, sometimes, at the crack of dawn, went by horse and dray to take the produce to market.'

IN THE COUNTRY

'During the 1940s, when our father was away at the war, my mother and grandmother took us three children to stay at a friend's cottage

at Great Comberton, near Pershore. The cottage was several hundred years old and adjoined the village churchyard.
We actually stayed in a prefabricated bungalow in the orchard, no electricity or running water and terribly spooky having to go across to the cottage at night for the toilet!
But how we all loved the countryside round Comberton. Every day we walked into Pershore for the shopping, a long two mile walk for little legs! What a treat, though, when the shopping was finished and we had tea and home-made cakes at the Green Door Café.
We often walked to Little Comberton a mile or so away. There was an old-fashioned bakery there and the baker made marvellous salty cheese biscuits.
In late August and September the orchards were full of bright red Worcester apples and we used to love watching the men picking the apples for market. One year we were told they were prisoners of war.
Even though facilities were very basic, no holidays ever compared with those times at Great Comberton and we returned every year until I was married.'

GAMES AND TREATS

We played in the roads when there was little traffic, and our games came round with the seasons as they always had, from bowling hoops to marbles, conkers to whip and top. Some were lucky enough to be able to join in more organised activities that broadened our horizons. We all had chores to do, though, before we could go out to play.

ALWAYS SOMETHING TO DO

'As a child at my grandmother's, we had oil lamps for illumination, and in the winter evenings would sit round the fire reading, sewing or playing cards at the table.
On Sunday evenings there was always singing round the piano. My aunt was organist at Upton church and also played for chapel and concerts at the "Union" (the local workhouse).

Going round carol singing near Christmas was fun, as we were allowed out in the dark. Sometimes we were given mince pies, but sometimes we had a bowl of water thrown over us from a bedroom window. A highlight was a visit to the pantomime at Worcester or Gloucester in a coach.

In the summer months we played "tracking" in the long grass in the meadows, paddled in streams, tore about on scooters, played with hoops or tops and were out in the open air for most of the school holidays.

On Saturdays I would have twopence or a penny to spend. There was a picture show in the Memorial Hall in the afternoon (admission twopence), Tom Mix cowboy films, or *Our Gang* usually. Music was supplied by a man playing the piano as the films were all silent. If the children were too noisy, stamping or shouting, a man would blow a whistle loudly, and anyone failing to heed this was turned out.

The penny to spend was eked out at various sweet shops, my favourites being a farthingsworth of aniseed balls, a farthingsworth of coconut chips or a gobstopper, and a halfpenny lunch bag or dab and sucker.

Occasionally a small fair, swings and roundabout, and a theatre company would come and park alongside the river for a couple of weeks. I was allowed to go and see *East Lynne* (what a weepie) but not *Maria Marten and the Red Barn*!

We were warned not to go too near the river, but there were not many Upton children who had not fallen in at some time or other, and been pulled out none the worse.

We never seemed to be bored, with so much to do and never hankered after expensive toys.'

ALVECHURCH CHILDREN

'In the 1930s Miss Atkinson worked at Alvechurch school as an assistant teacher; she had started at the school some 40 to 50 years earlier and stayed on afterwards. When the weather was fine she would have all the infants classes in a large circle in the playground parading around and chanting the multiplication tables. At playtime we would play tag, skipping games, "The farmer's in his den" or hopscotch. In 1934 a child died from meningitis; the whole school went to the funeral and lined the path up to the church.

Each evening workers from "The Austin" returning home to Redditch passed through the village in a procession of "charas" (coaches). These charas belonged to different companies in Redditch and were various colours and sizes. We used to sit at the side of the road and bet on the order in which they would pass by.

We walked a lot and played in local fields. A favourite walk was to the station at 11 am to watch the coal truck being shunted into the siding and the coalmen, the two Mr Taylors, would fill hundredweight bags and weigh their lorry on the weighbridge. The canal was always worth a visit with regular horse-drawn barges passing through.

Local farmers contended with children climbing ricks and making slides down to the floor. When spotted the farmer didn't go to the police but chased the children away. Should the policeman find the children being destructive he would wallop them. Many times my three brothers would race home and hide from whoever they thought was after them.

Most families of children had a truck or trolley made from bits of wood and old pram wheels. Ours had pivoting front wheels so that it could be steered. We had a "Cresta Run" from above the school, down School Lane and out into the main road! Fortunately there wasn't too much traffic around, but I look back at that particular pastime with horror!'

CHILDREN'S CAMPS

'In the early 1900s the Queenhill area seemed to be a popular one for children's camps. In 1910 a party of Boy Scouts from Upton spent a weekend at Pull Court but as it was too wet to camp out the boys were bedded out in the stables. In 1912 Cheltenham Boys' Brigade and Worcester Boys' Brigade camped at Moss Green, Bushley. In 1922 several detachments of Boy Scouts were encamped in the area. The 25th Cheltenham Troop, under the command of the Rev Canon Moyle, were camped at Moss Green – the summer home of the Dowdeswells at Bushley, whilst a troop from St Edward's Orphanage, West Malvern, the Upton boys and also a troop from St Paul's, Worcester were bedded down in the stables at Pull Court.

Early in 1923 Squire Dowdeswell of Pull Court was inspired to start a local troop of Scouts and invited boys of the required age to a meeting to see if they would like to form a troop of their own. About 16 responded and were enrolled on 14th October. Each Scout contributed half the cost of his uniform and very smart boys they looked on the first night they donned them.

Parents and friends were invited to the enrolment at Moss Green, when the Squire explained the objects of the Scout movement and appealed to parents to back him up in the training. General Johnson, the District Secretary, enrolled the Squire as Scoutmaster and G. Shaw and B. Bayliss as Patrol Leaders. Their first public appearance was at a church parade at Queenhill church on 26th November 1923.'

INTO THE WOODS

'We played the usual games at Broadway – marbles, hopscotch, conkers, skipping and whips and tops. I remember sticking coloured bits of paper on my top so that when it spun round it made pretty patterns a bit like a kaleidoscope.

At the age of eleven I was allowed to go on cycle rides with my friends, and we rode all over the district, visiting aunts at Offenham, Laverton, up on the Cotswolds, Chipping Campden, and Temple Guiting. Believe it or not, I even went as far as Redditch.

Another thing we would not dream of letting our children do these days is to go into the woods and play for the whole day. We took sandwiches and a bottle of lemonade and a gang of us would go to the woods about half a mile from the back of our house. We made ourselves dens out of branches and ferns and had a glorious time. We had a Summer Den, a House in the Hollow, a Fairy Den, and so on. We even had fights with neighbouring dens (boys, of course). My favourite pastime was picking primroses and bluebells, but of course that's against the law now. The woods where we played were an absolute carpet of blue in the springtime.

With my friends who lived near, I loved dressing up and doing little plays, making up charades on the back lawn, and we had a big box of fancy dressing-up clothes. They were wonderful times.'

GAMES WE PLAYED

'Our school playground at Himbleton was made of ashes and was a terrible mess when it was wet. However, we played hopscotch, Oranges and Lemons, and Drop Glove Tag. For the latter, the children all stood in a circle. One person on the outside of the circle ran round and dropped a glove behind someone, who picked it up and chased the outside person. They had to catch them before returning to their place. If caught, that child stayed in the middle of the circle.'

'The games we played in the 1920s included Jacky Five Stones, tip cat and buck stones. Tip cat was when the "cat" was a piece of stick sharpened at both ends. This was laid down on the ground and the children tried to hit or "tip" it by throwing other sticks at it. Buck stones was a similar game, when a large stone was placed on the ground and other stones aimed at it by the children.

Himbleton children in 1933.

There were not many toys for children at this time and whips and tops were quite popular. Children also liked to play games like rounders, cricket and football on open land.'

CHORES TO DO

'When I was a child at the time of the First World War, I would have to walk the three miles into Droitwich for the shopping. As a reward I would have a halfpenny to spend and my choice was always "scratchings". To prolong the enjoyment I would see how far I could get along the road home before they were finished.'

'When I was nearly seven and my sister five, in 1912, Dad was appointed as gardening instructor to the boys at Stoke Prior Reformatory, so we came to live in what was then considered a big house, surrounded by fields, in Shaw Lane. It had a large garden with beehives and we two each had our own little plot to be kept tidy, weed free and planted with lots of old-world flowers. The little paths round them were cobblestoned, with pebbles collected from the main garden. A big old walnut tapped its branches against our bedroom window, and owls called from it at night.

We had our jobs to do indoors, cleaning knives with a cork dipped in brickdust, brasses with Brasso and shoes on Saturday, ready for church and Sunday school next day.

We walked to a cottage along the lane to buy a dozen eggs for a shilling and were often given a bantam egg each as well. Then we went to the cottage shop to spend our weekly halfpenny on two things from the "farthing-box" – a liquorice pipe, aniseed balls etc.

In the afternoon we walked to Bromsgrove with Mother to do the weekly shopping and carry it home. The first to reach the milestone at Park Hall had the pleasure of sitting on it for a rest.'

SCHOOLDAYS: THE BEST YEARS OF OUR LIVES?

Long walks to school, wet clothes steaming round the fire, no running water, little equipment and a very basic education – memories shared by generations of Worcestershire children, and which go back to the start of the century.

TO SCHOOL IN 1902

'I was born in Pebworth in 1898, the youngest of seven – six girls and one boy. My school life started at four at the "Old School" in Dorsington Lane. The infants sat in tiered rows of desks with tip-up seats, presenting some discomfort for short legs. There were over 30 children to a class, the older children up to 14 years being taught in a separate room by one of the three teachers. Girls wore long dresses and pinafores and the boys wore cloth caps. My husband wore a dress until he was three as this was the fashion in those days.

No water meant carrying water from the tap in the washhouse of a house two doors away, and two earth closets were used. Playtime was in the road opposite the school – no traffic then.

The new school was built in 1902 so I went there after a few months (it is still open now). The old school was then used for night school and a youth club, but the girls had cookery lessons there on a Tuesday – making bread and cakes firstly in the oven of the coal fire and later on an oil stove. It didn't seem like "school lessons" so we looked forward to this. The boys did gardening at the new school.

Lighting was by oil lamps and heating by a coal fire. There were no games lessons, but knitting and sewing from seven years. We used slates and lead pencils, and managed as we didn't know anything different, then a small blackboard about a foot square and coloured chalks, and a sand tray with a piece of stick to draw patterns. We had movable desks and seats with inkwells at the new school. I remember a travelling Punch and Judy show coming to the village school when I was three, and we had a concert each year. The "School Boss" Mr Hobiss had a cask of beer in the porch and often in an afternoon he would be drunk, having supped away all day. Children walked to school from about two miles away.'

TRENCH LANE SCHOOL

'I was born in 1909, lived in Brownheath Common and went to Trench Lane school about two miles away. The headteacher was a woman whose title was "School Governess", but was known to the children as "The Governess". We sat on long forms at long tables. Discipline was strict and the cane well-used. Once I "guarded" the gate whilst my companions went into a garden to steal apples. We were seen, and all caned the next day.

In school, sand trays were used for letter formation for the youngest children. The playgrounds were segregated by sex – the front one for the boys, the back one for the girls. Every week a child who had done well was chosen for a "treat" by the Governess. The treat was to clean the brasses in her house – a prestigious task sought after by the children, but the chosen one was always derided as "teacher's pet" by the other children. The girls wore white pinafores over their dark-coloured dresses, and all the boys wore boots. Sandwiches were taken for lunch – mine were usually paste or jam. Water was from the pump outside. I always had to sit beside a "well-off" child who had to be coaxed to eat her tasty and beautifully-cut sandwiches, which I longed to eat myself.

When the rector visited the school, the children had to be very respectful. In the street the boys touched their caps and the girls curtsied when they met him.'

CANING WAS FREQUENT

'I got up at 5 am to help my father prepare two horses for the waggon, went to the mine with him and filled up with coal for delivery later, and when I got home milked six cows before walking to school at Heightington. We took our dinners with us – bread spread with lard and sugar. The teachers made us cocoa at twopence each. There were 135 children, aged five to 14, and three teachers. Caning was very frequent for bad behaviour in school and outside. The boys would lay horsehair across their hands to stop the cane cutting the skin.'

KIDDERMINSTER HIGH SCHOOL

'At the age of eleven I gained a scholarship to go to Kidderminster High School for Girls. Rules at the school were very strict, and school uniform of navy gymslip, white blouse and navy knickers, and black shoes, had always to be worn. We must not run or eat in the street when in school uniform. If reported doing this you were given an order mark, which was shown on your end of term report.

Most pupils took sandwiches for midday lunch. These had to be wrapped in a white table napkin with your name pinned on. You placed them on a table in the hall when you went into school. At lunch times you were supplied with a plate, a knife and a glass of water and you sat at a long table to eat your sandwich, with grace said before eating.'

SCHOOL IN BROMSGROVE

'In 1916, during the First World War, my father decided it would be safer for his family to stay in Bromsgrove with my aunt because he thought Birmingham might be dangerous.

My first school was a small private one, somewhere at the top end of Bromsgrove, exactly where I cannot remember but I didn't like it. We had to use slates, and one afternoon I was kept in because my twos were written backwards. I cried, and was rewarded with a rap over the knuckles. At that time I was aged three and a half! My sister, who was four years older, was most annoyed with me, as she was ready to go home and had to wait until I finished my task.

I remember the winter was bitterly cold and there was heavy snow which prevented me from going to school, no nonsense of being taken to school, you walked. However, after that winter my sister and I left, and went to another school, which was very different.

It was kept by, I believe, the daughter of the manager of Lloyds Bank, and there the dear lady taught me to read. I remember going from "Bill is ill, give him a pill" straight on to reading anything and everything that came my way. At the end of each afternoon, the school books were tidied away, a fringed cloth was brought out to

WORCESTERSHIRE COUNTY COUNCIL.
EDUCATION COMMITTEE.

Examination for County Secondary School Free Places, Local Exhibitions, &c.

SATURDAY, MAY 7TH, 1921.

ARITHMETIC.

(For children *under* 12).

$1\frac{1}{2}$ hours allowed.

Do all, or as many as you can.

---

1. 85 poor people were given a day's outing, and the cost per head was £1 19s. 11d. What was the total cost of the outing ?

2. Divide (by factors) £19485 13s. 6d. by 132. If you had to share £19485 13s. 6d. equally among 264 persons what sum would each receive ?

3. In selling an article, the shopkeeper read the price as £9·175 instead of its real price £9 17s. 5d. How much money did he lose by his mistake ?

4. Mount Everest is 29,002 feet high. What is the height of the mountain in miles, furlongs, yards, feet ?

5. A farmer took a horse, a cow, some corn, two chickens, and two dozen eggs to market. He sold the corn for £5. The horse sold for four times as much as the corn, and the price of the cow was twice as much as the horse and the corn together. Each chicken sold for one twentieth the price of the corn, and each egg for one twenty-fourth of the price of a chicken. How much money did the farmer receive altogether ?

TURN OVER.

An arithmetic examination paper for under twelves in 1921.

cover the big central table where we did most of our work, and our teacher then read to us for a quarter of an hour. She read us *Kidnapped, Treasure Island, Ivanhoe* and some of Dickens, and gave me a love of literature that has lasted all my life.

The garden of the house was next to the old *Messenger* office and we were warned not to go on that side of the garden in case we got splashed with printer's ink when the presses were running.

I wore school uniform, navy blue in winter and check dresses in summer, and always a hat with the school band and badge. Gloves too, and button boots. I hated my boots and longed for the day when as a "big girl" I could have shoes, black of course. We had thin pumps with cross-over elastic for dancing and black plimsolls for games. Knickers with a pocket in each leg, and elastic at the knee, quite useful really, you could tuck all sorts of things there.

As I went to private schools, the cane was not used, but being kept in, and given lines, were the usual punishments. As this meant you were late home, you often got a good telling off there as well, so it was sometimes a twice-over punishment.'

HARVINGTON SCHOOL

'The school at Harvington was established by the Church of England and opened (it is believed) in 1852. Obviously, no one "in living memory" can recall that event, but there are some villagers who can remember back to the pre-1920s, and others who are able to repeat stories told them by their parents who were at school at the turn of the century.

In the very early days there was a large room (the hall), one smaller classroom and a small cloakroom, which had one washbasin. The seniors, taught by the Head, were in a smaller room; all the other children were taught together in the hall, infants being separated from juniors by a curtain. Across the yard (gravelled, but later asphalted) were earth closets, the boys' closets (and playground) being separated from those of the girls and infants by a wall. One resident tells how her father, with remembered glee, often told the tale of having sneaked round the back of the girls' closets and nettled the bottoms of the girls sitting on the seats by opening and reaching up through the clearance (night-soil) doors along the back of the building.

By the turn of the century another classroom had been added for the infants and an organisation of classes was set up which continued for many years. Standards One, Two and Three were taught together in the smallest room by the assistant teacher (who, for many years, was the headmaster's wife) while Standards Four to

Seven were taken by the Head in the hall. Four and Five did written work (and were expected to be silent while doing so) while Six and Seven were being taught verbally and vice versa. The boys did "drill" (this having been made compulsory after 1902 when recruitment for the Boer War had revealed the unfit condition of the "lower classes").

The boys also were taken by bus (which had replaced the cattle truck of earlier times) to Prince Henry's Grammar School in Evesham to do woodwork. The girls, meantime, did needlework and/or knitting, all taught together by the assistant teacher, and laboured over sticky, grubby articles with needles which are remembered as being "always rusty".

The school was electrically lit in the 1930s but previously had only oil lamps, and is remembered as having been dark – cold, too, because the only heating was from an open fire in each room. The headmaster had his desk placed centrally in front of the fire in the hall, which, to the children, seemed grossly unfair.

Great use was made of the blackboard, especially during "object lessons", while geography meant frequent references to the maps on the wall – the map of the world being recollected as having the British Empire coloured pink. Music was taught from the tonic sol-fa chart.

Children stayed at school until they were 14 years old though certainly in the early years boys and girls were allowed to leave earlier if they had made the requisite minimum number of attendances and could convince the headmaster to provide them with a Labour Certificate. Also, in the early years, a few girls might stay and train as pupil-teachers, later, perhaps, becoming uncertificated teachers, and earning (in the 1920s) £6 14s a month.

In those years, and throughout the 1930s, two or three children were chosen every year by the Head to take the examination which would entitle them to a free place at the aforementioned grammar school. The system was seen as unfair (which it almost certainly was!) partly because the children felt it was not always "the brightest" who were selected. Nevertheless, the candidates obviously had to attain the standard necessary to cope with examination papers.

The connection with the church was very strong and the children were taken along to the church "in crocodiles" on important festival days, particularly on Ascension Day. The rector was a regular visitor to the school and when he arrived they all stood to attention and chanted, "Good morning, sir".

Absenteeism was always a problem; illnesses such as diphtheria, chicken pox, measles, scarlet fever and whooping cough were rife in the early years and these absences were augmented by the children being kept away from school for hop, pea and fruit picking. Even as late as the 1960s and 1970s the headmaster toured the village "collecting" boys for school. His authority was recognised as extending beyond the school and his Friday warning, "Whatever you are doing this weekend, remember that *I* shall be here on Monday!" was no idle threat.

All the children looked forward to the annual hunt meet on the village green in autumn and were all allowed to go out and watch, but some boys, not content with this simple treat, sneaked off after the hunt and did not go back into school. Needless to say, retribution followed the next day.

Memories of school are linked closely with memories of the village, of course – going down to the Misses Stratton at "The Limes" for milk or to the baker's for bread and lardie cake; passing the Coach and Horses where the publican was also the village undertaker; walking along the road referred to, locally, as "the back of the town"; engaging in name-calling and stone-throwing with "posh kids" who went (by car!) to the private school in Evesham; and being summoned into school, morning and afternoon, by the bell which hung (and still hangs) over the main door.

All in all, time having dulled the pain of bad times, memories of school and childhood are very happy ones – "life seemed very simple in those days".'

THE 3Rs AND NOT MUCH ELSE

'We moved to Bentley in 1919. The old Squire, Mrs Cheap, died near Christmas. After a service was held at the Manor, her coffin was carried on a farm waggon to Bromsgrove station. She was buried in Scotland with her husband. We schoolchildren were lined up in the playground and we had to stand to attention as the coffin passed.

John Henry Hopkins was the name of the headmaster. The pupils came from a large area of Webheath and Ham Green as well as Upper Bentley and Lower Bentley. The school was built by the estate in 1882. It had three classrooms. There were about 70 children. Miss Phibbs and Miss Thomas taught the younger children. We stayed at school until we were 14. We were taught the 3Rs and not much else. The girls had sewing classes from Mrs Hopkins two afternoons a week. (The headmaster and his wife lived in the black and white cottage next to the school.) She had a big basket with the girls' work in. For some reason it always seemed to be pillowcases.

I can remember two pictures in the school. When Mr Rowlens took over he asked why the glass was broken. Someone told him Mr

A class at Crowle school in 1920.

Hopkins broke them, throwing chalk at Blanche Stitch who talked too much! One picture was *When did you last see your father?* There was also an oak tablet, a memorial to the scholars who died in the Great War.'

A NEW SCHOOL

'In 1927 a new school was built in Wolverley village, provided by the Sebright Trustees, a village charity, at a cost of £10,000.

An elementary endowed school, it catered for pupils from five to 14 years and was considered extremely modern, having as well as normal classrooms and offices, a domestic science room and a woodwork room.

These special rooms were also used for the benefit of visiting pupils from nearby villages and had specialist teachers. All the older girls had a grounding in cookery, laundry, housewifery etc, whilst the older boys learned simple woodwork skills and also gardening. Because of this, few children left at 14 unable to work towards maintaining their own families at a later date. As the headmaster was heard to remark on many occasions, "You may not shine academically, but at least you'll have the knowledge to budget, grow vegetables, make things and cook so that your own children will be provided for!"

The main attraction of the school was the novelty of flushing toilets. Probably the first ever seen by the children – for these were the days, even until the 1940s, of the bucket privy.

Although modern, the school had no electricity. Gas for lighting – oh, the broken mantles – and a coke boiler below the school to provide heating and dry damp garments. The "teachers' room" had a range-like grate on which the kettle for cuppas was boiled.

No school dinners in those days, although in 1939 it was one of the first in Worcestershire to begin school meal provision. This was for the benefit of evacuees who had been placed with foster parents in the village at the outbreak of war, increasing the school roll by at least one third.

There was poverty, but most children were unaware of deprivation. Their homes were happy in spite of many problems, lack of money, damp etc. Several had cause to be grateful for the Police Boot Fund, having to walk miles in all weathers! A cup of hot Horlicks was served mid-morning – a weekly payment being made for this, but, magically, a welcome drink seemed available to all. Even in those days, teachers ensured that all were cared for as much as possible. The headmaster's wife often delivered a large pan of soup and bread for those who had "forgotten" their lunchtime piece on a cold day.

The numbers of the school were swelled again in 1946 when ex-internees from the Far East were housed temporarily in the area, and their children entered school.

In 1947, all children over eleven were transferred to senior schools in the Kidderminster area – a sorry time really for this thriving village school. In later years the school was "modernised" and, in 1958, electricity was installed and the old gas lighting was removed.

A good grounding was given to all children in the 3Rs. Respect for the teacher was expected – and received, and few children left school without a basic education not only in schoolwork, but also in a caring, courteous lifestyle.'

SCHOOL DOCTOR?

'About 70 years ago at Far Forest, one of the pupils fell off a swing, the "Giant Stride", one of those with a centre pole from which came rods supporting a circular seat. He cut his nose very badly and was taken by a teacher to her father who was an animal castrator, to have it stitched. A novel form of school medical service!'

CATSHILL SCHOOL

'A lady of 87 remembers her school days at the old school on the Stourbridge road where the dairy now is. Girls wore long dresses, white pinafores and boots. Boots always had to be clean, and any child with dirty boots was sent home. Apparently she and her 15 brothers and sisters had to wear bags over their boots when Little Rocky Lane, opposite the war memorial, was muddy.

Our mothers have some amusing stories about their schooldays. One day a lad decided to get his own back on one of his least favourite teachers who was on her way to the privy. The ladies and gents privies backed onto each other, and the lad found a gap just big enough to push a piece of holly through. On another occasion on a dark night at midnight a prankster rang the school bell and frightened the life out of the nearby sleeping residents!

In 1914 the school moved to a new building in Gibb Lane. In those days and for the next few decades the 3Rs were of paramount importance. "The cat sat on the mat" was how we learned to read. We had mental arithmetic (with weekly tests), arithmetical problems and spelling (again with weekly tests), and we each had a report on them to take home to our parents.

Apart from classroom work there was gardening for the boys and needlework for the girls. There was "drill" in the playground and stoolball and netball. At playtime the children took part in the old games such as "The farmer's in his den", "In and out the Scottish bluebells" and "I wrote a letter to my love".

As the seasons changed, so would the games – marbles, skipping, whip and top, hopscotch and a ball game called "sevens" played against the walls of the school hall. In icy weather there was the fun of long slides in the playground.

In summertime, Miss Free taught country dancing and "Gathering Peascods" etc, and then they would go and dance at local fêtes. The girls would be proudly dressed in blue short sleeved frocks with a white collar and cuffs and white ankle socks and white plimsolls.

Catshill school choir was formed by Miss Trim, a very popular teacher who filled the children with enthusiasm. They always started with "warming up" scales and sang the traditional songs, *Summer is a comin' in*, *Come lasses and lads*, *Trelawney*, and, especially for Empire Day, *Land of Hope and Glory*. The highlight for this choir was when they competed in the Three Choirs Festival. Miss Trim took them to Malvern and their final rehearsal was on the hills above St Anne's Well. The choir's rendition of *Come lasses and lads* won them the banner for their school.'

LITTLETON SCHOOL

'I started school in Middle Littleton in 1920 when I was five years old. I lived in South Littleton, so I walked through the fields, a distance of about a mile. Several of us walked together, but a girl called May Bickerstaff, a little bit older than me, was in charge.

There was no school uniform as such in those days. A collar and tie was a must and short trousers. Long trousers were not worn until boys reached the age of 14.

The school day started with prayers. We all sat at our desks in rows with two boys to a desk. The headmaster was extremely strict, almost cruel at times, especially if one was caught talking or misbehaving. A box around the ears was a regular occurrence.

Lessons consisted of the 3Rs and geography. Some of the older boys travelled by coach to a neighbouring village once a week for woodwork lessons. We also played games and football on the field opposite the school. Occasionally the football team played other village teams.

The poor children who were not so bright were given the tasks of sweeping the playground and other menial jobs. I remember one boy walked home after such duties. He thought his school day was over. Needless to say, he was in terrible trouble the next day.

The school was heated by open fireplaces and stoves. An old lady (she seemed old to me at the time) used to clean the ashes from the fires and fill the inkwells with ink. I left school when I was 14.'

IMPORTANT DAYS

'In the 1920s I attended Malvern Link church school. One of the important dates in the year was the one on which the summer fête was held on the vicarage lawn at which we danced the maypole. We had to practise for weeks beforehand and our teacher was a very strict disciplinarian, so woe betide the one who made a mistake and so threw the whole lot into disarray.

On Empire Day (24th May) we all wore little bows of red, white and blue ribbon and sang patriotic songs.

At the end of the summer term we had a sports afternoon, which was held in a field in Church Road, opposite St Matthias' church, now a housing estate. Various races were run – egg and spoon, three-legged and sack, to name just a few.

Two days in the year which I remember from my schooldays at the church school are Ascension Day, when we all went to church in the morning and had the remainder of the day as a holiday, and Armistice Day (11th November) when we all proudly wore our poppies and had a service in school. The two minutes' silence was observed and all the names of the former pupils who were killed in the First World War were read out from a board which hung on the school wall. One of the names should have been that of my uncle, but unfortunately a mistake had been made and the name on the board was that of another uncle, who was still alive, so each year the headmaster asked me what the name should have been.'

OUR SCHOOL OUTING

'I wonder what schoolchildren of today would think of our annual school outing. We left Upton on Severn by train at 9.40 on a Saturday morning, complete with sandwiches, bound for Tewkesbury. Leaving the station we walked through the town to join the river path to Deerhurst, where we looked round the Saxon church and nearby chapel. It was then time to eat our lunch which we throughly enjoyed, seated in a row along the river bank. Feeling well fortified, we retraced our steps – all four miles – back to Tewkesbury, where we were shown round the abbey. That left us a short time in which to spend our pennies (maybe sixpence or a shilling if we were lucky) on presents to take home. Catching the 5 pm train, we were back in Upton by 5.30, having had a very happy day.'

NO SHOES

'In the 1920s children were admitted to Kempsey school as early as three years old, when they had a rest in the afternoons on canvas cots. In inclement weather there was much absenteeism, and sometimes the reason was "no shoes".

In 1929 many older children were transferred from Pirton and Norton schools to form a senior top class. They were transported on an unreliable lorry and often ended up walking most of the way.

We were taken to the river for swimming lessons, where the girls were allowed to change behind a screen tied to two trees.'

SCHOOLDAYS FROM THE 1930s

Little changed for the next generation of children, though the war brought its own dangers and pressures.

SCHOOL IN REDDITCH

'I was born in 1923, and when I went to school at the age of five it was to Bridge Street council school (now Holyoakes Field) in the infants department, which was co-educational. Some children started as young as three, and these – in the "baby" class – had a nap on a small camp bed every afternoon.

In those days we moved on up to the "big girls" or "big boys" department at seven and stayed there until we were 14. The teachers we had in each class taught all subjects, but for the last year or two a few specialised and always taught geography, history or physical training. This last took place on the asphalt covered playground, but for Sports Day we walked to the communal playing fields not far from the school.

The curriculum included singing, country dancing, poetry (we learned a poem a week), and acting plays. All the girls learned to knit (a winter occupation), while in the summer we learned needlework, first embroidery then dressmaking, by hand until we reached the top class where we had the use of two hand machines. I was lucky as we had a treadle sewing machine at home and I could take my work home to do. We also had art as well.

For the last couple of years we attended a domestic science course once a week at a separate centre and learned cookery, laundry and CDS (Combined Domestic Subjects). We had old-fashioned flat irons, which had to be heated on a large gas-fired, pyramid-shaped construction in the middle of a room. We were carefully supervised as we walked round in single file, returning cooling irons and picking up heated ones. CDS was a practical way of learning housekeeping and cleaning, as we practised on the flat lived in by the two domestic science teachers. We also did their washing in with whatever we had brought from home. This was a mixed blessing, as it was all too easy for a novice to put a hot iron on a delicate piece of underwear!

While we were doing housework the boys were in another part of the centre learning woodwork and metalwork.

Our day started at 9 am, went on until noon, and then from 2 pm to 4 pm in the infants school, and 4.30 for the over-sevens. Everyone walked to school and most walked home again for lunch and back again for the afternoon session. Only those from as far away as Webheath brought sandwiches and stayed on. The distance I lived from school must have been at least half a mile.

For a while I joined the Brownie pack at my Sunday school, which took place in the evening. So, even in winter, I walked from home and back again, probably three-quarters of a mile each way, quite alone and unafraid.

During the summer holidays we usually had a day trip by rail to our nearest seaside town – Weston super Mare – and it cost five shillings. I well remember adverts on the station stating fares were one penny per mile!'

'St George's infants school, Redditch, was opposite the church and next to the junior school. The infants department consisted of one large room, divided into two by a curtain, and one small room (called the Baby Room). Both rooms had large black stoves with fireguards. On one was a picture of a camel, *The Ship of the Desert*.

The headmistress was Miss Ida Oates (she was called "The Governess"). She was very strict, and those of us who had more than two sums wrong had to stand in a line with hands outstretched for a smack with a ruler.

We always had a half-day's holiday on Shrove Tuesday and Ascension Day. On the morning of Shrove Tuesday we joined hands and ran round the playground singing, "Pancake Day is a very happy day, If you don't give us a holiday, we'll all run away!" On 24th May, Empire Day, the Union Jack was unfurled and we all sang the National Anthem. At harvest time we went in procession to church with our harvest offerings. At Christmas we decorated the rooms with lanterns made of paper which we first coloured. They were hung across a string. The vicar came every week for religious instruction. I once got into trouble because he told my mother that I had yawned in his lesson.

The three year olds were in the Baby Room. They slept every afternoon on the floor on straw mats.

Our first attempts at writing were on slates with chalk. We were then promoted to paper and pencil. We learned to sew and knit before we left the infants school. I remember making a kettle-holder. We also did "corking" (now called French knitting) on cotton-reels into which four nails were knocked. Those of us who could afford it bought penny balls of rainbow wool.

We could take "lunch" for our morning break. The most popular snacks were little sweet apples called "Doddins". There must have been a lot of poverty because the poorer children would beg our apple-stalks to eat. They called them "Storkels".

Times must have been very hard; discipline was strict; but I have the happiest of memories of my schooldays.'

HAPPY DAYS AT HEADLESS CROSS

'The buildings were Victorian and we did not have flush toilets, but the teachers made our schooldays very happy. Discipline was quite strict, but from the reception class right through to the highest class, we were well taught. The subjects included arithmetic (and mental arithmetic), English with literature, compositions and spelling, history and geography and, as we got older, domestic science (cooking, cleaning and washing) for the girls and wood and metalwork for the boys. Our handwriting and spelling was taken into account in our various examination papers, but we also had an examination in those subjects separately. I left school at 14 years old because of financial circumstances, but that education stood me in good stead for work and for life.'

A PACKED LUNCH

'Our village did not have a school so we had to walk to either Fladbury or Wyre Piddle, both a mile away but in opposite directions. We took a packed lunch with a small tin of cocoa and sugar to make a drink. It was a bit weak sometimes as we liked to eat the dry ingredients on the way to school.

It was a church school and we had services in the church on certain occasions, such as Ash Wednesday and Ascension Day when we were allowed to go home afterwards. The local rector came once a week to take scripture classes and to test our knowledge.

There were no uniforms for school until we "went up" to the senior school at Pershore at the age of eleven. We generally had hand-me-down clothes and clothing in general was poor, especially shoes. There was parish relief for some but people were proud and did not ask. To have something new was exciting.'

Country dancing at Wichenford school in 1935.

WICHENFORD SCHOOL

'We had a two mile walk to school and I remember the joy of Monday afternoons when we were allowed to go early to catch Owen's market bus home. Not only did we appreciate the ride but it was interesting to hear the farmers and their wives gossiping about the day's events.

There was a bell on the roof of the school which was rung at nine o'clock, and how the dawdlers ran when they heard the first peal!

I vividly remember our teachers, on cold days, heating up the icy milk in a saucepan on the school stove and making cocoa for us.

At Christmas time the local Squire's wife gave red cloaks to girls and tweed jackets to boys of large families. My sister had a cloak, and how I envied her, and looked forward to having it when she had outgrown it!

In the summer the teachers organised coach outings for all the children, parents and siblings, to Bristol, Bishop's Cleeve or Weston super Mare. Many children would never have seen the sea had it not been for these outings.

Being a church school the clergyman took scripture once a week and there was a yearly inspection by a church official to find out if religious instruction was being given properly – it always was! Then there were the dreaded days when the HMI visited. How we trembled in case his eye fell on us to read or say our tables. We knew we would be letting our excellent teachers down if we failed to come up to standard. Achievements were usually high and our school managers encouraged us by giving prizes at Christmas, not only for good work, but also for good attendance and appearance.'

STRICT BUT FAIR

'Ombersley and Sytchampton endowed schools both flourished, as indeed they do today. The endowment is from Lloyd's Educational Foundation, founded in the 18th century by Richard Lloyd for assistance in education and administered by a trust. There was a high pass rate of pupils to grammar schools and help was given by the trust for uniforms and books. In spite of this, in those days some were unable to take up their places for financial reasons.

Mr Tommy Styles was headmaster of Ombersley endowed school from 1918 to 1952. He was highly regarded, strict but fair. Children were expected to be clean and tidy. On occasions they were sent home to clean their shoes. A girl who had the temerity to come with a Bette Davis hair-do was sent home to comb it out. Discipline was strict. The playground was divided by an iron railing to segregate boys and girls. No one dared to break the rule. Misbehaviour was punished with a cane for the boys or a flat ruler on the palm for the girls. Hands were sometimes blistered. As he was known to be a fair man, this was regarded as just retribution.'

IN TO THE REGIMENTAL MARCH

'At Honeybourne, children were marched into school each morning to the regimental march of the Worcestershire regiment. Before going home for the midday meal they sang a hymn requesting the Lord's presence at the table, and they finished each day by singing the National Anthem. Boys and girls went in by separate entrances though classes were mixed. Every other week the boys were taken, by train, to Badsey school for woodwork lessons, and in the alternate weeks the girls went for cookery lessons. And those were the days, too, when the headmaster lived in the school house. In 1940 Blackminster school opened and from then on Honeybourne served five to eleven year olds only. A gentleman who was with the first intake of students to go to Blackminster remembered what a revelation it was with its own science block, gymnasium and domestic rooms.

A particularly vivid memory of those who attended Honeybourne school before the war is of the sports days in which Honeybourne, Bretforton and Pebworth schools took part. The sports days were held each year at Honeybourne and Bretforton and always finished with a tea in the village hall. Besides the races there were fairground rides and other entertainments to make a remarkable day.'

DUDLEY SCHOOLS

'Dudley Girls' High School, which I attended from 1930 to 1938, had a *very* forward-looking headmistress, Miss Sybil Frood. We had a "School Court", where matters of moment or misdemeanour were discussed by the Head Girl and prefects. The classes all had a form room and form teacher, but moved into other rooms for lessons. A bell told us when to move from one room to another. After she had won the Ladies Singles at Wimbledon, Miss Dorothy Round came to visit us – she had been a pupil of the school. She said she had always wanted to ring the school bell and was, of course, allowed to do so.

The uniform was unlike that of any other school. The tunics were cornflower blue with V-necks and a small inverted pleat from the waist on either side. A narrow self-material belt with a buckle – just the thread-through variety – finished it off. The tunics had to clear the calf when we knelt down and so were almost a mini-skirt! Long, black, woollen stockings, navy pants with a pocket to hold a handkerchief, a blouse in pale blue gingham with neat, pointed collars and buttoned cuffs, together with a cornflower-blue tie with white diagonal stripes completed the indoor uniform. There was a cornflower-blue blazer in a substantial cloth bearing a badge with the Castle and Staffordshire knot embroidered in gold. The school took fee-paying pupils, of whom I was one. Quite a number of scholarships were awarded to Dudley children and a few from neighbouring Staffordshire – hence the badge. Summer term saw us free to wear our own choice of summer dresses.

One memorable day was when we rushed out of school to cheer the Duke of Kent and Princess Marina on their way to Dudley Civic Centre. They were on their honeymoon at Himley Hall at the time. Someone must have been on the look-out because the exodus wasn't official.

Schooldays and childhood over, with war looming on the horizon, in 1938 I became a student at Dudley Training College for Teachers. The foundation stone had been laid exactly 30 years before, in September 1908, by the Countess of Dudley, and the college was opened in July 1909 by Mr Walter Runciman, Minister of Education. It was built to last and life inside was well ordered and disciplined. The principal's room was on the first floor and had a balcony – an admirable place from which to hear the feet of late students crossing the gravel beneath and note whether a man student had neglected to shave!

The outbreak of war at the beginning of the autumn term 1939 made return to college late because the whole building, including the hostels, had to be blacked out. Local students were summoned to help and it must have been hundreds of yards of blackout material that we machined. The college must have felt vulnerable because Ere Hill, where it was built, stood high above sea level (1,000 feet, it is claimed) and, as the biology lecturer used to say as she gazed out over "The Vale of Tipton" – her words – there was nothing between us and the Ural Mountains. The college added First Aid to its courses, which caused the men students to faint and have to be carried out.

Conscription had already been announced at the end of the first year, and many of the men in our year were called up at the end of their college course and, sadly, did not return from the war.

The war caused more radical changes in the years that followed – the Maria Grey College was evacuated to Dudley from London and the classrooms along one wing became dormitories.

Dudley Guest Hospital didn't escape wartime changes either. Two of their wards, Messiter and Georgina, were taken over for casualties from D-Day and the area of the Wilhelmina Canal. As a Red Cross nurse putting in her 50 hours at that hospital, I became involved in these changes.'

A DAY TO REMEMBER

'At the end of the war, when I was ten, all the Church of England primary schools in the Worcester Diocese were invited to take part in a service at the cathedral.

There was much activity to learn the chosen hymns, one of which I remember was *Sion City*, and the day out was anticipated with mixed feelings. It would be a day away from lessons, but would we remember the words and what if we got lost? We were just country children from Wichenford who had never been far from home before.

The day arrived and we travelled on Price's coach, an adventure in itself. We must have been late because when we arrived we were ushered into a cathedral jam packed with children and we just managed to squeeze onto school benches at the very back. It was awesome, I had never seen so many children before!

I think some of us were too excited to sing at first, but the cathedral was soon filled with children's voices echoing round the vaulted roof. The Bishop told us the story of the donkey carrying a load of salt who fell into a stream and discovered that his load was suddenly lightened. He did this on many journeys until he found he had a load of sponges! There must be a moral somewhere.

Later we picnicked on the cricket ground with all the other schools then returned home very tired, but excited, ready to tell our classmates who hadn't made the outing of our day in the big city.'

AN EVENTFUL SCHOOL YEAR

'The whole of the school year, in the 1950s at Broadwas school, was eventful. On May Day, whatever the weather, the maypole (once a telegraph pole) was brought out of storage and bedecked with new brightly-coloured braids. To the accompaniment of records played on the His Master's Voice gramophone, the boys and girls took their braids, bowed to their partners and away they went, dancing round and round and in and out, encircling the pole, enjoying every moment. It was great fun, on a special day, and the summer had come!

Fields, woods, lanes and hedgerows were all ours to explore. On sunny days we took our crude home-made fishing rods to Mr Skan's pond and, crouching over the edge, found scorpions, caddis, snails, boatmen etc to stock the school aquarium (a large glass accumulator).

All kinds of butterflies were brought to school to be fed and

Children at Broadwas school in the early 1950s.

watched until they spun cocoons, and later emerged from the chrysalis as beautiful butterflies or moths – to be released into the sunshine. This involved recording and illustrating, but was full of wonder!

Mr Taylor, from the local garage, made us a double-sided glass anthouse (called a formicarium). We filled it with damp soil and put in a few ants. It was fascinating to see through the glass the intense activity that went on inside. The boys put in some red ants and wondered if they would fight the black ones!

The hedgerows provided a profusion of wild flowers to collect, identify and label for the "Nature Table". We went for walks up Stoney Ley where there were badger setts, a woodland and, in the May time, a whole orchard full of marguerites – a lovely scene!

The village fête was exciting. There was always a children's fancy dress parade, maypole dancing and sports, arranged by the head teacher and so we all took part.

There was the Music Festival at Alfrick in July, where we met children from neighbouring schools. We were not all "nightingales" but all the juniors sang and enjoyed the occasion. We also went to the Three Counties Show for a whole day of sight-seeing.

The highlight of summer was the outing. The Elan Valley was the favourite venue. We sang with the vicar in a church at Nantmel on the way to the reservoirs, had a swim (or paddle) in the river Wye, a packed lunch in Birmingham's model village and tea in the Elan Valley Hotel. After fourpennyworth of chips each at Leominster, we sang all the way home. We were very tired.

On Harvest Festival morning we processed from school, laden with gifts of all kinds of produce. Mammoth marrows had to be taken in a borrowed barrow. The rector met us at the church and we had a special service.

Hop picking days were memorable. Most mothers and friends picked hops, and the children enjoyed their lunch hour in the hopyard, returning to school with arms full of trailing hops to decorate the classrooms, which were soon filled with a delicious brewery, sleep-conducive fragrance. There were always gypsies in the adjoining field in September, colourful and interesting. We saw a big caravan being burnt when the Gypsy Queen died.

At Christmas we performed our Nativity play in the church. Props and costumes were improvised and we all took part. The school party was a rollicking affair with plenty of jelly and cakes. There was also a party at Broadwas Court by invitation of the Squire. That was a more subdued occasion as our host was not known to us and perhaps we were somewhat overawed by the splendour of the setting.

THE WORLD OF WORK

ON THE LAND

Generations of Worcestershire families have made their living from the land, though that way of life has changed in so many ways over the last 50 years. Yet still within living memory, the hop pickers came every year, horses provided the power on the land and farm work was labour intensive, involving whole village communities. It was not an easy life, and hours were long and hard from an early age.

GROWING UP ON A FARM 1910

'My first impressions of our farm near Hadzor and Oddingley, in about 1910, were of watching life in the farmyards from our upstairs nursery windows, one of which looked over the carthorse stables and the other one the cowsheds, piggeries and poultry pens.

It was wonderful to see the beautiful horses, mostly pedigree shires, coming in from the fields of a morning, usually coming to the yard pool for a drink. The pool was directly under our window and was the remains of the moat which surrounded the house and quite a large area when, in the past, it was a moated manor house.

The horses would go into the stables (eight or ten of them) to be fed, groomed and harnessed and would come out geared for work in the fields or round the farm. For the ones that were going ploughing a nosebag each of food for the midday snack would be slung above the harness, also the ploughman's fraile with his bait (ie lunch) and a small barrel (about 16 inch circumference by 6 inch diameter, so quite small) of cider likewise slung over the harness.

From the other window we would see the cows come in for, I expect, the afternoon milking, the morning one being *very* early.

We kept shorthorns, which were dual purpose, quite good milkers and quite good for beef, but the milk output was far below that of the Friesians of today. When the bull was let out to do his duty with a cow, it was exciting to see him being got in again. There would always be two men with sticks, or a short hayfork if he was being "a bit awkward".

Pig feeding was a noisy time. At the first sound of a bucket being moved when the pigs' mealtime was near, it would set off the squealing, knocking about of troughs and jumping up on hind legs to look over the wall or gate. If the trough could be filled from over the wall it was easy, but going amongst them with a bucket of swill the man was lucky if half of it was not spilt.

As we grew older and were allowed out in the yards and buildings on our own, "looking the eggs" was always popular. We called it "looking" rather than "collecting" as the hens loved to "steal" their nests and lay in buildings or haystacks and sometimes in hedges. The guinea fowl like to lay amongst stinging nettles. They used to roost in the elm trees and were excellent watchdogs as they would set up a proper clatter if a prowling fox came round at night. There was a belief among country folk that a fox could "stare" a bird like a pheasant or guinea fowl down from a tree, the theory being that the fox would walk round and round the tree, often looking up, and the bird, unable to take its eye off the fox, would get so giddy it would fall to the ground and quickly meet its end.

Each season as it came along had its pleasure and its interests. The run-up to Christmas was more than busy. Two or three women would come to do the plucking of the young cockerels, geese and turkeys. My father or a farm worker did the killing. Then my poor mother dressed them, which was really hard work. The turkeys' innards were always hard to draw.

After the birds had all been collected or delivered we were free to enjoy our own Christmas, doing the decorating, which had to be done on Christmas Eve and not before because it was considered to be unlucky to do so earlier. Logs had to be got in for the fires and so on. After the excitement of our stockings and breakfast, church was the order of the day before we were allowed to open our main presents. After Christmas dinner we were sent off for a walk on our own, so that the maids could have the rest of the day off and my father and mother, no doubt, would have a good sleep.

Boxing Day we all went rabbiting with several ferrets to bolt the rabbits from the holes, a couple of dogs and one or two men with guns. Sometimes the rabbits would bolt well and sometimes a ferret would kill a rabbit in the hole and lay up, so it had to be dug out if the hole was not too big. When there was a decent "bag" we would have lunch. A fire was lighted and we would cut a stick from the hedge and thread a piece of home-cured bacon on it. What a lovely smokey taste it had cooked on the wood fire. You held a piece of bread in your hand and dabbed it with fat from the bacon. This was followed by mince pies and cider and cheese. We were supposed to eat apples but managed to steal a drop of cider too.

In January and February there was usually frost and snow, so there was sliding on the pools if the frost was hard enough, or making a slide somewhere; snowmen to make; and tobogganning on a tray from the house until we had a proper one.

March brought the lambing when the ewes were brought to the fields near the farm to give birth. Cold and weakly lambs were brought in and put in wicker hampers lined with hay and placed in front of the hearth fire to warm up. Some revived, some died and the orphans were reared with milk as pet lambs. They soon became very tame and if they could manage to get themselves into the house again later, they would lie down in front of the fire like a dog.

April brought an abundance of wild flowers, violets were the first and to find some white ones was a great treat because there were very few of them. Primroses, bluebells and cowslips followed. Very good home-made wine was made from these, they were so plentiful it was no sin to pick them as it is today.

In the same way, birds' nesting was the pleasure of practically all country children. There were so many birds about then that an egg or two would not be missed especially a blackbird's, they were very numerous. Moorhens and coot were everywhere, on ponds, brooks and canals, not eaten up as they are today by mink.

In June came the haymaking. There were mowing-machines by then to cut the hay and swath turners to turn it, a job that women used to do in the past. Actually very few women worked in the fields in our area, as there was always plenty of gloving work to be done from the comfort of home, sitting by the cottage door in the sun or by the fire in winter. We children loved to take the men's tea down to the fields. Sometimes visiting aunts, uncles and cousins made a special journey from the town to join in haymaking teas.

About this time of year the travelling shire stallions would come round, led by their groom (often the owner's son). What a splendid sight they were for children, great beasts 17 to 18 hands high and weighing two or three tons, their manes often plaited with coloured ribbons and shining brasses on what harness they carried. They were greeted with great excitement and pleasure by us as the groom was a great favourite of ours. He and the horses often stayed overnight.

The mating, too, was exciting with more than an element of danger attached. Several men would be helping, one or two to hold the mare which would kick and squeal and prance around, while the horse became restive, pawing the ground, neighing, rearing up, probably frothing at the mouth and making himself a real handful, prior to mounting the mare. How naturally mating, birth and death came to country children and perhaps more so to farmers' children as they saw more of it.

Harvesting took much longer before the days of combine harvesters, when the sheaves of corn had to be left out in the field to dry out, often being propped up in stooks of six or eight, done by hand. The binder of those days cut the corn and arms very like a windmill lowered the corn into the knives. Then it fell onto canvas sheets which lifted it up so that it was pressed and tied in bundles (in sheaves) and thrown out every few yards. The village children were always around when there was a field of corn to be cut for the chance of getting a rabbit for dinner and all the fun.

Rabbits at that time were so plentiful as to be a nuisance to farmers, but how almost life-saving they were as meat during the First World War a few years later. The rabbits in the corn would run towards the centre of the uncut corn, frightened by the sound of the binder. Just a few would leave early and often a fox or two would slink off, but it was towards the end that the rest would run off with the children after them, often falling head over heels over the sheaves that the stacker hadn't had time to stack. The big boys with sticks would manage to kill some and my father and a friend, who always had to be a good shot and *very* responsible with all the children about, would account for quite a number.

Next came the cider making when the cider apples and the perry pears were shaken from the trees with long hook poles, and those poles did have to be long for perry pear trees were often 25 foot tall. They were left on the ground to ripen (it looked more like rot) until being collected and made into cider or perry. We used to make three or four hogsheads, for farmhands of those days were given a little barrel or stone jar of cider most days and there would be six or seven regular hands on a farm of 400 to 500 acres at that time.

Threshing was done chiefly before Christmas. The machine was hired from nearby farmers or, in our case, a jack of all trades type, a resourceful chap who could mend machines, sharpen knives of all kinds etc in order to make a living out of season. It's many years since I last heard the "hum" of a threshing machine but it still lingers on my memory.

So Christmas has come round again and another year of fun and collection of knowledge of all kinds has come to an end.'

FARM LIFE IN THE 1930s

'No combine harvester! On our farm at Barnt Green a man had to cut a path all round the cornfield by scythe before the horses and binder could come in to cut the crop, then all the sheaves had to be stood up in eights, by hand, and left to dry for about three weeks. If it rained in the meantime you had turn all the sheaves to dry out as soon as the sun appeared again.

Sheaves were loaded on waggons and taken to be built into ricks.

Later the threshing machine arrived and each sheaf had to have its string cut, hard on the fingers, before going into the machine. The corn fell into sacks, up to two hundredweight which a man had to carry to the barn, often up steps, to the granary. The "cavings" (husks) had to be dug out from under the machine and bagged, very dusty work, to be used in feed mixes, or as bedding. The straw was bundled by the machine, but then had to be rebuilt as a rick!

Horses could turn hay to dry it, but often hand turning was needed as well. When dry, the hay was loaded loose onto waggons, taken to the rickyard, unloaded and built into ricks, all by hand. When you needed the hay, you took a huge hay knife and cut blocks out of the rick and carried it to the animals. If you sold hay, you got the hay trusser (or presser) with his machine. The cut blocks were compressed and tied with string in the machine, when each weighed 56 to 60 lbs, easy to load onto waggons and take to market.

Swedes, potatoes etc had to be picked up by hand and put into carts or sacks in the field, then carried to clamps (straw-lined pits) or put on straw in sheds. In either case, more straw went on top as frost protection. Clamps had soil put over the straw, to keep rain out if possible. Very cold on the hands and back!

After milking, again usually hand done, the warm milk was carried to the yard near the dairy to be cooled by filling a container which allowed milk to trickle over metal tubes (through which cold water flowed) and into a churn. If a commercial dairy bought the milk, the amount in the churn had to be measured and recorded. If for the farm's own retail sales, it had to be measured into cans for each customer (who supplied their own cans). For cream, butter or cheese making at home the churns were carried into the dairy.

Hedges had to be cut with a slasher, a heavy long-handled hook-shaped knife, used upwards from ground to head height – very hard work.

Keeping animals indoors was also hard work, as they had to have straw as bedding, and at least once a day all straw, wet with urine, soiled with manure, and the manure itself, had to be removed and piled into a well-shaped heap to rot until ready to spread on the land. Then new straw was mixed with what was left. Food had to be carried to them, and, unless there was a big yard outside the building with a water trough, you carried water to them in buckets. Several times a day.

Poultry was usually free range and was looked after by the farmer's wife. The money from egg sales was often the only money she had for herself (including for clothes for the children).

Animals usually walked to and from markets, when the drovers heartily cursed folk who left gates open, as animals always shot into gardens if possible. You tried to have extra hands (your children usually) who went ahead and shut gates, or, if there were none, stood guard in gateways to minimise trouble. Once Father bought a bull at Bromsgrove that was so tired it kept lying down on the way home. Each lie-down lasted ages, so Father sat on it till it was ready to move as he was weary standing waiting for it!

Ailments of people or animals were usually treated with home-made remedies. Not only were doctors and vets expensive but without modern drugs they could do little more than anyone else. To call on their services was a last resort.

Blacksmiths were plentiful. Barnt Green people could find at least six within three miles of the village!'

A DREADFUL MEMORY

'A dreadful memory of 1936 or 1937 is when our farmer neighbours at Overbury were affected by foot and mouth disease. All their cattle and pigs (cloven-footed animals) had to be shot and burned in deep trenches with lime. It was heart-breaking for us all, especially the village shepherds, cowmen and labourers, and the tearful farmers saw their established 20 year old herd destroyed.

We had no birds singing, no dogs were allowed off their leashes, our chickens had to be kept inside their houses. We had straw and buckets of disinfectant everywhere. Fields were completely out of bounds because neighbouring Overbury farms had huge pedigree herds all over their large estates.

Fortunately, this outbreak was contained and did not spread. The fires were visible six miles away (it was wintertime) and the pungent smell permeated everywhere. Prayers were said in our churches. It was a miracle indeed when Greaves Brothers were finally permitted to start a new herd of cows and to buy in some sheep and pigs again.'

HAGLEY HILL FARM IN THE 1950s

'In 1951 the farm was about to be compulsorily purchased by the government. We were given leave to buy it and start farming. We married in February 1952 and work started on 25th March. There was no electricity, no gates or doors on the buildings and only a feeble water supply. The alterations to the cottage were done on permits; coal was on dockets and neither of us knew anyone! The farm tracks would only take machinery in bottom gear.

We had a new Grey Fergis, a secondhand iron-wheel Fordson tractor, an ancient mower, a tip-up trailer, a secondhand combine and a fiddle. We employed two workers – one youth of 17 and one woman.

We grew corn, wheat, barley, oats, potatoes, sugar beet (drilled with a horse called Blossom) and grass seed. We kept beef cattle, hens (Rhode Island Reds and Light Sussex) and pigs. All the fields were referred to by names eg Big Stocking, Little Stocking, Top Shutt, Bottom Shutt. Our livestock markets then were at Hagley, Kidderminster and Bromsgrove.

Seed potatoes, fertilizer and machinery were delivered to Hagley station, then we had to collect frozen seed, dented machinery and burst fertilizer bags! Pig and hen food arrived on flat-bedded lorries, in hessian one-hundredweight sacks. Grass seed came in beautiful linen sacks.

We made silage in a pit and were the first in the area to do so. We planted potatoes which were harvested with help from the locals and women from Lye (in the Black Country). Their van always returned heavier than when it came.

Children from the local school came to picnic in the meadow and play games. Their voices could be heard: "In and out the windows" and "The farmer wants a wife".'

HOP PICKING 1920

'Country life was ruled by the seasons and hop picking heralded autumn. Camp Hill and Clay Hill were two hopyards in Hallow and being small there was not the influx of outsiders as in larger yards elsewhere. Women from the local villages were the main pickers and children would help, picking into open umbrellas stuck into the ground. They tired quickly and would soon be off to gather nuts in a nearby coppice or climb to the top of a steep bank from where they could watch the steamer from Stourport on its way down the Severn to Worcester. At Camp Hill the grassy bank was so steep that the children rolling down the slope couldn't stop until they reached the bottom. Clay Hill was different – no steep hill – but nuts could still be found along the banks of a nearby brook. Rabbits, scuttling out of the fast dwindling corn, were chased but never caught. The midday meal was a picnic with a fire built with wood collected by the children. An S-shaped iron bar called a sway was pushed into the ground at an angle over the fire and the kettle hung to boil. Several families would share a fire and enjoy a gossip before work began again. Hop picking was fun – but not picking hops! Fingers got stained and bines were so rough that arms and legs became badly scratched. Hops were picked into cribs, heavy wooden frames with hessian slung between, divided into two so friends could share.

Hop picking at Hallow in the early years of the century, a time for all the family to work together.

Workers were paid by the bushel. Twice a day the cribs were emptied and a card marked to keep tally of the bushels picked. When the oasthouses where the hops were dried became full the farmer would call, "Pull no more bines" and work ended for that day. The last day was a fun day. Pickers, whilst waiting for the final bushelling and payment, would play jokes on each other. Most popular was cribbing – two or three would pick a victim and dump him into a crib among the hops. When picking was over and the labourers paid, home they went – happy that their children would have stout boots for the winter; most important as transport was non existent and all children walked to school whatever the distance.'

HOP PICKING IN THE 1940s

'Thank heavens it only took place once a year, one had to spend so many man-hours preparing for this event. Hop pickers' quarters or barracks had to be whitewashed and partitioned off with hessian to pass the Health Inspectors; hop kilns put in order after having been idle for eleven months; and the cribs all prepared. Then I got in contact with four "ganger" women representing Great Bridge and Tipton, Blackheath, Newport and Worcester. Some of the latter were resident on the farm, the rest coming daily by bus or lorry.

We had about 400 pickers, some no doubt babies in arms, but they all counted in the gangers' count at a shilling a head. I paid for the rail tickets, they paid the return fare. I always ended up with about a 100 spare return tickets.

Horse or tractor-drawn drays or waggons met the Black Country pickers at Leigh Court station and the Newport pickers came to Bransford. By the time all the pickers had arrived for the seven farms from Leigh Court to Pidgeon House there were up to 2,000 extra people living in Leigh not counting those in Bransford or Leigh Sinton. Leigh was transformed from a rural village into a small town almost overnight.

One or two extra policemen were resident; one nurse was drafted in, holding a morning and evening surgery at the Great House. Church Army sisters were resident, some staying with Mrs Bought, who, it is said, never served the same pudding twice in a month. They held services and Bible classes.

A man called Jim Clark kept a shop at the Great House and had about 2,000 registered customers; he coped with the ration books. He sold fresh milk daily and gave each picker two pounds of potatoes on a Sunday.

Some farms had to engage extra staff to work in the kilns and measure the hops, and booking staff. Wood and coke was supplied by the farmer for cooking. Wages could be paid on Monday, Wednesday and Friday nights, care being taken that no one was overdrawn.

Nothing was safe, from fire risk to unpicked fruit, so constant patrols were needed. Weekends were the worst time, when busloads of visitors arrived and apples and potatoes would disappear by the sackload. Most farms would have one meadow set aside for gypsies and their caravans.

Picking on a Saturday was almost a waste of time as so many would go by train to Worcester. Most of the pubs opened special bars for hop pickers. On Saturday and Sunday nights, gangs could he heard singing on their way home. There were just too many people to control though this is, of course, a biased point of view from one grower. My young family loved the excitement of it all and looked out for old friends who came year after year. Nearly all pickers referred to the district as Leigh Court as that was the station's name.

Normal farm work, like the grain harvest, came to a complete halt, when hop picking and kiln work was one's only thought.'

'Around the Shelsleys, a group of villages in the Teme valley, the ground is agricultural, used for the growing of hops and cider apples and soft fruit. The most important crop in the 1940s was the hops. There was a Land Army hostel in a local farmhouse and land girls were also billeted in village homes, and prisoners of war also helped on the land. Extra pickers were brought in from the Black Country by lorry, as many as 200. They brought their own bedding, chairs, tables and cooking pots, ready to start picking in September. Open braziers were provided by the farmer for cooking. The farm buildings had been cleaned out ready for them, the pigs and horses moved to temporary sites.

To provide for the pickers a small shop was manned in a garage at the church house. The Salvation Army sent a contingent down and they took surgery twice a day at all the farms. They lived in a wooden bungalow provided by the farmer.

Tea and cake were taken down to the hopyard morning and evening. The day started at seven o'clock and finished at six. It was all piece work, and lasted about three weeks. Cash could be subbed or kept until the end of the hop picking. A favourite place to relax was the Stanford Bridge Inn. Whole families would come for the hop picking, from grandparents down to the littlest.'

A PARADISE

'Holdfast in the early 1900s must, indeed, have been a paradise for Miss Hilda Hemus, residing at Holdfast Hall, who cultivated sweet peas in an area known by that name. The perfume must have been a delight and a far cry from the odours which often hang in the country air these days.

After school the children went to gather the flowers, which were then left overnight. In the morning, the women of the area went along to pack the blooms, fan shaped, into boxes which were then taken to Upton station for transport to London.

Hilda Hemus was famous for her sweet peas, gaining two silver medals from the National Sweet Pea Society and two first class certificates, in addition to three awards of merit for new varieties in 1907. At the Royal Agricultural Society meeting in Gloucester, attended by Edward VII, she received royal acclaim. While inspecting the flowers the King was so impressed by the beauty of Miss Hemus's exhibition that he called for her and graciously shook hands, expressing his admiration of her blooms.'

THOSE WHO WORKED ON THE LAND

'One farmer at Salwarpe in 1920 with a farm of about 300 acres had 17 carthorses (all bred on the farm) and employed a waggoner and boy, a stockman and a pigman. Waggoners rose at 5.30 am, breakfasted at 6.45 and finished their work at 3.30, after which they cleaned up and tended the horses. Three or four casual farm labourers were also employed when needed at harvest time. There were a housekeeper and two maidservants in the house.

Farmers had the services of a blacksmith on the main Worcester road, and he employed four or five men.'

'Casual work was to be had on the farms around Storridge. Most of the villagers went to the small farms to work up to the 1940s. Some mothers and small children went picking up potatoes, pulling swedes and picking sprouts. Hop picking was done on two farms in the village. Sometimes all the occupants of a household would go and pick from eight o'clock until four o'clock and the rate was sixpence a bushel. The children loved hop picking as it was done in September and the school had a whole month's holiday. Many mothers went to get extra money to help clothe the children for winter. A farm worker's wage was only 28 shillings and sixpence a week, with rent to pay out of that.'

Land clearing at Eckington – and typical working clothes of cloth cap, moleskin trousers, leather belt, shirt and waistcoat.

'The majority of people at Great Comberton worked for the Squire. In addition to their wages he would give each employee a row of potatoes from the potato field. This would keep a family supplied for a year. His men worked six days a week and on Sundays were expected to be seen in church.'

'Most of the men at Kington and Dormston worked on the land and the women in service until a decline in farming in the 1930s forced the young lads to cycle to Redditch some ten miles away to find work in the needle industry, where the pay was much better than the 30 shillings offered to farm workers.'

'Officially boys started work on the family farm at 14 years of age but they had, of course, been working hard on the farm long before that. One gentleman remembers milking at five years old. There were certain jobs the boys could do, such as putting hay up in the loft and cutting the chaff, short for the horses and long for the cows.

On market days the men and boys walked to Worcester with the cows. They started at about 8 am and arrived in Worcester by 11.15 am. The market was held then in the Farrier Street area.

At haymaking time they often got up at 3 am to cut the fields while the dew was still on them and then went back home for breakfast.'

'The majority of the men at Norton and Lenchwick worked on the land (and many women at seasonal times like onion hoeing or pea, bean and plum picking). This all changed after the war when car manufacture in the nearby Midlands towns flourished to such an extent that many men travelled to work in the factories. So many deserted the land that one farm which had a labour force of ten in 1939 was eventually reduced to four. This also coincided with mechanisation so that the horse, too, was seen less and less on the land.'

'Farming in Ombersley used to be far more intensive and productive than today. A large share of the land in the 1940s was used to grow vegetables and soft fruits. There were also extensive apple, plum and cherry orchards and still some dairy farms. Many more farm hands were needed, most of them taking home about £11 a week plus much of their food to their rent-free tied cottages. This weekly wage of £11 was above the national average. Regular overtime increased this. They did not go home at midday but brought their "bait" and a bottle of cold tea with them. Most never took a holiday longer than a day trip to the seaside. Holidays abroad were out of the question but many said they had seen enough of that during the war.

Apart from the regular workers, casual labour was required as crops matured. This was done partly by gypsies and partly by women fetched by lorry from Worcester, Droitwich, Stourport or even Tipton. At 4 pm the lorries took home the women and their prams and toddlers but the gypsies needed somewhere to rest their caravans. By then they were all of the type towed by motor vehicles and not so attractive a proposition to have near your house as the old Romany type. There were a few complaints chiefly about the late-night revelries or fights. Sanitation was another bone of contention. Some people believed that what a gypsy might do in the relative privacy of a hedgerow was unhygienic but they thought nothing of having 100 sheep in the field who did the same thing in full view and more frequently. It was quite illogical but in time the Droitwich RDC began to press for some amenities. Corrugated tin latrines were provided but old habits die hard and at first many were turned on their sides and used as tables.'

'Mum worked on the land at Bentley. One year I remember she was pea picking and she had my baby brother with her and was he cross, he didn't like it. I can see it now. Rather than she went home and lost an afternoon's money, the other women pulled the peas up and stacked them round her, and there she was, surrounded by peas, with this cross baby.

I started work for Mr Impany, from Norgrove, in 1924. Dad didn't have enough work for me at Bentley Forge. Mr Impany started farming at Upper Bentley farm and Norgrove in 1919. He was a go-ahead farmer and the first person round here to have a tractor. It was an Austin. People told him it would be too heavy for the ground – folks just didn't like them.

I helped Mr Badger with the portable bail. Mr Badger went to Wiltshire, where they made them, for a week to find out how it worked. We milked 50 cows with it, around six at a time being brought into the bail. The vacuum pump was run by a little paraffin engine that also ran an electric light. The milk was collected in churns and taken to the dairy with the horse and cart. The tractor moved the bail once a week. We got wet when it rained and cold in the winter.'

'Farming was the main work in Hanley, mostly mixed farms employing a cowman, shepherd, ploughman, woodman, gamekeeper etc, each skilled in their own job. Land workers had very low wages, but generally had perks such as, perhaps, free rent, free milk, sometimes a row of potatoes in the field, or fruit.

There used to be a milk factory in Sink Lane, where the local farmers sent their milk. Also gone is the estate yard of the Lechmere Estate, which employed a blacksmith, carpenter, plumber, painters and bricklayers. Mr Jackson was the village blacksmith at Hanley Castle, who retired in 1915.'

'My father was what was termed a rough carpenter; he worked on his own account and employed one son at Broughton Green to help him. His work consisted of fencing, gate hanging, hedge laying and thatching, both ricks and farm buildings. He was never without plenty of work and was much sought after by farmers for miles around. He always gave value for money; he walked hundreds of miles in a year to work, it was a must in those days. There were very few people who possessed a bicycle and motor vehicles were only invented in the 1890s. I have known him walk to Hewell, Tardebigge, Bentley, Webheath, Bradley Green, Feckenham, Inkberrow, Astwood Bank and as far as Studley station. It was a case of being up about five in the morning and not getting home until seven or eight at night, and sometimes later. For that reason we always had our cooked meal at night. These journeys had to be done in all weathers, or there was nothing coming in.

We never had milk, only when Mother made a milk pudding; we got a large can full of skimmed milk for which we were charged a penny, or if we had anyone call in on Sunday afternoon for tea, we would fetch a pint of fresh milk, price a penny, otherwise we did not have milk. When a baby was weaned it went on to bread soaked in water and perhaps a pat of butter and gradually went on to solids. If a mother had no milk for her baby and had to put it on to cow's milk it was considered the baby would have a poor chance of survival.

I left school at 13 (in 1899) and I kept asking my father to get me a job; of course there was only farm work which I was quite happy to do. Father kept on saying I didn't want a job yet, but I myself asked Mr John Petford who was cowman at Little Lodge Farm to ask Mr Maunder, who was bailiff, if he could find me a job. He gave me a job to look after the poultry and his nag, so I started work at four shillings per week for 72 hours a week, six till six, no Saturdays off in those days. Men's wages were twelve shillings per week for casual work, 13 to 16 shillings for shepherds, cowmen and waggoners, with house. Of course one could not dress like a lord on that wage; it usually meant a clean pair of corduroy trousers for Sundays. Even that wage was better than when my father and mother got married; he was then getting nine shillings per week.

The only transport was your own two feet. When I started work I had to be waggoner boy for the second team and occasionally we went to Worcester with perhaps a load of wheat or straw and would bring back a load of grain from the brewery or a load of soft wood timber, so that meant walking there and back, a distance of 18 to 20 miles.'

VILLAGE TRADES AND CRAFTS

Villages were busy places, with local shopkeepers, tradesmen and craftsmen providing services for the local community. Many people worked locally, or even from their own homes, and village work could be as varied as that of the banker or blacksmith to that of the nailer and scythe maker.

THE CHOICE OF WORK

'At Fairfield during the 1920s and 1930s men worked on farms or market gardens. Some were nailmakers or did glass blowing, which entailed intricate glass work, and were often helped by the women.

One 86 year old veteran started work at 13 years old at Cook's post office, Bromsgrove. She earned three shillings and sixpence a month, and walked four miles from Dordale every day, but later she lived in. Girls went into service, and some worked their way up from scullery maid to housekeeper, while others worked in shops or the clothing factory, and the better educated took up nursing or office work.'

'Most people in Hanley Swan and Hanley Castle were in work connected with the land. Boys leaving school hoped to be apprenticed to a "trade in your hands" otherwise you were a labourer. Parents did everything they could for their children, including paying for an apprenticeship. For girls it was domestic work or shopwork until the war opened up new jobs to them. Many people had more than one trade. Frank Jarret was the organist and pigsticker (slaughterer). Mr Williams was basket maker and shoe repairer.'

'Living near Kidderminster – a carpet town – most villagers at Blakedown, both men and women, went to work in the carpet factories. In some of the larger houses domestic help was employed and these maids nearly always lived in on the premises, probably enjoying a much higher standard of life than they would have done in the often overcrowded cottages. A good cook might be paid £1 a week and a general maid ten shillings a week.

In the Blakedown area there were a lot of mills, powered by water running down from the Clent Hills; ironwork, glassmaking and corn mills. Most of them are derelict but we still had one corn mill working until 1930, at the bottom of Mill Lane. The miller, John Wilson, had an unpleasant horse that bit you if you gave him the chance when passing!

Every year a group of clog makers from Lancashire came as campers by one of our streams, by the entrance to Wannerton. They cut the willow trees back and fashioned clogs from the wood which they piled up in a sort of pyramid before taking them back to Lancashire.

Apart from the carpet industry, farming provided work for a large number of men. There were no tractors or mechanised agricultural implements, all milking , harvesting sugar-beet and haymaking was done manually and farmers employed several labourers to cope with the work.'

'A lady born in 1900 had to leave school at twelve years old in order to earn money for the family. She went to work at the flour mill and slept with the other children working there, on the mill floor, in a sleeping bag made by the miller's wife from old flour sacks. A few years later she found a job waitressing at a café in Bewdley. She worked until 10 pm the evening before her wedding, stayed up all night making the food for the guests and walked to church at Far Forest. A horse and cart had been garlanded to take the couple home. Her father walked a sow with 14 piglets down the lane and installed them in her pigsty as his wedding gift.

Another lady walked to Kidderminster market from Bliss Gate village (nine miles) twice a week to sell her eggs, cream and butter. She had to leave at 4 am in summer so that it was still cool when she got there. Life must have seemed very good when she got a pony and trap after the First World War.'

LOCAL BUSINESSES

'The local businesses in Callow End in the late 1930s included the bakery in Bush Lane, owned by the Brickell family – the bakers being Arthur Smallman and Sid Stone. They were always fun for us children to talk to and sometimes they let us have a go at making the bread. The post office was run by Jack and Alice Cubberley, and the newsagent's was owned by Mary Thomas. She also hired out bicycles at threepence a day and Bill Horniblow, who lived next door, maintained them. The local garage was owned by the Dallow family and they combined garage duties with shoeing horses. Mr

Walton was the village cobbler who lived next door to the newsagent's. There was also a slaughterhouse in the village.'

'At Chaddesley Corbett there was Mrs Hunt who had a small drapery shop in her cottage and always had a hat displayed in her bow-fronted window. Charlie Raybold was the shoemender, known as "Crutchy". A room at Miss Perrin's cottage was used by the Midland Bank once a week to transact business. Jukes stores and post office was then also a family run business. Bread was made in the bakehouse at the back of the stores and farm workers on their way to work would buy a batch loaf and a lump of cheese for their midday dinner, carrying it away wrapped in a large handkerchief. The carpet trade in Kidderminster employed people from the village. The butcher's shop was only a quarter of the size it now is, and had removable, bolted shop windows for use in the summer. There was a slaughterhouse in the yard.

Of the two public houses, it was to the Swan that the local cider maker travelled to make the brew for sale to the thirsty. Villagers, including children, would also come along with bags of apples and pears for pulping and pressing. Everyone helped with the process. Jars or small barrels were filled to take away. Fresh cider was a grand taste – but the next day was spent on the loo!'

THE VILLAGE BAKERY

'There was only one bakery in Salwarpe, which was run by three generations of the Dovey family. It was started by the grandfather of the last baker in 1890. The bread oven was built in the lean-to at the side of the cottage in Brownheath Lane. It was the old type of bread oven that was heated by piling burning faggots inside to heat the brick lining. Experience was necessary to indicate the reaching of the required temperature. The ashes were then raked out and the loaves put in to bake. The end result was tasty, crusty loaves. The yeast used was "brewers' barm" obtained from the nearby Pear Tree Inn where beer was brewed. Bread was delivered round the parish by pony trap.

The bakery carried on during the First World War when bread could only be sold if it was a day old – stale bread went further and reduced consumption. After the death of the grandfather his two sons ran the business. A Model-T Ford van was bought and the bread round extended. In 1924 new ovens were installed in the bakehouse. The ovens were heated by steam tubes with the furnace fired on coke obtained from Droitwich gas works. A third generation was now prepared to enter the family business. He entered his

'Master baker' Eric Dovey, following the family trade at Salwarpe bakery.

apprenticeship with Cadena Bakeries in Worcester in 1938. To obtain this his father had to pay a lump sum of £25. Young Dovey was paid five shillings a week for the first year, ten shillings for the second and 20 shillings for the third year of his apprenticeship. When Cadena Bakeries moved from Worcester he obtained a position with De Greys Bakeries in Droitwich under Mr Burgoyne, a first class master baker.

Mr Dovey joined his father's bakery in 1940, but was called up into the army the following year. He returned to the bakery in 1947. To gain further qualifications he attended a bakery school part time at the Victoria Institute in Worcester. This school was intended to help the bakery industry regain the standard and quality reached in pre-war years. Later he did a year's course at the Birmingham College of Food Technology.

In 1954 as a master baker, he took over from his father and continued the thriving family business. The specialities were crusty home-baked loaves, including cottage, twist, open tin and sandwich loaves. Plain and fancy cakes, sponges, buns, malt bread and scones were made by his wife, who worked full time in the bakery. There was part time general assistance given by a 15 year old boy and a full time male assistant concerned solely with deliveries over a wide country area. Wedding cakes were a speciality, as were loaves for the Harvest Festival.

A 72 hour week was worked by the baker and his wife. Work started at 4 or 5 am with tending the fire. The oven furnace was only let out once a year, on Christmas Day. The bread was baked in three batches producing 300 to 400 loaves a day. This was carried out in a bakehouse 17 feet by 10 feet. The main ingredients for bread-making were flour, yeast, salt and water. Yeast was supplied by the United Yeast Company, and, even in 1960, the only flour available was a government controlled mixture of Australian, Canadian and British wheats. The loaves were still put in and out of the ovens with the original baking peels.

This bakery in the parish of Salwarpe was one of 52 small bakeries still operating in Worcestershire in 1960.'

COAL AND BREAD

'My great-grandparents lived at Bridge House, Upton on Severn, and ran a thriving business as hay and coal merchants. Most of the hay and coal was transported by boat up the river.

If any boat was too tall for the old swing bridge, a section had to be opened. The boats would sound blasts on their horn as they approached the bend in the river and the bridge would be opened by men turning a large wheel by hand. A section would swing open. This was closed after the boat had passed.

Upton was no stranger to floods and the water would come well up the walls of Bridge House, sometimes into the kitchen, and cover the meadows and roads, and even some distance away from the river cellars could be flooded. At times of bad floods everyone took boats to get about.

My grandmother was left a widow early with five children and a country bakery to run. Her house was at the bottom of Old Street with the bakehouse in the yard at the back of the shop. There was a pump for drinking water and two large water butts holding rainwater for washing and laundry. No taps, and no hot water. Up the yard and across the backfields was a stable for the horse, and a long garden.

As a child I remember the lovely warmth of the bakehouse and smell of bread and cakes, also the long-handled peels for removing the hot bread from the oven.

On Sunday mornings there was a steady stream of people carrying their joints of meat to be cooked. These were placed in the bakehouse oven and were fetched in time for Sunday dinner.

Grandma would go out with the horse and baker's van, the wooden shelves at the back piled high with all kinds of loaves. She would drive far into the countryside, all alone, summer and winter, in all weathers. In the winter she had two big hurricane lamps.

On rare occasions in summer I was allowed to accompany her perched beside her on the hard bench seat, and once or twice fearfully held the horse's reins. Deliveries of as many as ten or twelve large loaves would be made to the farm labourers and other isolated country dwellers.'

THE BLACKSMITH

'Frank Dyson, my father, was the last in a long line of farrier blacksmiths, having learnt his trade when there was at least one smithy in every parish. He was also a well-sinker and a repairer of pumps and wells. He came to Wichenford in 1920.

He rose early to light the forge fire which later on I had to keep going by pumping the huge bellows. Besides shoeing horses he mended farm implements and fitted iron rims on cartwheels. I often had to ride a horse and lead another back to their farm once they had been shod, returning home on foot no matter what the time or weather. At times when my father was called out to mend a pump he would often walk several miles along the footpaths carrying his toolbag, no vehicle in those days.

Frank Dyson, blacksmith at Wichenford in the 1920s and 1930s.

My father was also the church sexton, maintaining the churchyard and digging the graves and Mother cleaned the church. In winter evenings he allowed my brothers, myself and other lads to meet in the warm forge and play darts or quoits on home-made boards as we were not old enough to join the men's club.

By 1939 trade was dwindling and finally when war broke out he went to work at Heenan and Froude's factory in Worcester, as a blacksmith. The forge was closed, never to be opened again. He had been at the forge in Wichenford for 20 years.'

'My father, the village blacksmith at Overbury, also had to ring the pigs' noses to stop them rooting! He would take his shoeing tools to the dairy at the farm to trim the big bull's feet. He was also a keen bellringer, so he used to mend the stops and replace the clappers. He looked after the church weathercock and he was responsible for the church flags.

He tolled the bell when a villager passed away. He always helped at village funerals, and I remember he was always discreetly approached by a specialised firm in Birmingham (Stubbs) when a villager hoped to buy household goods etc "on tick". He received a few postage stamps for his information!

He kept his blacksmith's "daily records of work done" from 1917 onwards and they relate many stories of work done in those days for a mere pittance by a country craftsman, who had to leave school, aged twelve, in 1900, and go into a seven year apprenticeship under his father's guidance – and he never really enjoyed shoeing horses!'

SCYTHE MAKING

'Belbroughton village sign depicts a man with a scythe and four village views. It was painted by Miss Barbara Bate, and was presented to Belbroughton by the WI on 12 June 1938.

The man with the scythe does not, as many suppose, represent agriculture in Belbroughton but the trade for which Belbroughton was once world famous – the manufacturing of scythes, hooks and other edge tools.

The scythe industry began here as long ago as the 16th century, but its peak was from 1860 to 1960, when it was the centre of village employment. The little stream, Belne Brook, which still flows through the village, was the source of power used to drive the many mills along its banks, at one time numbering 28. The man who made the biggest impact on the trade was Isaac Nash, and Nash scythes were sold world-wide.

A scythe was not made by one man but included many processes such as forging, plating, grinding and setting, carried out by different craftsmen, each process calling for a high degree of skill. Not the skill of using complicated machinery, but the skill and dexterity of hand and eye, acquired by years of experience.

Generations of village families followed each other into the scythe trade, often three generations working together. In the 1930s Nash works employed some 135 men and boys, all local people. The High Street would echo to the sound of hobnailed boots and men's voices as they made their way to Forge Lane to begin work at 6 am.

Soon the thud of the tilt hammer would be heard across the meadows, this the only indication an industry was being carried on, so well-hidden were the forges.

Those who lived near would return home at 9 am for breakfast, emerging into the High Street, hands and faces already blackened and smoke-grimed, and hurrying home, the smell of frying home-cured bacon already in their nostrils. Half an hour for breakfast and half an hour for dinner, and work ended for the day when the required number of scythe blades had been completed.

The average wage earned there in the 1930s was £2 10s per week, while an experienced foreman could earn £3. They were paid so much per dozen and an average week's work would number 70 dozen. They were not paid for work which was considered not perfect, so it was no wonder they learned to be quick and accurate.

With the invention of modern farm machinery, the demand for the old fashioned hand tools slowly declined and, sadly, one by one the mills closed, until finally, in 1968, Nash works closed its doors.'

KNIGHTON ON TEME

'Knighton on Teme is a parish of scattered houses and farms on a south-facing slope to the north of the river Teme, four miles from Tenbury Wells and 20 miles from Worcester. It has been traditionally a farming community and so most of the memories of people who have spent their lives working in the parish concern the production of hops, apples of all kinds, damsons, plums, together with arable crops, sheep and cattle. There are also two large estates within the parish, with their big houses, tenant farmers and woodlands where pheasants are reared for shooting parties in the autumn.

The other major influence upon life in the village was the railway line from Kidderminster to Woofferton, which passed through Newnham Bridge station on its way to Tenbury Wells, the local market town. At its busiest time in the autumn, it employed ten porters in addition to the stationmaster and signalman. It enabled produce to be taken the comparatively long distance to market in Kidderminster, the farmers' wives riding to the station with their eggs, butter, fruit and vegetables by horse and trap.

The village had its own school, in a suitably bracing situation at the top of an exposed hill above the Teme valley. The older children, attending the school to the age of 14, travelled by train to spend a whole day each week at Goffs School in Tenbury Wells which was run by twin spinster sisters, the boys to learn woodwork and the girls to learn laundry part of the year and cookery for the other. They wore long pinafores over their dresses and carried their ingredients or items to be washed in baskets as they walked down to the station from all parts of the parish.

The station was at its busiest in the autumn when the hops and fruit had to be picked quickly. Long trains full of workers came from the Black Country, so many carriages that they had to draw up to the platform several times to allow people to get off with their families and all their equipment. They lived in lines of low, roughly-built barracks by the Talbot Inn, Field Farm and Bickley Farm and provided a colourful addition to the village for a month or so each autumn. The women wore long dresses and large hats when working in the hopyards. They were joined by gypsies who came with their Romany caravans and horses to join in the harvest. The local policeman was kept busy keeping an eye on all these extra people, particularly when they went pheasant stealing, but the local gamekeeper, Joe Jones, was more than a match for their tricks, knowing every inch of his estate and able to frighten them off with a few well-timed shots in the air!

The number of trades carried out in the village was infinitely greater then than now. The blacksmith, who played such an important part in life before cars were common, shoeing horses and mending agricultural implements and machinery, also kept cows and supplied milk to the villagers.

The wheelwright's shop produced wheels for the carts and traps, and the wheelwright also made the coffins. There was a baker at the New Inn. A man travelled around from farm to farm with a portable cider press. Some of the village men remember teasing him by painting his cider press white one day when his back was turned. The local pig-killer came round when it was time to kill a villager's pig. Coal arrived at the station from Bayton Colliery and was delivered by horse and cart.

Work for girls when they left school was often in service. Doris Hurds, who worked as a parlourmaid at Newnham Court before she was married remembers all the work involved in the rent dinners, held for the tenants each year in autumn, three dinners on three successive days, first for the gentleman farmers, then the smallholders and finally the cottagers. Extra help had to be brought in to manage all the work involved in cooking and preparing the house for all the visitors.

The following people out of many in the village with vivid memories, have recalled in more detail some of the events in their working lives: Joe Jones, the gamekeeper, Ida Jones, who worked making bricks for her father, and Albert Griffiths, who worked for Mr Evans, the blacksmith.

Joe Jones (in his eighties): "I went to Lindridge school and our holidays were the main thing. It was always working holidays, fruit picking, hop picking. We went to the Moor Farm at Lindridge then, the blackberries and the redcurrants and the peas. Then we carried on from there to Christmas, which was just an ordinary holiday.

"When I left school, the first job which I had was pole pitching, with my father and another fellow. My father was on the iron bar, making the holes and that was on the Low Bank and I lifted them up to my father's friend, Mr Teague and he put them in the holes and they had all got to be fixed. If anyone was out of line in those days, he was told about it by his workmates.

"Then after about a week there, a job came along in the coal pits at Bayton. I had nine months there working under two feet high and you pulled the sledge with about a hundredweight of coal on and you worked a length about 200 yards long by the end of the week. You had a rope around your stomach and legs. I was paid half crown a day. After about nine months the pit closed. It had a notice on the office door saying 'contract day by day'. That meant that they could sack you that day or the next day, and it went to the Saturday and finished because it had fallen in and we were given our pay.

"There was another pit, just started. I went to see Mr Moody because he was the manger of the pit at Whinricks then and he said, 'Why do you want a job, Joe?' I said, 'Well, it's like this. Our pit has fallen in and they are being soaked every few minutes with the water coming in.' He looked at the newspaper and he looked at me and said, 'I've just been reading the paper and it's going to be wet for several days.' I said, 'Thank you very much Mr Moody and good day!'

"On the following Sunday, Nash the keeper, John Nash's father, heard that I had been laid off and he came for me for a job keepering. I took the job and for two years and three months I was never out of work. Then I came up to Bickley in Knighton on Teme and I lodged at the Trapnell with Mrs Ryder. I had 23 bob a week at 17 and worked every day, seven days of the week, every hour that was possible, no holiday at all.

"If I wanted to go home to see my parents at Frith Common, I had got to ask. You were not allowed off the place. I paid 18 bob for board and lodging and had five bob for myself.

"I was there for five years before I moved up. When I got married, I moved down to the cottage at Cainey, a great mansion, one room up and one room down!"

Eastham Brickyard – Ida Jones (in her seventies): "We three sisters worked in our father's business, making bricks, Ida, Doris and Elsie.

"I started when I was 14. We all did our own jobs. I made the bricks. The clay was brought from the hole on a small railway and it was shovelled into a big mixer above and it came out in a big 'log' with oil on each side. I had to cut it off into bricks with a cutter with nine wires like a cheese cutter, then I loaded the bricks, about 50 at a time onto an open barrow with a back and no sides and my sister used to stack them to dry in the yard and cover them to keep the rain off them.

"They dried by the sun and the wind. Then they had a big shed shed with coal fires underneath (the coal came from Bayton pits). They stacked the bricks on planks to dry, with ten fires on each side of the shed. My Dad used to burn the dried bricks, day and night for a fortnight. Some were blue, the ones that had been too well baked, but they were used too for houses and covered with rough cast. The bricks were used locally, at 'Frog's Hall', the vicarage at Eastham and many other local houses and cottages.

"I hated the job, it was so heavy and such hard work. I worked in it from 14 until after I was married."

Albert Griffiths (in his seventies): "I went to work at Newnham Bridge smithy when I was 14 when I left school. I had to light the fire and work the huge bellows and take the shoes off the horses, although only Mr Evans the blacksmith nailed the shoes on. We repaired the agricultural implements as well and I often spent all day hammering out the metal. We mended ladders, and made the metal bands to go on the cart wheels which were made at the wheelwright's shop at Bickley. The bands had to be made slightly smaller than the wooden wheel and then they were heated in the fire and expanded enough to fit. As soon as they were in place, we poured water all over the band to cool it rapidly so that it would fit.

"I left the blacksmith's because his son was going to work with him and he said that he got more work out of one boy who concentrated than out of two who spent their time looking for mischief together!

"Then I was called up at the beginning of the war. The blacksmith's shop became a garage and that shut in 1973."'

CATSHILL

'Until the early 1900s nailmaking had been Catshill's main cottage industry for about 200 years. The nailmaking cottages that had been built around 1830 were square red brick cottages, one room up, one room down. The children slept along the upstairs landing, and usually there would be ten or more of them – just imagine it! Not only was it crowded, but often damp as well.

These cottages had a tiny square building on the end, serving as the nailshop. The children worked with their parents in the nailshop: the more children there were, the better the production. It was said that a man was likely to marry a woman firstly for strength and child rearing capabilities – looks came second!

The nailer's staple diet was a thin meatless soup that was cooked over the nailshop fire, and as a treat a rabbit or fowl was also cooked over the fire, the animal having probably spent its life in the nailshop!

There was a privy at the bottom of the garden with a wooden seat that had to be scrubbed every day. The privy had to be emptied every so often into a large hole in the garden. At the Plough and Harrow (Stourbridge Road) three privies had to be emptied and Mrs Nora Wheeler (now aged 92) who was the landlord's daughter, says

Stanley Wheeler's baker's van, on the Stourbridge Road, Catshill. There were five bakers in the village, each delivering to the door.

that this was an event that everyone in Catshill knew about! There were plenty of volunteers to do the job as the payment was ten bob.

In 1920 villa-type houses were built because people were more prosperous, thanks to the employment offered by the Austin motor factory at Longbridge. In 1921 Woodrow Cottages (Woodrow Lane), the first council houses, were built.

During the first half of the century, the majority of shops were situated on the Stourbridge road from the church and the war memorial. This was known as The Village. It was not unusual for a cottager to take down the front room curtains, purchase bottles of sweets, tea, etc and the room would be transformed into a shop. There was J.B. Wilson's, the grocer's, Mr Perry who sold sweets and shoes (previously the undertaker's establishment). Mrs Sheward, who sold sweets, grocery, newspapers, magazines, haberdashery and children's clothes. Lewis Liddell owned the butcher's shop and here the animals were always slaughtered on the premises, and hung up on hooks from the ceiling. All the children would come and watch!

By the side of the butcher's was the last nailshop where Mr Alf Stokes could be found at work over his fire of glowing embers. Each nail was made individually, with the skill of a true craftsman. The children would stand at the door and watch, and it made their day when Mr Stokes allowed them to operate the bellows.

Next there was Juggins' the bakery, with their shop on the opposite side of the road. They also sold groceries. There was also Fisher's, a general store, and a barber's shop (Loynes). In later years, Mrs Thompson, the architect's wife, opened a babywear and wool shop from her lovely house near the butcher's.

A lady of 87 tells me that at the end of Billy Street (now Westfields) there was a public house called the Vine which was the nailers' favourite haunt. Money was extremely hard to come by, and the wives were very unhappy about the men wasting their money on drink. One day the women got together and made a united protest, and won; for soon afterwards the Vine closed.

It then became Bunnigars the tuck shop and was also known as the shop that sold "useful things". Latterly it was a ladies' hairdressers's and a betting shop before being demolished completely in the 1970s.

In the early days, Catshill garage was owned by Mr Giles. He sold bicycles, petrol, lamp oil and charged batteries (called accumulators) for radios. I remember my late father in law used to speak of dirty cars being washed down with petrol instead of water! Petrol was a shilling a gallon.

Many people kept a pig in their garden, and this was a great asset, especially during the war years. Mr Liddell was employed to do the killing. No part of the pig was wasted, and great excitement came when the bladder was removed: this was washed, dried, blown up, tied and used as a football.

Nailmaking was a harsh life for the whole family and wages were always at starvation level. During this period there was a shop at the end of Church Road, known as Cannister Corner. It was called the "caddy" or "fogger's" shop; the fogger was the nailers' middleman who owned the shop and very often the nailer was forced to buy his groceries from there too at inflated prices. After the decline in nailmaking, this little shop became the "corner shop" until it ceased trading in the 1980s.

Each Saturday morning the nailers collected their orders and iron rod from one of the three warehouses. They were Banners in Meadow Road (formerly Dog Lane and now the site of the working men's club), Waldron's in Golden Cross Lane and Parry's in Church Road. This is now the site of a disused metal factory, and on the wall next to the factory there can be seen a small metal ring. This ring was used to tether the donkeys that were used to fetch the nailmaster's supplies from Halesowen.

The nailer, assisted by his wife and children, from as young as the age of seven, produced thousands of nails each week. This work was undertaken with great skill and the men eventually ended up handling the metal working tools and machinery for the car industry. They worked very long hours from early in the morning to late at night, especially if there were older children to take over when father or mother stopped for a break.

After the decline of nailing, those nailers who did not go to work at Longbridge took up market gardening and loaded waggons would be brought to the brook to wash root vegetables. The water from the brook was so clean and unpolluted that it was possible to catch trout from there until 1930. There were watercress beds across the "Butch" – Butcher's field, alongside the Crown Inn. The market gardeners took their produce to Birmingham and returned with their carts loaded with manure.

Pea picking was usually done by women, and the charwoman from the Plough once asked if she could come and do her work at 6 am as she wanted to go pea picking. After her work she walked to Burcot with her empty pail. She could earn fourpence for 40 lbs!

Cattle droving was a familiar sight in Catshill. The cattle were sold in Bromsgrove market on Tuesday, then a firm of drovers collected the cattle, walked them to the horse trough at the end of the Strand for a drink, then along the Stourbridge road. The cattle were destined for butchers in Catshill, Romsley, Halesowen and surrounding areas of the Black Country.

The drovers timed their arrival at Catshill to coincide with the children leaving school and Ron Wood and his pals from Wildmoor helped them by running in front of the cattle, shutting all the gates and guarding holes in the hedgerows so that the cattle could not escape. By the time they reached Wildmoor the tongues of the cattle were hanging out and they were much easier to manage for the last seven or eight miles of their journey. The reward for the help was a piece of liquorice cut from a stick and shared out. One of the drovers, a character called Keck Field, was a local man and you could hear him shouting at the cattle as soon as they left Bromsgrove some two miles away!

Ron worked on a farm at Chadwick from the age of 13, and used to take the pigs to Bromsgrove market in a pony and trap with a net over the top to stop them jumping out. In the very hot weather he came back up the Stourbridge road and walked the horse and cart through the brook at Washingstocks to soak the wooden wheels so that the iron rims didn't come off.

Another character of Catshill was Biddy Manning, the scrap iron man, on the corner of Golden Cross Lane facing Green Lane. He would give you a penny for a dried rabbit skin and a copper or two for any scrap iron.'

OTHER WAYS WE MADE A LIVING

From going into service to running a hotel in the Malvern Hills, from market gardening to motorcycle manufacture, the ways we made a living cover such a variety of experiences that the following can only be a sample of days past.

IN SERVICE

'I am now aged 88 and remember my early working days in service as a maid at The Croft, a large house in Astwood Lane, Wychbold, owned by two spinster sisters. The staff were expected to attend morning service every Sunday at St Mary de Wyche church and any absences were noted with displeasure. I confess I slipped away occasionally before the end of the service and ran across the fields to see my mother at Stoke Works.'

'When I was 16 years old in 1925 I went into service at Salwarpe rectory and was there for five years. There were three staff – a cook, a housemaid and a nanny – for the family of four. The rectory was huge with 40 rooms. The rector there at the end of the 19th century had had 16 children.

My duties began at seven o'clock with early morning tea to be taken upstairs. Not so simple when the fire had to be lit first and the kettle persuaded to boil. Next the breakfast table was laid, and then the cleaning started. There were more fires to be lit and tended during the day. Tables had to be laid and then later cleared away and the washing up done. My many duties did not finish until 8 pm.

I wore a white cap and apron in the morning, and a coffee coloured apron and cap over a brown dress in the afternoon. I had half a day off a week, when I would walk over to see my mother a couple of miles away. Later on I owned a bicycle – a great event in my young life.'

'I was brought up at Stanford on Teme and left school a fortnight after I was 14. Dad always told us girls that when we left school we had to put our feet under someone else's table! In 1924 Mum got me a job at Hartlebury, ten miles away, with two elderly ladies. They were what you termed "real gentry". They were ladies of private means and entertained a lot. They were what we called "county people" and had several titled relatives. They kept a cook, a parlourmaid and I was the housemaid. We all lived in. It was a large house; there were nine bedrooms and lots of big rooms downstairs.

I was the first one up in the house at 6.30 am and my first job was to light "Jumbo" – the hot water system. Very often the sticks wouldn't catch hold, which used to upset me as I had to have the tapwater hot for the ladies and visitors to have their baths before breakfast. When the cook had the breakfast ready she sounded the big gong and whichever lady came down first rang a hand bell and we all paraded into the dining room for prayers. After we had our breakfast it was all work – with no electric gadgets to help us.'

FISHING TACKLE AND AIRCRAFT PARTS

'When I left school my first job was with a fishing tackle manufacturer. There were many in Redditch in those days but this one, S. Allcock & Co, claimed to be the "Largest in the World". Almost everything was made there, very little was bought in. Rods were mostly made of split cane – no fibreglass then. Lines were often of linen and royalties had to be paid on several patented items – like the Allcock-Stanley reel, which could be reversed, or an ingenious bait, made by treating a real little fish so that it appeared solid and varnished. This was invented by the foreman of the Bait Department. Some of these fish were mounted on brooches as a sideline and proved quite popular.

Fly dressing was, of course, a real art and one of the things outworkers, all women, could do at home when they left to start a family. Women in the works could stay on as long as they liked, married or single, but on the staff, if you married you had to leave. This continued until the war in 1939. Everyone worked five and a half days a week, till noon on Saturdays, as a matter of course.

I was 16 when the war started and before long Allcocks, as a leisure industry, had to slim down its workforce. After a short spell at the BSA factory, where they had changed over from making bikes to guns, I started working at a new factory, High Duty Alloys, not far from where I lived. The main product was aircraft parts. In the works they worked in shifts round the clock. In the office I was in we worked long hours, working out wages and doing all kinds of calculations of the kind done by computers today.

Saturday morning working was the norm, and for a time we had to work Saturday afternoon one week, Sunday morning the next and Sunday afternoon the next, with one weekend free.

One of the operations carried out in the works involved a huge drop stamp, known locally as "The Big Hammer". It would strike three times and then rest for a moment or two. This sound could be heard all over the town and for several miles around! Living close to it as I did, the sound was deadened by the railway embankment which was between our house and the factory, but we could feel the vibrations. Eventually, cracks appeared in the plaster on walls and ceilings, and, about twelve years after the war ended, two of our ceilings came down. The hammer was on a bed of clay, which finally cracked beyond repair. The machine was dismantled and moved elsewhere in the late 1940s.'

HOTEL LIFE

'My brother and I were brought up in the early 1900s in a small hotel, high up on the Malvern Hills. As my father's health had broken down through asthma he was forced to give up his business in a low-lying town. But my parents were able to take over a small hotel as a going concern, where it was hoped that the dry air would improve his health.

Soon after he and my mother had settled in, my brother and I, who had been staying with our grandmother, were put on the train, and were met at Great Malvern station by my mother. I can still remember vividly our drive in an open landau. As Church Street was too steep for the horse, the coachman turned our carriage to the left by the Exchange Buildings. We went past the theatre, then sharp right and through the Abbey gateway. Again we took a sharp bend, to the left, to go up a steep rise onto Wells Road. To ease the load for the horse at this stage, the coachman and my mother got down and walked up the hill. After going some distance there was another sharp right-hand turn, which brought us on to Foley Terrace and an exciting drive along a narrow tree-lined road, till we finally arrived at Aldwyn Tower, which was to be my home for 33 years.

The house, which had four storeys, plus two bedrooms up in the tower, was lit by gas; "fish-tail" burners on the landings and small mantles in the rooms. There was, at first, just one bathroom, on the top floor. The water was heated by a coke-burning stove in the kitchen. For washing, each bedroom had a wash-stand with basin and jug, a bowl for face-cloths and a jar for toothbrushes. Each item had a pretty hand-made mat underneath. At eight o'clock in the morning the housemaid would take a can of hot water to each room and knock on the door, leaving the can outside. At 9 o'clock a big bell was rung to summon the guests to breakfast, which was served in the dining room on the ground floor.

Postman Willis of Droitwich at the turn of the century, remembered by his daughter as smartly turned out, with brass buttons and cap badge always well polished.

There was a washhouse with a curved brick roof, partly under the road, running the length of the building, with a window at the far end. It was fitted with a cold water tap, a stone sink and a brick-built boiler with a fireplace below. There was also a large wooden dolly tub which stood on the floor, and a peggy with a cross-piece handle to swish the clothes around. A mangle with wooden rollers stood nearby, and a large galvanised bath to catch the water.

On Sunday, the white linen table napkins were put to soak in the boiler which was filled with cold water, and shredded soap added. On Monday morning the fire beneath it was lit, and the water was quite hot by the time the weekly washerwoman arrived. She was a big fat woman with rosy cheeks and a broad Worcestershire accent. She lived in West Malvern and walked over the hill and down the Happy Valley. She and her husband had brought up ten or more children in their one up and one down cottage by the roadside. She usually brought a gift from the allotment where her husband grew the vegetables for their family.

All the personal clothes were washed at home, but sheets, pillowslips and tableclothes were sent to the laundry in a big wicker hamper. The clothes were hung out to dry on long lines in the garden, brought in and sprinkled with water, then rolled down ready for ironing in the afternoon.

When lunch had been served and cleared away, several flat-irons were put on top of the Eagle range, heated by a coal fire. Then everyone – the housemaids and parlourmaids, the cook and kitchenmaid and my mother – all set to and tackled the ironing. The clothes were hung to air on wires strung high up across the kitchen. Everyone enjoyed this get-together, and tongues clacked merrily.

The maids in those days were paid £10 a *year*! – "all-found" – and the cook a little more. They relied on tips from the visitors during the season, that was from Easter to late September, and they usually managed to spare a half-crown for a postal order to send to their family back home in the mining villages of South Wales, each week.

In the winter, when there were few visitors and only two or three permanent residents, none of the staff were dismissed. As tips were few and far between then, Mother would occasionally give them a half-crown "to go to the pictures".

Preparations for Christmas were soon under way. For the Christmas puddings there were six pounds of currants and sultanas to be washed, dried on racks and picked over for stalks etc. Juicy big raisins were soaked in hot water, cut in half and pips taken out, then they were dried and chopped. Six pounds of butcher's suet was shredded, seven or eight basins greased and cloths and string put ready. An extra large earthenware basin or "steen" was placed on a kitchen chair. All the ingredients for the puddings were weighed and mixed together in this bowl, with a large wooden spoon. Then came the stirring ceremony. Everyone had to come in to give the mixture a stir, have a taste and wish. The mixture was then packed into the basins, greaseproof paper and cloths tied into place with the corners knotted firmly over the top for easy lifting. They were carried out to the washhouse and cooked in the boiler for six hours, with one person put in charge to see that the fire was replenished and the water topped up. When cooled, the puddings were stored away for six weeks, to mature for Christmas, and for any special occasions, not forgetting one for the faithful washerwoman.

There was a happy atmosphere in the hotel, which was advertised as a "Home from Home". Many of the visitors came year after year, especially at Christmas, which was celebrated in the good old fashioned way. Visitors were roused from their slumbers by the playing of the piano and the singing of the hymn *Christians, awake! Salute the happy morn*. The midday Christmas dinner was followed by toasts to "The King", "Absent Friends", "Our Hostess" etc, drunk in ginger wine or lemonade, as this was a teetotal household.

A special home-made and decorated Christmas cake was served with afternoon tea in the drawing room. A cold buffet supper was followed by party games and general conversation. For Boxing Day, guests had been warned that there would be a fancy dress party in the evening, and most of them came prepared. Again, there was a midday dinner, with goose instead of turkey. After the cold buffet supper, preceded by a fancy dress parade, there was much hilarity as we played charades and other family games till the early hours of the next morning.

Sadly, after four years in Malvern, my father died of his illness, but Mother carried on with the business. There was no widow's pension in those days, but she made sure that my brother and I had a good education. With the help of bursaries and scholarships, we gained entrance to college and university. In this way we were enabled to pursue useful careers, and, in our turn, to support her in her old age.

In her working life she did not subscribe to the "Lloyd George" sixpence-a-week Old Age Pension scheme and so she was never dependent on the State, though she lived to the age of 88.

Looking back, I am tremendously grateful to and very proud of such a high principled, determined and gifted Victorian mother.'

MOTORCYCLE SPECIALISTS

'Approaching Worcester from the west, down London Road, you come into Sidbury. On the left-hand side, close to Royal Worcester Porcelain and opposite the Commandery, is the building which houses W.J. Bladder & Son, motorcycle specialists.

I went to work there in the 1930s, as did my future brother in law, and, apart from war service, I stayed there until I retired in 1986.

At that time old Mr Bladder still took an interest in the business, and I often had the job of driving him home at five o'clock to his house in Bath Road, for his tea.

He had come to Worcester from Castlemorton in 1880, with just ninepence in his pocket, to work for Bowcott's, cycle agents and repairers, who were the original owners of the premises. In 1898 he set up in business in the same place on his own account.

These were the years of the cycling boom, following the appearance of the pneumatic tyre and the "safety" machines. Even the wealthy people and the gentry cycled, and, like Lady Sandys and Lady Cobham, bought their machines from Bladder's.

However, the internal combustion engine was appearing on the scene and Mr Bladder became an enthusiast. The Thousand Miles Trial was routed through Worcester in 1900 and soon Bladder's was selling Humber cars and, by 1904, Mr Bladder was driving round in his own car JFK 14.

At that time petrol was delivered by rail in two-gallon cans. Two railways served Worcester at that time. The Great Western would only accept petrol for delivery on Tuesdays and Thursdays, the Midland would not accept it on a Saturday.

More motor agencies followed and Bladder's was firmly established in the motor trade.

His son, Albert, who joined the business in the early part of the century, was always keener on motorcycles. After the First World War he scored successes in motorcycle trials, usually riding a New Imperial, often a big V-twin sidecar machine, in which his wife accompanied him. From that time the emphasis of the firm was clearly towards the motorcycle.

It was a real family firm, with service second to none. All the local doctors bought their cars from Bladder's and the district nurses' bicycles were always repaired straightaway. It was that sort of firm. Customers knew they would get good service, and employees were loyal and worked hard in all capacities.

As young Mr Bladder and his wife grew older, we often drove them about. We took them to Torquay for their holidays – there and back in a day before there were motorways. After Mr Bladder died, my brother in law and I continued to run the business for his widow. On her death we bought it and ran it ourselves. When we retired in 1986, and sold it – to a former employee who had set up in business himself – we had done over 100 years of service, between us, to W.J. Bladder & Son.'

THE SALT WORKS

'In the early 1930s I lived in Stoke Prior and walked to school in the next village – Stoke Works. On the way I passed Stoke Works station and this was very busy in those days. After this I had to go under two rail bridges. The first one was for most of the passenger trains and the second was for express and goods trains (there was a small goods yard). The stationmaster's house was after the second bridge and opposite was a small row of cottages that were part of the salt works. This and farming were the main employers of the area.

The local landmarks that were attached to the salt works were "the big chimney" and a time bell that sounded twice in the morning, then at lunchtime and at five o'clock for the end of their hot working day. Brine was pumped into large pans and heated and salt was formed from evaporation. The men worked stripped to the waist, with towels round their necks to absorb the perspiration, raking the salt out.

The girls and women used to do the packing of these large blocks, then it was transported by barge and rail around the country. The canal ran through the salt works and the public house that I passed just before the school was called the Boat and Railway.'

GLOVING

'I was born in the early 1920s, one of six children, living in the country seven miles from Worcester. The only means of getting to town was by push bike as daily public transport did not exist.

Once girls left school, the most convenient way of earning a living was to undertake gloving at home, which was then a well established tradition. The work was brought to the villages weekly, but in irregular quantities and girls and women worked in their homes, often in small groups, on machines supplied by the manufacturers. The rate of pay at one time was two shillings and sixpence per dozen pairs, which would be a day's work for even the fastest machinist. Having become very skilled, the women continued gloving when they married and had families.

The gloving industry in Worcester consisted of many small factories but was dominated by Messrs Fownes and Messrs Dents which later amalgamated and eventually moved away from the city.

After the war, I worked firstly at the Stylish Glove Company for five years and then moved to Fownes. Here, the leather was brought in already treated and dyed and a team of men using long scissors would cut out the gloves using templates. Later developments resulted in machines stamping out these gloves in one operation.

At this stage, most of the gloves to be machined were packed into lots of either six pairs or one dozen pairs and delivered to the homeworkers, although the factory also employed expert machinists who were always girls and women. Depending on the style, the seams were either prixseam or pique or roundseam. Silk thread was used on ladies' gloves and a heavier, stronger thread for men's gloves. The gloves were then lined and finished and sent to the warehouse.

Hand-sewn gloves were always expensive and were mostly sewn by the outworkers. It took at least three hours to make one pair. The leather used, whilst being fine and supple, dried the sewers' hands badly, and dry, rough hands were always a great problem to the women.

Every pair of gloves, whether hand or machine sewn, had to be individually inspected and examined and had to show a high standard of workmanship. This was a very tedious job and could only be done by an expert glover.

When Her Majesty the Queen visited Worcester early in her reign, it was my privilege to sew the gloves presented to her by Fownes on this occasion. I remember one pair was champagne coloured and the other a delicate shade of pink.

Sadly, the demand for gloves declined. For a time, fur fabric hats were made at Fownes. Fur-lined mittens continued to be sewn by homeworkers until the early 1970s. All that remains of the once flourishing industry is the Fownes factory which has been converted into a first class hotel, and a small factory outside the city.'

'The main employment in Childswickham was market gardening or farm work. The young women went into service in pre-war days, although many women worked in the gloving trade, with one woman in charge who walked into Evesham with the finished gloves.'

KIDDERMINSTER CARPETS

'Kidderminster carpets were being made centuries ago on hand looms in cottages in Kidderminster. Then, in 1783, John Brinton had the idea of putting six looms in a shed – thus creating

Kidderminster's carpet industries. These reached a high standard in the world market which they have proudly maintained to the present day.

In the late 1890s an ugly riot between the workers and bosses broke out over working hours and conditions. Soldiers were camped on the outskirts of the town at this time, but were not used to put down the riot. The outcome of this dispute was that one firm – Whittles – took their factory lock, stock and barrel to the USA and nearly half of Kidderminster went with them.

In the First World War many men went overseas and there they saw cheap and loosely woven floorcovering, which helped to make rooms a little warmer. The Belgians took advantage of this interest and entered the British market, but the British carpet manufacturers did not follow suit and lower their standards.

There were about 20 carpet firms in Kidderminster at this time but, during the war, many of them went out of business. But the "gaffers", who ran the town council as well as their own firms, still adhered to the policy of a "closed town" – no other industry was allowed in. The sugar beet factory eventually came in and broke the monopoly.

Now down to single figures, Kidderminster's carpet firms still hold their renowned high status in the carpet world.'

APPRENTICED TO A DRESSMAKER

'I left school in the 1920s when I was 14 and was apprenticed to a dressmaker in Bromsgrove. I walked to be there for 8.30 am. The workroom was over a stable where a pony and trap were kept, used to deliver the finished work. There were six people in the workroom, which was lit by gaslight and heated by a stove which smoked badly. Stitching was by treadle machine. Flat irons for pressing the garments were heated on the stove. Garments were protected with muslin before pressing, to prevent marking with smuts from the stove.

Work finished at 6 pm Monday to Wednesday and at 7 pm Friday and Saturday. Thursday was our half day when we finished at 1 pm. After work I walked back home. There were no lights on the streets so it was very dark in winter. After ten years I set up my own business, working from home.'

INDUSTRIES OF THE WYRE FOREST

'During the 1930s and 1940s the Wyre Forest consisted mainly of oak trees, with small amounts of birch and ash. The forest supported many industries both nationally and locally. The heaviest timber was taken away for such uses as shipbuilding, pit props, rustic poles, fencing etc. The smaller timber had many uses which provided employment for local people.

One of the better known skills was charcoal burning. The burner lived in a booth, a rough tent-like structure made of tarpaulin sacks. The mound of wood in the charcoal pit was covered in turfs and carefully allowed to smoulder, but not burn, for four or five days, after which it was damped down and the charcoal removed. The whole area was permanently covered with ash, including the burner, but he would always have plenty of tea and cider to lubricate his dry throat. Even with the ash and the primitive conditions the burners seemed to enjoy their solitary lives in the peace and quiet of the forest.

The smaller branches were put to such uses as besom making, basket making, bean sticks and hurdles.

The bark was peeled from the wood for use in the tanneries. The local ladies, many from Bewdley, walked several miles into the forest and back each day to do this hard work.

The local people gathered the brushwood for their fires; and the ferns, which had been growing under the trees, were used for packaging fruit. In this way the whole of the forest's resources were utilised, and the forest floor was clean with nothing wasted.

With the advent of the Second World War, all of the hardwood was cut down for war use and softwoods subsequently planted because they grow and mature faster. Most of the traditional crafts of the forest have long since died out, mainly due to changes in technology and the introduction of more modern materials.'

OFFICE WORK

'I left Headless Cross school at the age of 14 in 1933 and I was very lucky to get a job straight away. It was in the office of a small spring firm and, although the floors were bare boards which had to be swept each morning and the room heated by a combination stove, the atmosphere among the bosses and the girls was so good.

Each morning at "lunchtime", mid morning, we did toast on the stove. Our day was from 8.30 am to 6 pm, with a break of an hour for dinner, and we worked on Saturday from 8.30 am to 12.20 pm. Any further education to obtain extra qualifications was at night school on two or more evenings and we had to pay our own fees. We had one week's annual holiday for which we were paid.

Wages were low. I started at seven shillings and sixpence a week and rises were small and only each January, but we enjoyed ourselves and were so glad to have a job.'

PYX QUARRY

'The parish of Welland and Little Malvern was much the same as most rural villages in that employment was in working on local farms. But, having the Malvern Hills adjacent, quarrying was an alternative employment.

Little Malvern estate in the early 1900s was owned by the Berrington family and the Pyx Quarry was part of their estate. Machinery for the crushers and quarrying of stone was then driven by steam engine. Transport was by steam traction engines and trailers, usually two trailers being used alternately to take the stone to the LMS railway station on the Malvern Wells to Hanley Swan road by way of Hornyold Junction.

Because of the continuing scuffing of the road by the steel rimmed engine wheels, causing deep ruts, blue engineering bricks were laid at the road junction. The stone, being of a granite nature, could be used in many ways – roads, local houses, churches and schools were all built with it.

As time went by the mineral rights were bought and the quarry was closed down in about 1924.'

MARKET GARDENING

'My father was a market gardener. There were several men who earned their living in the same way in Upton on Severn. They cultivated anything from five to 20 acres and it was a very intensive system. Each patch provided two crops every year. There was a pool of unpaid labour to call on, children of school age, wives, mothers and other near relatives.

The first job of the year was in the Christmas holidays when we tar-washed the apple trees. The wash was mixed in an iron tank like a box on wheels. A hose was attached with a pump and I worked the pump handle up and down all day while my father operated the spray at a safe distance from me. One's feet soon became blocks of ice and it was a good thing the winter days were so short.

In the spring, children were given the job of scaring the birds from the newly-sown radish seeds. Little birds would quickly strip a patch once the seed chitted. I walked up and down banging a football fan's rattle. I mastered the art of reading, walking and swinging the rattle very quickly. When the radishes were ready, all the women of the family got the job of tying them in bunches. After being pulled the radishes were soaked in a tank, drained and then spread on a table. You had to collect a tidy handful and tie them by winding a piece of string round and bringing the end down smartly through the heads of radishes – no knot actually, but it was necessary to pull the string quite tightly or else the bunch fell apart. The bunches were then packed ten dozen in a half-pot hamper with the last layer packed upright with their shiny red butts and little tails showing. Onions were bunched dirty on one's lap and washed afterwards.

From Easter to the end of October there was always something to be picked or gathered, fruit and vegetables and flowers too; gillies (wallflowers to the world), sweet williams, larkspur and chrysanthemums. Plum picking I loved, looking at the world from the top of a ladder and picking greengages, purple Pershore plums, yellow egg plums and the luscious Victorias. These latter were all picked with the stalk attached and the bloom unmarked. I had a basket with a hook which I slung from the ladder or a strong branch, as my mother would not allow me to wear a basket on a belt round my waist like the men.

Most of our produce went to the local auction market or to Birmingham. The apples we sent to Birmingham market were packed in round tubs and it was quite an art to keep the rings even, working from the outside.

This kind of living from the land has gone for ever. It was an uncertain existence and prosperity depended very much on good weather and the laws of supply and demand working to the advantage of the supplier, which they seldom did. Economic necessity has driven all the small market gardeners to sell to large combines. The only reminder of that life is to be seen when the gangs of women gather to harvest spring onions out in the fields. I think I regret most those beautiful Victoria plums. The chip baskets were lined with sheets of pink paper which came well up above the top of the basket. When the fruit had been transferred carefully from the picking basket, the tissue was folded down and tucked in at the ends, so that each side had about two inches of paper showing either side of the plums. Then the lids were put on, tied with string and sent off to the station 200 yards away on the cart drawn by the old pony, whose not very arduous duty this was.'

WEBBS OF WYCHBOLD

'Because of my father's long association with Webbs Seeds my early memories seem to be dominated by this company, which was founded in the latter part of the 19th century when the proprietors were William George Webb and Edward Webb.

As a child in the 1930s I was often taken on visits to Astwood Farm in Wychbold, where Webbs first had their agricultural seed trial grounds. Astwood Farm was near the railway line and a large board facing the railway informed passengers that these were "Webbs Trial Grounds". Here patches of agricultural crops were grown – cereals, root and grasses. A "Latin squares system" was used to compare varieties of cereals and regular observations were made on all crops. Sugar beet varieties were tested for their sugar content.

Webbs' vast warehouses, the majority of which were used for agricultural seeds and hops, were situated near Stourbridge. During wartime Sunday working was normal and it was between 1940 and 1942 that I assisted in the horticultural seed packing department. There was a special area for the pulses and the other vegetable seeds were arranged in alphabetical order. Only a very small area was allocated to flower seeds, food being all important at that time. The packers had their own tables and were responsible for checking and packing their orders. I remember well the feeling of apprehension when having to walk through the agricultural warehouses. Massive piles of sacks containing grain, trap-doors in the floor that opened to allow the hoists to operate and large metal doors controlled by weights and separating the different departments that clanged behind you. One felt rather as a small insect must do when traversing a potting shed.

By the greenhouses there were pigsties where pig club members were allowed to keep pigs to complement permitted rations, each member contributing as many food scraps as possible. After the slaughter the produce was divided equally.

In the late 1930s Webbs Trial Grounds at Wychbold were opened. These were cultivated areas of ground where every hardy variety of flower and vegetable seed offered in the Webbs Horticultural Catalogue was grown. As a child I was allowed to visit these trial grounds and I always looked out for "Henry" (the name we children gave him) who would cycle along the trial grounds fence with his Walls' Stop-me-and-buy-one tricycle – an icebox in front containing ice cream. We always bought a triangular-shaped water ice in its blue and white chequered wrapper. I seem to remember that the absence of a base meant that the ice melted and trickled down your hand.

Many people, individually and in organised groups, visited the Wychbold Trial Grounds. Here they could purchase seeds and plants and during summer months inspect and enjoy the magnificent display. This was of special interest to all keen gardeners, particularly those who liked to compete at horticultural shows. In the early 1950s I was responsible for coordinating these visits.

The greenhouses were full of tomatoes, melons and cucumbers all grown for seed and large quantities of flowering plants for exhibition at leading shows. The tomatoes which had had their seeds removed were not wasted but distributed among the staff.

Charlie's story is also tied up with the early days of Webbs at Astwood Farm, where his father was farm bailiff and where Webbs kept a herd of pedigree Hereford cattle which used to win many prizes at agricultural shows. Charlie and his brothers grew up at Astwood Farm and became very skilled in building and thatching ricks after harvesting. They won many awards in this activity.

Charlie well remembers the early days of harvesting before the advent of combine harvesters and I also remember being present when a crop of stock wheat was being harvested at Astwood. It was very important that the seed was "true to variety" and workers familiar with a certain variety would precede the binder, removing rogue plant as they went. They converged on the crop working towards the centre. There were also one or two workers in the outfield waiting for the rabbits. I remember being alarmed to be given charge of a whippet and being told to "let him go" if a rabbit emerged.

Charlie and his parents moved from Astwood and purchased Ridgeway Farm in Crown Lane. Here they kept a herd of pedigree Shorthorns of such excellence that they often swept the board at shows. Sadly both the Hereford and Shorthorn breeds are seen less frequently today having been largely superseded by European breeds.'

WAR & PEACE

THE GREAT WAR 1914-1918

Though the fighting was far away, families in Worcestershire waited and worried as the war dragged on. The armistice was greeted with relief and some sadness, with celebrations across the county.

WHITE FEATHERS

'My father, later blacksmith at Overbury, was then working for a master blacksmith at Wednesbury, shoeing horses for the British Expeditionary Force in Flanders, working on night shifts. Father tried seven times to join the army, but he was refused as his work as a smith made him in a reserved occupation. My mother, in 1915, was the recipient of three white feathers because my father was still a civilian. He remembered seeing the Zeppelins bombing the armament factories and chemical factories in Birmingham.'

Munitions workers in 1918 from the Queenhill area: M. Jones, E. Bates, N. Bates, E. Isaacs and F. Walpole.

Celebrating the end of the Great War, outside the Ring O'Bells in Droitwich Spa.

TOLLING THE BELL

'During the war, my mother (the vicar's wife) went across to the church in Wichenford each day at noon and tolled a bell to remind people to pray for our soldiers.'

PRISONERS OF WAR

'On 16th April 1918 a prisoner of war camp was opened at Holdfast Hall, Upton on Severn, which housed 40 German prisoners. It was disbanded a year later, but not all the prisoners returned home to Germany, at least one man preferring to remain in the community.'

THREE WHEN IT STARTED

'I was three when the war started. Food must have been a nightmare to our parents, as there were no ration books until 1916. There were queues for everything and rumours of deliveries spread quickly through Worcester, folk being prepared to wait in hope and good humour for hours, only to be told "No more". Margarine, when you got it, tasted as though it was mixed with a pencil. We were fortunate, as my father, being an engineer, was not allowed to volunteer but had to teach officers to drive one day a week. That meant he would return with a piece of meat, a few potatoes or loaves of bread.

Well I recall the noise of the Zeppelins on their way to Birmingham and my older brother scaring me with the story that they were after a naturalised German who lived nearby.

To this day I can hear the bells and the factory hooters blaring away the day the war ended, and we sped out of school. There were victory parades in the pouring rain, all the girls in white dresses, and presentation of medals. Then, and for the inter-war years, there was a two minute silence – a complete silence when the traffic stopped and everyone ceased work, to say "Thank you".'

THE SECOND WORLD WAR 1939-1945

Less than 20 years later we were again at war, and this time we had to get used to air raids and gas masks, disturbed nights and strangers in our midst, from the Free French to the BBC.

BOMBS IN SOUTH WORCESTERSHIRE

'At around 8 pm one night a bomb was dropped on the village of Eckington. It fell in a field known locally as The Piecing and the crater still remains, quite close to the railway line, which is on the mainline route from the West of England to Scotland. The children still call it the Bomb-hole Field! It was presumably dropped by a plane en route to Birmingham or Coventry.

Two or three other bombs fell nearby at Bredon's Norton, again not far from the railway line, early in the war. They fell in a field, so no damage was done, but they did make a big noise and we all got out of bed and sat in our kitchens waiting for more!

We had plenty of incendiary bombs dropped in the Ashchurch area of Tewkesbury, where the army RAOC/REME etc were based. We lay in bed and listened to the German bombers flying over, for their engines had a distinctive sound, different to British planes. Also we had several searchlight companies all round here, and we used to watch their beams of light interweaving as they attempted to "fix" the raiders.

Several aeroplanes came to grief in this area – on Bredon Hill and at Pershore (British/Canadian airmen). Defford and Pershore and Honeybourne airfields were in great use and many allied airmen were stationed at those bases. At Pershore cemetery flowers are still placed on the war graves every year by the local ATC youngsters.

We listened to Lord Haw Haw as he broadcast from Hamburg and other German wireless stations, telling us what was going on in England! Our own newspapers were very limited in what news could be published – in fact, we were very much "in the dark".

Another vivid memory still remains. Every Sunday evening early in the war, the BBC broadcast the national anthems of all the Allies and it was a very moving programme indeed.'

THE NIGHT COVENTRY WAS BOMBED

'The time that stands out most in my memory is the night that Coventry Cathedral was bombed (14th November, 1940). The house where we lived in Broadway was one of an avenue of white-painted rough-cast exteriors which, on the night in question, were showing up far too well in the bright moonlit night sky. The Royal Observer Corps had a post on the top of Broadway Hill near the Tower and from there our houses could be seen very clearly. They sent a message round to the houses by the air raid wardens warning us that when the German bombers came back from their raids on Coventry, they would just as likely drop any bombs they had left on the first thing they saw, which could quite possibly be our row of houses.

The planes were going over in hordes, directly above us on their flight path towards Coventry, and we were warned to take our few valuables and get out of the houses before the planes came back. We took to the fields which were behind our house and went across to my Dad's cousin's farm at Peasebrook which was about half a mile away. Here we stood in the cowshed doorway facing north to where the bombing was going on. The planes were going over all the time and we could hear the rumbling of the bombs, also anti-aircraft guns. Suddenly we saw the flames, getting more and more, and within the space of a few minutes the whole of the sky to the north of us was filled with this awful blood-red colour. I could see the flames from 40 miles away. Someone said, "My God, that's Coventry, the b– – – – – Jerrys are burning them down!" We stood and watched those flames in complete silence and a feeling of absolute desolation. Until my dying day I shall remember that night.

We were told next morning on the radio of the raid on Coventry the night before, but the BBC didn't give much away on the news, because of course the Germans were listening, weren't they? It wasn't until later that we heard how the cathedral had been destroyed, and it turned out that this was one of the worst air raids throughout the whole of the war.

We did have a few bombs dropped around this area, but usually because they dropped their bombs anywhere on the way back from raids, just to get rid of them. I remember there was one dropped on the main road from Broadway to Evesham, which ruptured the water mains and made a large crater in the road. This meant that the school bus couldn't get through so we were overjoyed to have the day off from school!'

'In 1939 my father joined the Local Defence Volunteers, which became the Home Guard, and he was on night duty at the top of Bredon Hill when Coventry was bombed. He was unable to talk about what he saw for security reasons, but he came home deeply shocked.'

HABBERLEY VALLEY AIR RAID

'My vivid childhood memory while living in Habberley Valley was connected with an air raid on a beautiful moonlit night, 16th/17th May 1941. The air raid siren had sounded, followed by the low droning sound of enemy aircraft on their way to the northern cities of Manchester or Liverpool.

My father, a member of the ARP, was very apprehensive and stayed awake. Some time later, at about one o'clock, my parents and I dressed and went downstairs. Soon we heard the easily distinguishable drone of the enemy aircraft returning from their deadly mission, immediately followed by one of our fighter planes.

Suddenly there were two enormous thuds as high explosive bombs dropped on the Harry Cheshire School (Kidderminster). At this point, my father, realising that danger was imminent, went upstairs to insist that my grandmother came downstairs with the rest of the family.

This proved very fortunate because, just as my father reached the landing at the top of the stairs and was about to enter her bedroom, an incendiary bomb burst through the roof and dropped at his feet. He had the presence of mind to throw it down the stairs, at the same time shouting to my mother to smother the bomb, which by now, had started to smoke.

My mother grabbed a home-made woollen hearthrug and managed to smother the bomb. Eventually my parents moved it into the kitchen where, unfortunately, the back door being bolted delayed proceedings. Flames went higher and higher, and were very near to the paraffin cooking stove. After a few seconds or so (it seemed like hours) the bomb was thrown outside into the garden by my father to burn itself out. We all heaved a sigh of relief!

By this time, and after all the confusion, my grandmother decided to join us downstairs. We went out into the garden to see what other damage had been sustained. To our horror a small fire was starting to blaze in the dry bracken of the nearby wasteland. My father tried to extinguish the fire, but with little success. Members of the local ARP and soldiers nearby, on seeing the blaze, hurriedly came to assist with the fire-fighting by beating out the flames. The fire spread relentlessly over a large stretch of tinder dry wasteland. Fortunately, the fire was kept away from our cottage and large shed used for catering by the efforts of the fire-fighters and also because my father always cleared three or four yards of bracken away during the summer months as a precaution against fire.

When the drama had subsided my mother made cups of tea for everyone concerned, which was very much appreciated in the circumstances. Our family spent the rest of that moonlit night sitting in the garden, in an alcove hewn out of the sandstone rock!

Next morning, on investigation, we found that two more incendiary bombs had damaged the roof of our cottage, but had fortunately bounced off into the garden, otherwise our troubles would have been greater. There were also many unexploded incendiary bombs embedded in the garden and the remains of a Molotov basket with even more bombs had been scattered in our adjoining field.

Apart from my father receiving burns to his hands, our sheepdog having his coat singed when he became involved with the bomb at the bottom of the staircase, our roof being damaged in several places, and one or two charrred items, we had a miraculous escape. This was especially so, as our old cottage with its oak beams was a great distance from any adequate water supply. (In fact, our water came from a spring in the woods.)

Although we were shocked that night, it was an unforgettable experience to be sitting in our garden on a moonlight night warmed by a fire started by the German bombs! Who would ever have thought that the tranquillity amidst the beauty of the Habberley Valley could have been shattered in such a way!

Soldiers of the Royal Essex Regiment, billeted in a large house situated in Low Habberley, could often be seen on manoeuvres in nearby Habberley Valley. This large area of trees and natural heathland with its heather and bracken, and sandstone outcrops, provided marvellous camouflage for their exercises. Bayonet charges on straw dummies were very realistic.

To witness these soldiers scrambling about, clothed in heavy khaki uniforms, in the wet undergrowth seemed rather a strange occupation to us children. Of course, we realised the significance of their actions as being a preparation for the serious business of warfare which, for them, most probably would soon be a reality.

On another occasion, an Avro Anson training aircraft on a flight over farmland in the Low Habberley area had a lucky escape. The Polish pilot successfully landed his aircraft after hitting a line of elm trees bordering a field.

When necessary repairs had been carried out, an attempt was made to get the Anson airborne again. The first attempt failed due to lack of adequate space for take-off so the aircraft was towed back to its original position. Next day, another pilot was successful, and so the Anson was flown away, much to the relief of all the Air Force personnel concerned.

This unscheduled visit of the Avro Anson and its crew was much appreciated by the local schoolchildren, especially the boys, but was later followed by disappointment at its departure. The aircraft's visit had proved an interesting distraction from ordinary village life in wartime!

During a blinding snowstorm, on the morning of 19th January 1945, an aircraft crashed into the trees on high ground in Wassell Wood. This aircraft, an Airspeed Oxford 655, was on a normal training flight from Halfpenny Green airfield when it suddenly flew into a blinding snowstorm over the Bewdley area.

The pilot made an unsuccessful attempt to crash land. Unfortunately his aircraft hit the tall trees of Wassell Wood and was totally destroyed. Flight Officer Frank Reid Miller was the only fatality for, miraculously, Flight Lieutenant N.B. Worswick and Flight Sergeant J.R. Payne survived the crash.

Wreckage from the stricken aircraft was scattered over a large area of Wassell Wood especially near its proximity to the steep field between Habberley Valley and Trimpley. With great difficulty, due to inaccessibility, the large pieces of wreckage were removed by RAF lorries. For months after, smaller pieces of wreckage could be seen wedged among the branches of the trees.

Once again, with our cottage situated less than half a mile away from the crash, we had another lucky escape!'

LAND MINES

'Castlemorton is a very scattered parish with large areas of common land. During the war several acres were fenced off and ploughed and planted with cereals. The north-west common had tall, twelve foot high poles erected all over it to stop aircraft landing, and a searchlight was sited on the south-west side as a decoy for enemy aircraft.

One morning, around 6 am, a German plane came very low along the range of the Malvern Hills and a few days later two land mines were dropped, one at Upper Welland, Malvern Wells and one at Bromsberrow. Some of the parachute material was salvaged and the local ladies made use of it for underwear.'

GIs ON CRUTCHES

'Hanley Swan was put on the map because it became the centre for four or five hospital camps. Convoys of ambulances came through the crossroads.

One villager tells of GIs on crutches coming to the Ewe and Lamb. When the lookout called that the MPs were coming there was a mass rush across the fields back to camp and, later, a jeep would come for the crutches. It seems they were delaying going back to the front line, poor things!'

THE FREE FRENCH AT RIBBESFORD HOUSE

'During General Charles de Gaulle's broadcast over the BBC on 18th June 1940, calling on his defeated countrymen to continue the struggle he declared, "Whatever happened the flame of French resistance must not be quenched and will not be quenched." Frenchmen from France and from all parts of the world answered his call and so the Free French Movement came into being.

However, it is of the arrival of young French men who eventually became part of the exiled Military Academy of Saint-Cyr at Ribbesford House, Bewdley, that I write.

The Military Academy at Saint-Cyr was founded by Napoleon in 1808 in the village near Versailles. General de Gaulle himself had graduated from this academy in 1911. His son, Philippe, now a retired Admiral, was a cadet at Ribbesford House as was Pierre Lefranc, who later became Chief Secretary to the Cabinet in General de Gaulle's government after the liberation of France.

The General visited the academy on many occasions during the war to present medals and awards and to attend passing-out parades. It is known that he stayed at Ribbesford House the night before leaving for the North African campaign.

A unique memento of this period is an invitation sent to Miss M. Wraight, a land girl in Bewdley during this time. It is interesting to note that this Passing-Out Dance took place on the evening of the D-Day landings – a night for great rejoicing.

Also of poignant interest is a poem written by Jean-Claude Diamant-Berger in memory of his friend Jean-Claude Camors who was killed by the Gestapo on 11th October 1943, after a brilliant war career. Diamant-Berger was himself later killed on 18th July 1944, during the battle of Caen. It was translated into English by Michele (née Finas) and Merryn Howell in 1994, the daughter in law and daughter of Wing Commander A.J. Howell, who bought Ribbesford House in 1946 and who still owns this lovely old house.

In Memoriam Jean-Claude Camors.

It is not our empty tears
nor our regrets nor thoughts
which will make us eternal
There is no need to weep.

You are no longer even a memory,
but a legend and your death
has fallen like an axe on our youth.
Who will give back to us our early years
and Summer in Bewdley, and the
tranquil Severn, and your beloved heroism,
Camors; and the setting sun near us
while under the great tree we listen
to the Second Symphony?

It is neither a sad poem, nor a dream, nor nostalgia
but life, life beyond this world
Why sow death and sorrow when death
in its entirety is enclosed in a single corpse,
and in his passion all suffering is resolved.

It is the Wing Commander, his son, Columb, and daughter, Merryn, who have dedicated so much time and effort into researching this important period in the history of Ribbesford House and indeed of Bewdley. It was they who planned and organised the great event which took place in the grounds of Ribbesford House on 25th May 1994, to commemorate the part the Free French Forces and Ribbesford's young men played in the D-Day landings and the liberation of France. It is sad to record that of the 211 young cadets who passed out from Ribbesford House during the years 1942/44 some one-third gave their lives in the service of their country.'

US INVADES HAGLEY

'One night in April 1944 Hagley was startled to find that the United States Army had arrived in the village. The troops had crossed the Atlantic in the *Queen Elizabeth I* liner, landing at the Clyde docks in Glasgow, and then come on a crowded troop train into the sidings at West Hagley station. They were going to an old house in Middlefield Lane whose large gardens extended down into Park Road opposite the village school. The house was called Oldfields, and in its grounds had been built a number of huts forming a depot and stores for a US Army Field Hospital. The new arrivals, about 200 to 300 of them, were medical staff, nurses, orderlies, stretcher bearers and caterers. England at that time was filling up with foreign troops of all nationalities ready for the D-Day landings and there were Poles, French, Czechs and Canadians as well as the US troops in this area.

Hagley was quite a small village in those days and the sudden arrival of these "foreigners and yet not foreigners" made a great impact. I was 15 at the time and at school in Stourbridge. I remember how we were all amazed at the gentle thud, thud of the Americans' boots on the roads as they marched along – their boots were soled with rubber, not the leather and metal studs of our boys who could be heard well before they came into view! There was no "left right, left right" either, just "hup two three four, hup two three four". Very strange! We admired their beautiful uniforms, so different from the rough khaki our soldiers had to wear, and chuckled at the request to local shops to provide coat hangers! And they were supposed to be on active service in a battle zone!

Trucks, lorries, jeeps and ambulances soon arrived in Hagley by road and the next day one family in Woodland Avenue were surprised to find the police sergeant from Clent knocking on their door and asking how many people were in the house. When hearing there were two adults and two young boys there was a shout up the road, "One here!" and a large GI detached himself from a US army truck and entered their home. He was dirty, unshaven, laden with full military kit, tin helmet and all, desperately tired and, on being shown to the small back bedroom, collapsed onto the bed and promptly went to sleep for twelve hours, while the family crept about wondering what on earth had arrived!

But Private (1st Class) Joe Gullo was a gentle giant of a young man, just 21 years old. Trained as a nurse by the US Army, he was from Buffalo, a kindly and caring personality happy to fit in with English family life, making friends with the two young boys, helping in the garden in his off duty hours, homesick for his country and family, but conscious that a job had got to be done here in Europe. He was only one of several young men who were billeted here in houses in Hagley at that time, and they stayed until just after D-Day in June 1944 before going off one night with their ambulances, medical equipment and supplies to set up hospitals in France and Germany to look after their wounded.

Once a soldier was billeted with a family, the billeting form issued by the army (obviously a left-over from the First World War) insisted upon certain provisions being made by the occupier, which not only included "ten ounces of meat, three ounces of bread, ten ounces of potatoes, eight ounces of other vegetables, four ounces of pudding" for his "hot dinner", but also a "stable room, ten pounds of oats, twelve pounds of hay and eight pounds of straw on every day for each horse". I hope Joe Gullo didn't have too many of those tucked into his capacious kit bag! The remuneration received by the family from the army for the "hot dinner" was one shilling and fourpence, and for the horse two shillings and threepence. A footnote to the same billeting form states that: "The manure remains the property of the War Department which is entitled to any benefit rising from its disposal."

My future mother in law became so fond of Joe Gullo that she kept in touch after he went back home in 1945. He had been following most of the major battles through France, Belgium and Germany and, indeed, had been at the opening up of a concentration camp which affected him for the rest of his life. He became an active scout leader in his home town in California, and one of the last things he did before his death from cancer in 1970 was to open a camping centre in the desert. He had always intended to come back, but the cost was too great while they were bringing up their family and he died before he was 50.'

THE BANK AND THE BBC

'The BBC came to Wood Norton, just outside Evesham, in August 1939. Mr Stanford Robinson, conductor of the BBC Light Orchestra, rented a cottage in Conderton and often visited our blacksmith's shop and gladly accepted home-cured ham or fatty bacon. Mr (later Sir) Charles Groves and his singers provided concerts in our church for wartime funds.

The Bank of England came to Overbury village (Overbury Court and the village hall) also in August 1939.'

'At the turn of the century, Norton and Lenchwick was mostly part of the Wood Norton estate, once owned by the French royal family who escaped to England at the time of the French Revolution. One sign of their occupation, even in the 1930s, was a part of a ten to twelve foot high corrugated iron fence erected to enclose the deer and wild boar imported from France so that the family could enjoy their sport. The estate was eventually sold off to local farmers, and just before the war some land came into the possession of the BBC. It was used for regular broadcasts all through the war, and was mentioned from time to time by "Lord Haw Haw" though it was meant to be secret.'

BENTLEY MANOR

'Bentley Manor was taken over at the start of the war. The Essex Regiment was billeted there. We lived at Upper Bentley Farm, next door. Our cats migrated en masse to the cookhouse. One even had her kittens at the farm and carried them one by one over the meadow to the manor.

We had a lot of enemy bombers come over. One night a stick of incendiaries were dropped. One hit a new hayrick at Raglis Cottage. The men formed a chain with everything they could find that could hold water from the brook to the farm cottage and put it out.

Winters when it snowed were always hard at Bentley. The lanes filled up. From Windy Harbour to the crossroads the snow-in soon makes it impassable. The first winter they were there, the Essexes had to dig out the lane so the milk lorry could get to Bentley.

The Americans were next. They played baseball on a field still called the baseball field. They sang at "The Brook" Sunday night and made Pumphouse Lane wider driving their lorries into Redditch.

After they left the prisoners of war were the next occupiers. They worked on farms in the area.

In 1947 dry rot was found and the Manor was pulled down.'

IT'S MILES AWAY!

'The thing that frightened me more than anything was when they dropped the atom bomb. The news was on the radio. I thought the world would explode. One hadn't been dropped before and I thought this would be the end of the world. My mother said, "Don't look so worried, it's miles away." I'd been in London and had bombs drop all around me, but it was nothing to what I felt then.'

LIFE GOES ON

Families still had to be fed and clothed, and that became an increasingly difficult task as the war went on. We all suffered hardships and longed for the day when rationing would at last be over.

EXTRA RATIONS

'During the war, land workers had special or extra rations, which in our case were supplied at the village shop at Chaddesley Corbett. As most country people kept a pig, hens and possibly a house-cow, rationing problems were somewhat alleviated. Every part of our gardens was used to grow vegetables.'

THE RITUAL OF THE NEWS

'As 1940 progressed the ritual of listening to the six o'clock news became important in our lives. We heard of the invasion of France and the Low Countries, the Battle of Britain and the daily scores of enemy planes shot down, and our own losses, and it became part of our lives.'

DELICACIES

'A searchlight and sound detector was positioned on the golf course at Blakedown, manned by GRA personnel. Then later on a large US Army stores depot was set up by the station. A lot of the soldiers were black, which few of the villagers had encountered before. They were most generous in handing out huge tins of apricot jam and other delicacies, unseen for several years here, and they laid on a wonderful Christmas party for all the children.

Fuel was desperately short and I remember fetching sacks of coal slack from the coal yard at Hagley and bringing them home in the boot of my Austin Seven.'

GETTING WED

'My sister was married in May 1943. My father was a gardener at a large house in Barnt Green and his employer gave us some pretty pink rhododendron heads to make a bouquet. We needed some white ribbon to tie round them and to make a streamer. I went into Bromsgrove and starting at the top where the road divides for Birmingham and Stourbridge I went into every shop, both on the main street and in all the side ones (and there were many small shops selling haberdashery in those days). I had reached the last one, nearly a mile along the Worcester road, when I finally managed to obtain two yards of two inch wide ribbon – it was like finding gold.'

NO MORE VESTS

'I, and all my friends, stopped wearing vests because they were on coupons, preferring to use the coupons we had on outer garments. There was a black market in coupons and I remember someone who sold secondhand dresses requiring a few coupons as well as cash when selling.

Net was not on coupons. I made a very pretty blouse from ordinary blue net, with a ruched neckline, for dancing. I also made a coat from a blanket. Parachute silk was, of course, wonderful for blouses and underwear – if you could get it.'

A WARTIME COOKERY BOOK

'In 1940, long before the last boundary changes, the County Borough of Dudley was part of Worcestershire; in fact it was an island of Worcestershire completely surrounded by the county of Staffordshire. It was an industrial town and, therefore, much involved in the production of the munitions of war.

One of the Dudley firms that played a great part on the Home Front was called Goodwin Foster Brown Ltd, famous for self-raising flour, packed in bags with the picture of a baby and therefore always known as The Baby Bag. The firm was founded in 1880 and in 1940 celebrated its Diamond Jubilee.

Mr Goodwin said, "Since Goodwin's Extra SR Flour was first packed in the now famous Baby Picture Bag, our beloved country has fought two major wars and is now engaged in a desperate struggle against the most brutal, tyrannical regime in the history of civilisation."

Therefore, to celebrate the Diamond Jubilee of the company, Mr Goodwin decided to publish a *Wartime Cookery Book and Guide,* and give a copy to all housewives who bought Goodwin's SR Flour. Goodwin Foster Brown were major producers of flour at that time, so that the book was likely to reach to the far boundaries of Worcestershire and beyond.

The Goodwin's Baby – a familiar advertising sign brought into the war effort.

Having spent two years at a domestic science college, specialising in cookery, I was now cookery demonstrator for the SWS Electric Co in Dudley and I was asked if I would write the cookery section, which was the main object of the book.

I knew that it was going to be a challenge. It was wartime; we lived far from the sea and so fish would be scarce, but near to the Vale of Evesham, so vegetables, fruit and rabbits would feature more in our diet. Every householder who had a small garden was growing vegetables, especially onions. Most recipes had to include flour because this was advertising the product as well as helping on the Home Front.

The book, when finished, had 68 pages, and included other helpful information. The subjects were: Emergency, such as first aid; Child Welfare; General Information, such as identity cards; Rationing; Blackout; Household Hints and Safety in the Home.

The cookery section started with Food and What to Eat – Group I Body building food – Group II Energy foods – Group III Protective foods. Each group had a list of the foods that were available to help the housewife when planning meals and to help her create a balanced diet. When food is plentiful we do not have to think about these groups, but little did we realise at that time that rationing and scarcity was going to continue for a whole decade. Finally there were 36 pages of recipes.

In 1940 the book was launched and I was invited to have lunch with Mr Goodwin and the publishers at the Dudley Arms Hotel, which was then in the centre of the town but has long since been demolished.

Mr Goodwin said, "For our part we hope that this book will be of great assistance to the wives and mothers at home, on whose shoulders rests the heavy responsibility of feeding properly our workers and our fighting men's children in the face of restricted supplies, and, in the great majority of cases, depleted purses."'

HARDSHIPS AND RATIONING

'We were quite lucky in our family and always had plenty of fresh fruit and vegetables, my father being a market gardener and fruit grower, but we didn't get the meat to go with it too often. I believe the ration of meat per person was four ounces per week; if you had meat you couldn't have bacon and vice versa. We had two ounces of butter or margarine, two ounces of lard, also sugar, but manual workers and land workers had an extra allowance of cheese. We kept poultry so were all right for our own eggs, but I remember my mother using the dried egg powder, trying to make scrambled eggs by mixing it with water, and trying to bake a cake. Dried fruit was also very scarce as were oranges and bananas, because they came from abroad. I think it was during this time that the carrot cake came into its own, and has been a favourite ever since. I remember we used to have rabbit stew quite often as my father used to shoot the poor little blighters on his crops; pigeons and pheasants were also caught on our market garden.

As far back as I can remember we always kept a pig, up until about 1950. Every year when the pig was killed we lived on the fat of the land! Faggots, chitterlings, scratchings, rosemary lard, hams and sides of bacon, these latter being stored away under the stairs in the "glory-hole" as we called it. The end of our pig keeping days came very drastically about 1950, just after my father had had a new cider shed built. The sides of bacon and hams that year were stored up in the rafters of the cider shed to dry off, and one morning when Dad went to the cider shed he discovered the locks had been broken open and all the hams and bacon had been stolen! He was dreadfully upset about this and swore he would never have another pig. No

Housewives found themselves the target of much government advice on how to cope with the rations and to 'make do and mend'.

trace of the items was ever found, but Dad said he hoped it would choke them!

Occasionally we would have a boiled fowl. So long as they kept laying eggs they were spared, but as soon as they got a bit long in the tooth they were due for the cooking pot.

Clothes rationing was a bit of a bind for me as I was just at that stage when I was growing up and beginning to take notice of nice clothes. I remember particularly one winter during the war when I needed a new coat and did not have enough coupons! The lady next door to us was a dressmaker, seamstress, upholsterer, anything in the sewing line she could do. She had a winter coat which had become too small for her and just fitted me, but, sadly, it was very faded. On inspection it was found that the reverse of the material was a lovely pink and blue check. That dear lady unpicked the whole coat, including the belt and completely reversed it, thereby making a lovely new pink and blue check coat which fitted me perfectly. I thought I was the cat's whiskers in that coat and I wore it until it practically fell off my back, not only because I loved it so, but also because of necessity!

Another thing we did during the time of clothing coupons was to take the best parts of several garments and make them into one, blouses and dresses for instance. A bit like Joseph's coat of many colours some of them! I still have a booklet published during the war called *Make do and mend*, which gave you all sorts of tips and hints on how to make the best of what you had.

The rationing continued after the war and when I was married in 1951 some foods were still rationed. I remember my mother and mother in law saving up fat and sugar etc, in order that we should have a really nice wedding cake. My husband used to get an extra cheese allowance because he was a manual worker.'

'We used to get sheep's heads and pigs' heads. You could get some tasty meals off them. Pigs' trotters made lovely soup, then the dogs had the bones.

My aunt used to buy whale meat. I stayed with her and she kept telling me about this lovely casserole she made with it – and the next day we had it. If only there'd been a space between it, I might have enjoyed it more. Some people thought it very nice. It looked like braising steak, and you soaked it in vinegar.

We used to send my brother to the butcher's to get the meat as he was very thin and very pale and he always did well. We'd send him down for, perhaps, a breast of lamb and he'd come back with two.'

I TRIED TO RING THE KING

'On VE Day I was working on a telephone exchange and it was the busiest time I've ever known, because everyone was phoning each other. They were queueing up to make calls. I tried to ring the King. There was dancing in the streets at Upton on Severn.'

DOING OUR BIT

From the Women's Land Army to firewatching, from knitting socks to making jam, those who were left behind did their best for the war effort.

THE DAY WE RANG THE BELLS

'Perhaps the most unique, frightening and, later, humorous recollection of wartime in Bewdley was one from Sheila, only daughter of Mr Fred Bishop, then publican of the Talbot Hotel in Bewdley. Mr Bishop was himself a member of the ARP and had also a very special duty to perform in the event of an emergency. This duty was to ring the bells at St Anne's church in Bewdley.

And so it was that on Sunday afternoon, 30th June 1940, Sheila, a small girl at the time, remembers her mother answering the door to a messenger with a written message from Captain Harold Goodwin, MC, of the LDV (Local Defence Volunteers) instructing her father to go at once to ring the church bells. The time was 4.46 pm when Mr Bishop unlocked the belfry door of the church and commenced ringing. The notes, faint and very slow at first, grew louder and, by this time, members of the LDV were assembling. The town was crowded with visitors as it usually was on a sunny Sunday in June. After 15 minutes, Mr Bishop, together with Mr Tom Timmis, the local butcher, left, Mr Bishop to go home to don his ARP uniform and present himself, along with his other ARP colleagues, for duty.

The emergency was caused by several people in the area claiming to have seen what they thought to be parachutists landing in the area of Long Bank and Golden Valley following the flying north across the town of two low-flying aeroplanes. There had long been the fear that German parachute landings of this kind would take place and, with all the sightings reported, Captain Goodwin, who was in charge of the Bewdley division of the LDV, set in motion the warning of the supposed parachutists' landings and sent his message to Mr Bishop, as mentioned above, instructing him to ring the church bells.

However, at the end of that Sunday in June, the conclusion was drawn that, as no parachutists had been found, one explanation was that what had been seen to cause the events of the day were "Flying haycocks", a local phenomenon. These haycocks were stooks of hay gathered loosely together and left in the fields to dry prior to carrying for ricking. The remains of many of these had been found in the tops of trees and far from their fields, presumably due to some thermal activity on that hot summer's day.'

FIVE YEARS AS A LAND GIRL

'Peggy lived in Putney and in 1942, at the age of 17, volunteered to join the Land Army. She was signed on by Lady Denman, the Honorary Director, and was sent to work at Hanley Hall in Hanley Swan. The first year was very hard work and included hoeing, going up and down the corn fields cutting out thistles, and then haymaking which was all done by hand, no tractors, just a horse and cart.

She was very "green" and the men on the farm had fun by sending her to get the key to the mangold bury; asking her to go to the barn to get three round post holes and three square post holes; and on being told to clean out a pen containing one year old bulls, one bull put his head between her legs and threw her into the manger, luckily she was only badly bruised!

Peggy's pet hate was threshing, which went on for weeks. She was put on the "plugs", carrying them into a shed all day. The dust got everywhere and at the end of the day the men would push her into the pile and it took her weeks to get the plugs out of her clothes.

Next she moved to another farm as she wanted to learn to milk, which she enjoyed doing. However, there was still field work to do such as picking up potatoes, hedging, and yet more threshing!

Peggy then went to work at Powick Hospital's farm, which had a large staff as food was provided for everyone at the hospital. She worked in the dairy, milking the cows twice a day, then washing and sterilising buckets etc, and also looking after the chickens, even plucking and dressing them ready for the doctors' dinners. Her pay was then £2 10s a week out of which she had to pay £1 for her lodgings.

Peggy enjoyed her five years as a land girl, usually starting at seven in the morning and working until five o'clock, except at haymaking when work finished when it was dark.'

'Land girls worked all round the Hanleys. Few knew there was a Land Army Vermin Control Unit and a hostel in Upton on Severn. One Land Army member was paid elevenpence an hour, while the model farm paid £4 a week to another.'

I ENJOYED BEING A LAND GIRL

'I joined the Women's Land Army in 1940 and was "kitted out" with a nice, thick donkey-brown knee-length overcoat, a felt hat, fawn dungarees, green V-necked jerseys, cream shirts, knee-length socks and stout brown shoes and a badge. I also received brown corduroy breeches. These were baggy and badly fitting so I am afraid I never wore them, but used breeches of my own.

I began work on a farm near Warndon (part of which now has the M5 running through it). I had my own horse with me and so I used to ride round the sheep most mornings and sometimes more often in the lambing season. I liked working with sheep – they have beautiful eyes, all different, and of course the lambs were so attractive gambolling together in the fields. Sometimes there were orphan lambs which had to be brought into the kitchen and bottle-fed. In the winter months hay had to be taken to the cattle in the fields. I learned to cut blocks of hay out of the rick with a hay knife. This was a large bladed implement with a handle at right-angles to the blade.

I also helped to get a 17-hand hunter used to pulling a trap, or float as they were usually called. When being ridden on the road, he was used to walking near the gutter, and I well remember driving through Fernhill Heath where he kept trying to walk near the curb and the float wheel kept going up onto the pavement at intervals.

I lived in at this farm and after a very cold winter and the following spring, I moved to a large, mainly arable farm near Broome. I used to cycle seven miles to work then and seven miles back in the evening. This journey entailed negotiating the steep Hagley hill, much easier to go down than up!

There were four land girls on this farm plus four men who were Jehovah's Witnesses and therefore conscientious objectors. We girls used to get very annoyed with them because when we asked if they would protect us if the Germans came they replied in the negative. However, the rest of the time we were on good terms!

It was on this farm that we had to hoe and single sugar beet in a twelve acre field. When you got to one end of the field it was time to start getting the weeds out back at the beginning again. What a boring, back-breaking job that was. The farm had a tarmac road running through it, and at intervals during the day the farmer would ride his bicycle quietly by, and if he caught us talking he would shout, "Bend your backs" – at five minutes before our lunch break, this could be a little irksome! Later on in October, November and December the sugar beet was lifted by the men and we girls, armed with big knives, cut off the tops. Mercifully my fingers are still all intact.

The potato harvest was important and I remember soldiers coming to help get the crop in. The tractor dug them up and we all picked them up and put them into sacks. When there was an east wind blowing it was a horrible job – your fingers were frozen and when you bent down the wind seemed to whistle up your back under your jacket.

Every year the ricks had to be opened and the sheaves of corn would be fed into the threshing machine, in order to separate the grain from the straw. This was a hot, dusty job and all the straw had to be put in another rick for bedding. There was work non-stop for us all then. Harvest time including stooking corn and learning how to stack the sheaves on the dray when it was ready to be put into ricks.

About this time I became engaged and moved to a farm nearer home – only four miles to work. I used to arrive at nine o'clock to do the milk round in Halesowen, which was then in Worcestershire. Some of the milk was bottled and the rest was in cans and measured with pint and half pint ladles. When the round was finished it was back to the farm, where the bottles all had to be washed plus the churns, cans and measures.

In the afternoon the 14 cows, plus the bull, had to be brought in from the fields. The cows usually went into their correct stalls and then had to be fastened with a chain round their necks and the bull had to be chained in his stable as well. I learned to milk on this farm and once milked all 14 cows on my own. After milking was finished and the milk cooled, the bottles had to be filled and tops put on. The rest of the milk was put into the churn and left in the dairy ready for the morning delivery. While working at this farm which was near Hagley Wood, I was married and later became pregnant, but I carried on until the eighth month carrying the milk cans and delivering the bottles as it was a government ruling at the time.

On the whole I enjoyed being a land girl. I loved the country and I learned a little about farming. I made some good friends and learned that whatever the weather, farming had to continue and animals had to be fed and looked after, every day of the week.'

WE ALL HELPED

'At Ombersley herbs were dried, jams sold and seeds for vegetable growing distributed. In May 1941, 122 eggs were collected and sent to Worcester Royal Infirmary. At that time the egg ration was one per person per week.

Children also helped. The top class of the school picked blackberries for the school canteen ladies to make into jam for school dinners, which for a time were supplied in the Memorial Hall. A local farmer collected older children with a trailer to take them pea picking or potato lifting. Children were paid and they were very glad to go.

Americans were based in Westwood Park. Families were able to invite soldiers to Sunday tea by officially requesting them at the post office.'

FIREWATCHING

'I worked at a munitions factory at Long Bank in Bewdley, owned by Mullers. I was obliged to take turns in firewatching in case any incendiary bombs were dropped. We stayed there the night and slept in our clothes, on camp beds. We were each paid five shillings a night with a free supper and breakfast. It was a relief when we woke in the morning and had not been required to attend to any emergency.'

JAM MAKING AND CANNING

'During the war I was a member of Elmley Castle WI. In 1940 the National Federation of Women's Institutes began to administer the Ministry of Food's fruit preservation scheme as part of the national war effort. Our president was Lady Davies and to support the scheme she called on members for fruit picked from their gardens and for volunteer jam makers. But there was a problem.

In those days there was no village hall as such at Elmley. All village activities were held in the old tithe barn near the church, but there was neither water nor power laid on, nor any cooking facilities. Because sugar was rationed the jam all had to be made uniformly in one place to comply with the Ministry of Food regulations. So we had to improvise.

On the appointed day members arrived at the "village hall" (tithe barn) with their picked fruit and jam kettles or large saucepans. The fruit was weighed, paid for and booked in. The weight of fruit per pan had to be recorded and then taken home to be cooked slowly to pulp.

The next day the pans of cooked pulp were returned to the hall where a motley collection of members' portable oil or calor gas stoves were brought. A sack of sugar had been delivered to the safe-keeping of the vice-president Mrs Snow, the vicar's wife, and brought to the hall. Sugar was added to each pan of pulp according to the weight of fruit recorded the previous day (a pound of sugar to a pound of fruit) and boiled to setting point. The setting point had to be carefully monitored by a qualified member, Helen Humphreys from Kerso, who was domestic science trained. The finished jam was packed in one pound glass jamjars with the approved Ministry of Food stamp on the base (saved and collected by members of the Institute)

The jars of jam were covered and labelled the next day, using WI covers and labels. The jam was collected by Ministry officials and distributed for sale in local shops in Pershore and surrounding villages, in particular, Derrett's at Little Comberton who baked and delivered bread around the villages by horse-drawn carts until the late 1960s.'

'The canning centre opened by the WI in Eckington was used by everyone in the village. From 1941 it was housed in the stables of the hostel for evacuated children (now Elm House). During 1941 and 1942, 3;393 pounds of jam were boiled, jarred and labelled and 3,301 cans of fruit were sealed. The enterprise went from strength to strength and became a daily occupation until the end of the war.'

FROM LAMBS' WOOL TO CAMOUFLAGE NETS

'Wartime, 1939 – evacuees – headlice – WI to the rescue! Find a big dinner plate and some old sheeting. Draw a circle around that plate, cut out the material and machine/sew a hem around it and insert some elastic. Then, in the old Scout hut, deal with the unwanted visitors with Lysol or Durbac or that purple dye-stuff! Cover hair with mob-cap. Then give the little ones a little present of sweets for being so very good.

1939 again – *Polish* refugee children, who were in Allied territories, needed knitted garments such as little vests, socks, gloves – and the men in HM Forces (Navy) needed sea-boot stockings, balaclavas, mittens, gloves, socks, scarves etc. We all knitted whatever we could manage.

Rose hips were collected for syrup; lambs' wool out of the

hedgerows for some special purpose; silver paper for the Cheltenham hospitals for sale for money; pies were made for the men in the fields who worked until moonlight in double summer-time.

Camouflage netting was made in our WI, too, and, with the 1940 Dunkirk evacuation, the County Federation appealed for, I believe, 2,000 pairs of socks in a few days, as those poor, tired Dunkirk soldiers were minus shoes and socks after their terrible ordeal. (I was at Prince Henry's Grammar School then, and one June morning, as we walked to our Evesham school, there were crowds of bare-footed soldiers on the pavements near Evesham GWR/LMS stations – they were exhausted but, oh, so relieved to be back safe in "Blighty".) Needless to say, more than enough socks were soon knitted by the womenfolk.

Living at Conderton Forge we always kept two or three pigs, from baby piglets to pigs weighing 20 stones (280 lbs). We also could get rabbits very easily, so we lived on pork or rabbits mainly. Fish could be purchased – fishmongers used to visit our village, selling whatever was available. Bread was delivered, as were all our groceries, and, between the wars, milk was delivered. (Yoke with the two buckets of milk.) We had family evacuees, too, and, at one time, Mother was catering for 16 people.

We salted runner beans and we dried apple rings on wires or strings in the airing cupboard. We made jelly, jams, chutneys, pickled walnuts, mushroom ketchups, and preserved eggs in waterglass in pottery vessels. We made home-brewed ginger beer and lemonade and elderberry wines, as well as parsnip wine, beetroot wine, cowslip wine, potato wine, and any other fruit/vegetables were similarly processed if we had some sugar.

Our WI ladies were also asked to machine some special bandages, emergency dressings, very carefully eliminating seams if at all possible, and those bandages were for "amputees".'

'Our first project at Crowle was jam making and the vicarage laundry was used as this had fire grates on which we could use our jam kettles. Later we were able to buy two oil stoves which were a great improvement.

The Australian WIs sent us food parcels and our Institute shared them amongst the older villagers. There were tins of corned beef, luncheon meat (unheard of before), fruit and some dried fruit.'

A CHILD'S WAR

Children came to accept wartime life as normal, with all its dangers and shortages. Evacuees came to many parts of the county from the cities, and some formed lasting friendships in their new life.

MOVING OUT FOR SAFETY

'South of Birmingham are the Lickey Hills and I remember as a small child walking among masses of bluebells, climbing log-style steps and picking bilberries in a jam jar to be taken home and made into a pie.

My school, Colmers Farm, Rubery, must have been very modern and up to date in the late 1930s. It was certainly big and quite frightening. When the war came and the sirens sounded we were marched over to the air raid shelters. Sometimes we saw gunfire flak or even bombs falling on the Austin car factory. At home in Rednal we had our own air raid shelter and my brother and I were often put to bed in there to save getting up in the night when the raid began.

One of our pleasures was a tram ride into Birmingham. I chose a Christmas present in a store called Barnaby's and it was bombed shortly afterwards so I had to have something else.

As we were close to the Austin factory, our parents decided that for our safety we should move to a little cottage in the village of Hanbury. This was such a lovely time. The village school was a long walk away but a happy place. Once someone brought a lion cub on a lead to show the children. Our grandparents spent some time there with us too. We had to draw the water from a shared well which fortunately had quite a high wall around it. The memories evoke a sense of freedom in the countryside in spite of the war.'

OUR SHELTER

'Our school air raid drill at Kempsey was to run up the road and get under the hedge. That was our shelter. We had to practise doing it but luckily we never had to do it for real.'

SCHOOLDAYS DURING THE WAR

'My school, built in the late 1920s, was quite modern and had many windows. Returning there after the 1939 summer holidays one of the first effects of the outbreak of war was to see the windows in classrooms and corridors all criss-crossed with sticky tapes against shattering from falling bombs.

Gas masks were carried all the time at first. The cardboard box had a waterproof cover and when this wore out I remember that always I had to make room for it in my school case, along with homework books. Gas mask drills were carried out in the early years – the smell of rubber still reminds me of dragging it on over my head.

Eight brick-built air raid shelters appeared in the gardens surrounding the school. When the sirens sounded we dispersed to them, 30 or 40 to each one, but fortunately nothing disastrous befell us. Towards the end of the war flying bombs were coming into south-east England and it was realised that we would not reach the shelters in time. A new procedure entailed the teacher banging on her desk and we had to dive under ours instantly. We had many a practice and many a bumped head, but fortunately again nothing worse happened.

My home was about two miles from school and entailed a bus journey. I recall that, some time after Dunkirk, several buses came into use which had had their seats set lengthways down the sides. I believe they had been used as ambulances to transfer returning troops from the south coast to Midlands hospitals.

The "Dig for Victory" campaign had us digging up patches of ground surrounding the games fields and gardens. Vegetables were tended all spring and summer, mostly in our lunch hour. A farmer from a few miles away used to come and collect a few girls to help with beet singling and potato picking. Despite these back-aching jobs there were enough eager volunteers to have a bumpy ride in his trailer, sitting on straw bales.

We collected from the countryside foxgloves for digitalis and dead nettles, I think for chlorophyll. These were festooned on strings above our heads in the physics laboratory until dry. Then we had the awful job of stripping off the leaves into sacks. Rose hips were also collected for the extraction of vitamin C. Sheep's wool was gathered from hedgerows and fences and a member of staff washed it all then used it to stuff children's quilts. A very dusty job which some of us undertook was carried out in the Corn Exchange behind the Town Hall. There we made camouflage netting. A huge net was suspended from a pulley and rope system near the roof and strips of coloured sacking had to be woven in and out of the mesh to correspond with

We all did our bit – Joan joined the Girls' Training Corps and her younger sisters the St John's Youth in Upton on Severn.

the pattern behind. As we worked there was a handle to wind up more netting until the bottom edge came into sight.

Paper was in short supply and as the years went by it became thin and easily torn. No new writing books were issued until every margin was filled. Subsequently revising for exams became a nightmare with such cramped notes. Text books were loaned to us and we had to cover them with brown paper to preserve them. They were in such short supply.

The most senior girls undertook overnight firewatching duty, considered a great privilege for they were taught how to use the stirrup pumps.

The Free French had an HQ nearby and we were encouraged to write and practise our French. I remember some of them visiting the school. I still have a small badge bearing the Cross of Lorraine.'

LIFE WENT ON MUCH AS USUAL

'When I look back, as a schoolchild in the 1940s at Worcester, I can't remember feeling frightened as we walked to our local school with a cardboard box containing a gas mask slung across our shoulders and an identity bracelet with our own personal number engraved on our wrist. Isn't it strange – I can still remember that particular number and yet I have difficulty in remembering my current car vehicle number!

We sat quietly in class with gas mask at hand but there seemed no threat and although we went through the routine every week of practising with the awkward appliance, it never occurred to us that we might ever need it for real – it all seemed a bit of fun at the time. The air raid siren would wail out once a week in a practice run, and we would all troop to our air raid shelters, but apart from a homeward German bomber dropping his excess load on a factory in St John's, causing, thank goodness, no injury, just damage to the factory, we didn't ever feel threatened in our part of the country. I suppose living in a quiet place like Worcester during the war made all the goings on we read in the newspapers seem like another world. Occasionally, one of our classmates would come in to report that one of his or her relatives who was in the services was either wounded or missing, and although we could appreciate the grief involved, we were all so cocooned in our town and in our families it didn't seem like real life, but more like when we went to the pictures and saw the films.

Once a week I was despatched down the road with the accumulator (or battery) for our rather cumbersome bakelite radio, to have it recharged. One was left and another already charged given in its place. This was my weekly job, and I felt very responsible to have this job, as before television the old radio was the centre of home entertainment. I can remember sitting with my grandfather to hear the end of a show as the battery was getting fainter and fainter and just hoping it would last out to the final part – it usually didn't and I was despatched post haste to get it recharged!

Endless hours were spent listening to all the comedy shows like *ITMA* (It's That Man Again) with Tommy Handley and *Workers' Playtime* which every day came from a factory producing goods for the war effort, and was usually an hour long music hall show at lunchtime. A great many of our now well established and much loved entertainers started their careers in this show. I can remember first hearing Julie Andrews as a very young singer performing with her mother and father – Ted and Barbara Andrews – on this show. She must only have been around ten years old, but her voice was wonderful even then.

I suppose we all look back to our schooldays with nostalgia, remembering the good times, shutting out the bad, but during and towards the end of the war, Worcester wasn't a bad place to be living!'

Evacuees arriving at Great Malvern station on 1st September 1939.

OUR AMERICANS

'One day in 1940 a bundle of comics arrived in our classroom in Malvern from American schoolchildren. We grabbed them excitedly, even though they were probably intended for children who had suffered in the Blitz. In Malvern we shared our homes with evacuees, but we still had our homes intact. The sirens sounded often, and bombers throbbed overhead, but we were not considered important enough by Hitler for his bombs. Many of the comics had names and addresses of the senders on the front of them which added to the excitement. America was a far-away place of glamour and wealth, the home of Mickey Mouse and Shirley Temple films, far removed from our Worcestershire town.

Mr Mooney, our class teacher, pointed out to us that if we wished to write to the address on our comics it was quite likely that our letters wouldn't reach their destination, for the Atlantic Ocean was thick with submarines and the Merchant ships carrying food were the number one priority. However, in spite of the warnings, and the vagueness of the address on my comic, I wrote, and was thrilled to receive a reply a few weeks later. My penfriend was an eleven year old boy, the same age as myself. His name was Dana Morrill and he lived in a place called Benedict in Minnesota. He sent a photograph of himself with an enormous fish he had caught, and also a photograph of the ship-lap schoolhouse that he and his sisters attended. This letter was the first of hundreds that in the succeeding 54 years winged their way between Minnesota and England. Not only did he write, but so did his mother and sisters.

I learnt a lot about Minnesota and never ceased to be amazed by the coldness of their winters. The lakes froze to such a thickness that holes were cut in the ice to allow the people to harpoon fish through them, and timber wolves howled outside their homes, in the biting cold. In turn I told them about Malvern, our hills and healing springs and wells, and about my friends and the games we played. They were anxious to know if we had enough food to eat, and what we would do if Germany invaded.

Like all children we had become accustomed to the food available and didn't feel in the least deprived. I explained about the vegetables we grew and the chickens we kept and assured them that we weren't starving. As for Hitler invading – he wouldn't dare, and if he did . . . a German aircraft was shot down on the golf course one night and an airman was arrested single-handed by a lady with a bike. This incident related in a letter from me was no doubt embroidered for effect.

We didn't go out of Malvern much during the war, but in 1942 large contingents of American troops flooded into the area. The men and women wore smart brown and cream uniforms. They chewed gum and were confident and extrovert. The Military Police patrolled the area in jeeps with white stars on the side, and were not backward in cracking on the head any American soldiers they considered were misbehaving. The Ministry of Defence took over the boys' college and strangers poured into the town. It was a time of change and upheaval, and the air crackled with a sense of urgency and impending battle. Having written to my American family, I felt a real authority on Americans, although my impression of my homely penfriends in Minnesota didn't equate with the laughing, noisy soldiers I saw around.

Over the years we learnt a lot about each other's families and fortunes. We rejoiced when the war ended and shared each other's successes, disasters, births, deaths and marriages. At last, in 1976, when my husband and I were in America, we flew to Bemidji in Minnesota and visited the family that I had written to for so long.'

THE WAR IN WORCESTER

'I suppose my first memories of the war are of gas masks in black canisters we had to carry around with us – I hated having to put them on; the blackout with torches held low; and the garden railing to the front of the house being taken for scrap metal. Also evacuees – we had a full house so couldn't take any but later on when my brother left for college, then the army, we had a young man to lodge who was drafted into the area and employed at the old Archdales factory.

There were air raid shelters and concrete blocks at the side of the road, ready to be moved across to stop the Germans if they invaded us. We had an air raid siren, just about 50 yards away from our house, but as we had a cellar that was our air raid shelter, I can remember sitting on the cellar steps in my dressing gown finishing a Weetabix for my supper. Later on in the war my older sister, who was going to train as a nurse, was poorly in bed after the required vaccinations. The siren got stuck on the lowest note for several hours and Mum had to keep going upstairs to see how she was, huddled under her eiderdown.

My father used to turn out the lights and draw back the blackout curtains so that we could watch the searchlights over the river Severn. Sometimes we could hear the German planes overhead on their way to bomb the Birmingham area. Father was very involved with the Home Guard and when the Second Front began we had a map on kitchen wall and marked the progress of our troops.

The radio was much in prominence. Chamberlain's broadcast in 1939, Lord Haw Haw, and Richard Dimbleby's report on Belsen concentration camp are vivid memories.

We lived on a main road and for months, day and night, American tanks and troops passed our house on their way to the South Coast before D-Day. The pavements were all cracked from the heavy traffic passing through!

The Americans arrived and I remember when queueing for one of the first ice creams (speckled with brown, not like most ices today) we were treated by an American soldier. They seemed to have so much and used to throw us children chewing gum and chocolate out of the back of their lorries as they went by.

As I was only six in 1939, so just twelve by the time VJ Day arrived, most of my childhood was rationed with sweet and clothes coupons being quite important in my life. I was lucky that my father was too old to go and fight, he had more than his share in the 1914-18 war.'

THEY ARRIVED IN A CHARABANC

'The evacuees arrived at the parish room in Wribbenhall in a charabanc. They came from Birmingham, a place I had hardly even heard of.

The WVS lady brought the girl we had been allocated to our house. Her name was Joan, she was older than my sister and me and all she had was the clothes she was wearing. My mother had to ask other women in the village who had older girls for spare clothing.

She had never seen a garden. She did not know you could pick fruit and dig vegetables, and she had never seen wet fish, which my mother bought from the van that came to the village on a Tuesday morning. In Birmingham their milk was delivered in bottles, but we were not so advanced and our milk still came in the grey churns and was ladled out by the milkman into large china jugs.

At first we had many strange faces in school but they soon began to disappear as they drifted back to Birmingham. I cannot remember Joan ever receiving a letter from her parents but they did visit her once. Soon after that, she too returned home.

The spare room was not empty for long. We then had twin boys whose aunt in the village had no room for them. Their home in Birmingham had been bombed.

While most of the evacuees returned home, one or two remained and are still living locally.'

CHILDREN AND ADULTS

'As the area around Habberley and Trimpley was regarded as relatively safe from air attacks, there was very little evacuation from here except for some children who went to Canada to stay with relatives.

Instead, many children from Birmingham and its surrounding industrial areas were evacuated here. So, too, were many children from Clacton High School who were billeted in the Habberley and Trimpley areas. Several girls from Hong Kong and Austria attended Kidderminster High School. We had two evacuees (twins) from Clacton High School staying with us for over a year.

At another point in the war we had a family of six adults who had been bombed out of their house in Smethwick staying with us in our cottage. They came one Sunday afternoon and pleaded with my parents to give them shelter as they were all so terrified of spending another night of bombing. At first my mother refused, saying it was impossible to take six more people as our cottage had inadequate accommodation. They were so desperate to stay, they said that they could all sleep on the floor downstairs if only she would let them stay. Realising their desperate plight, Mother relented.

So, for over a year, they all slept in one bedroom, either on a double bed or on the floor with cushions – anything to get a night's rest. They were a delightful family.

Every night, they arrived, exhausted, about 7 pm, prepared and ate their supper and then chatted and listened to the wireless. The two women (the mother and daughter in law) washed up the crockery they had used and cut sandwiches ready for the next day. After a bedtime drink of cocoa they all went to bed about 9.30 pm, ready for an early start again next morning. In fact the family were gone by 5.30 am, as the four men (the father and his three grown up sons) all worked in a foundry in Smethwick or Oldbury.

A life-long friendship developed out of this simple act of kindness and compassion.'

MY SECOND HOME

'As an eight year old boy I had no notion of the immensity of the proclamation of the then Prime Minister, Neville Chamberlain that we were going to war against Germany.

The events that followed happened very quickly and I found myself with most of the other children at Alston Road school in Birmingham being evacuated.

The first thing to happen was that we were taken from the school in buses to Adderly Park railway station. Each of us had a label with our name on and also the name of the school that we came from. I can remember that we had our gas masks but I cannot recall that I had any other luggage (I must have had a change of clothes at least).

None of the children or their parents knew where we were going. The train left Birmingham and arrived at Evesham. I cannot remember how we left the station, only going into the hall at Bengeworth school and seeing rows of chairs and benches to sit on. It was here that the ladies of Evesham, who had volunteered to become foster mothers, came to select the child that they wished to care for.

Most of the children were picked out and I was taken by Mrs Huxley who lived at 76 Kings Road, Bengeworth. Several children were left in the school hall after all the foster mothers had gone. These children were taken by the billeting officer and went from house to house and the occupants were asked if they would take a child in.

The Huxley family consisted of Mr and Mrs Huxley and their two children, Joan who was about my age and Arthur who was about five. I was made to feel very welcome and Arthur had to leave his bedroom and share his sister's room, so that I could have a room of my own. I had never had a bedroom of my own before and so for me it was very exciting.

The following day I went back to Bengeworth school, along with the rest of the evacuees, where we had to write a postcard to our parents in Birmingham to tell them where we were living.

The next thing was to go to school to continue our education. From Bengeworth to the school, going down Port Street, I passed a cinema where some of the evacuees used to go to the Saturday morning matinee. Behind the cinema were some derelict buildings. It was in one of these buildings that a tramp lived. To me he seemed to be old, dirty, and bearded. All his worldly possessions were in an old pram and the only words he ever spoke were "yodel-ay-ity".

For some reason or another I had to change schools and was sent to what I call the "Green school" which was a little further and somewhere near where the telephone exchange is now.

Leisure time at Evesham was exciting to a "townee", lots of space and new places to explore. The park was a favourite, where games of battle were acted out using the old First World War tank that was there, as a fortress. Occasionally the battles would become more realistic when the townees fought with the locals. Wintertime saw the battles turn into snowball fights with the intention of making the rivals late for school. Also that winter the river Avon froze over with the ice being declared thick enough to be safe to go on. The river then became one huge slide with the children vying with each other to see who could slide the furthest. As the ice started to thaw strict instructions were given to stay away from the river, but this was totally disregarded by myself and my friends and a new game of crossing the river, by jumping from one piece of ice to another, was started.

I was very fortunate staying with the Huxley family and I was treated as one of them. Actually I became one of the family when identity cards were issued, as my identity number (QJEA/43/5) was the same as theirs.

I caught German measles whilst living with them. When the rash was over and I was well again I had to double up with Joan and Arthur while my room was thoroughly cleaned and disinfected. About once a month the family, including me, went to visit Mr Huxley's parents who owned a large house up Greenhill. We children were bathed and put into our Sunday best for these visits which included having tea there.

The months slid by and the evacuees gradually started to go back to Birmingham as there had been no really serious air raids.

Eventually I also returned home but for many years kept in touch with the Huxley family, albeit only by letter and Christmas cards.'

CHOOSE A CLEAN ONE!

'My mother looked tense as she pressed my Girl Guide uniform. Although there was no one to overhear, she spoke in a whisper: "I want a girl – and choose a *clean* one!" Then she added, "And don't tell anyone I told you!"

She need not have worried for when I arrived at Abberley school, ready to help deliver the evacuees to their officially allotted families, half the women of the village were already there, waiting to take their pick.

A row of frightened children sat quietly on the wooden chairs against the wall. Boys and girls, each with a name label, were dressed in a variety of clothing. Some were bundled up in layers, others had little extra except the regulation gas mask in its cardboard box. Two little boys sat close together at one end, a huddle of dirty rags.

I acted quickly and pointed at the cleanest girl. "I'll take that one!" I said, dragging the child to one side.

No one seemed to object. The children were soon sorted out and taken to their new homes – all except the two dirty little boys from the Birmingham slums. Nobody wanted them. They ended up at one of the big houses, banished to the servants' quarters. A protesting cook and housemaid had the job of bathing and de-lousing them.

Meanwhile little Hazel was settled into the spare bedroom. She had only the clothes she was wearing plus a very frilly pink party dress. Luckily my mother could use outgrown dresses belonging to my sister and myself. Hazel had never been into the country before and collected leaves and fir cones which she hid in her bed. As she also wet the bed, the mixture was quite horrid and my mother was at her wits' end.

After a few weeks Hazel's mother made the journey by bus from Birmingham to see her daughter. My sister and I had never seen a real "townee" before and were amazed at the jaunty hat, nipped waist peplum-jacket and high-heeled shoes.

My parents were not at all pleased at this sudden visit for there was no bus back for two days. My father, cursing under his breath, took Hazel's mother by car to Stourport station. This was not on his "legal" route and if found out, he would have been in trouble.

My sister and I were sent away to boarding school, and after a few months Hazel's mother fetched her daughter back home again.

Now, over 50 years later, the word "evacuee" conjures up not Hazel; but the uncomfortable memory of those two poor, dirty little boys.'

HALF TIME SCHOOLING

'At the very beginning of the war we had evacuees from a Catholic primary school in Birmingham come to Blakedown. They shared one school building. They, and the two teachers who came with them, used it in the afternoon and our own children in the morning. In the mornings the visitors were entertained in the front rooms of various houses. Gradually they all filtered back to Birmingham. Then, after a bomb had been dropped on Clacton on Sea on the east coast, the grammar school from there was evacuated to the Kidderminster area. The museum and art gallery in Kidderminster was used as a school for them. One of my evacuees complained of the dreadful hills he had to negotiate on his bicycle each day to get to school, Clacton being quite flat.'

'I came into Evesham from Broadway every day for six years from 1938 to 1944 to Prince Henry's Grammar School. Waverley Road Grammar School from Birmingham was evacuated to Evesham, and after being billeted in homes in the town it was decided they should come to school at Prince Henry's. Not having the space to cope with us all together, the day was divided in half and we went to school in the morning and they went in the afternoon. We had to go on Saturdays as well to make up for lost time, but we usually had sports then, playing them at hockey or football.

We also had to share desks, cloakroom pegs and everything else there was to share. After a few months of this, it was all utter confusion and as the bombing on Birmingham was getting less, gradually the evacuees began to go home. We then went back to a full day's school and the ones who stayed in Evesham joined in with us and we all went to school together. I became firm friends with the evacuee who lived near us but when the war ended she went back to Birmingham and we lost touch for 36 years. Then we met again through sheer chance and once again we are good friends.'

HIGHDAYS & HOLIDAYS

WE MADE OUR OWN ENTERTAINMENT

There was talent in every village, it seemed, and we found plenty to occupy our spare time, from whist drives to amateur dramatics. The radio was a part of all our lives and the cinema, from silent films to talkies, was often a weekly treat.

WORK AND PLAY

'To many at Hanley, leisure meant work, in the garden to feed the family or in the fields at harvesting to earn money. In season the whole village seemed to have baskets of blackberries. Many pounds went to a market gardener, Fred Parsons, who paid twopence or less per pound. They went to the jam factory or the dye works.

Before the war, gangs of boys and men with dogs and ferrets would go rat-catching on a Sunday morning, coming back with rats hanging on their handlebars. They were paid by the tail.

On Sunday afternoon, Jo Lanney from Worcester, first on a bike and sidecar, then in a van, would sell ice cream. As if by magic local youths appeared. Thick wafers were threepence each, small cornets a ha'penny. He would organise races round the green for small boys, prize a small cornet. A packet of cigarettes, elevenpence for 20, was the prize for a raffle of twelve people guessing the nearest number to the cigarette card.

Hanley put the first village pantomime, *Cinderella*, into production during the war through the youth and drama clubs. It toured villages up to Severn Stoke to raise money for the Russian Convoy. The football club and cricket club were sports activities.

The church played its part for many years, twopence a week at Sunday school meant an outing to Bristol Zoo and Weston, once a year by charabanc.

There was a lovely church choir, swelled by the boarders at Hanley High School and from the Home of the Good Shepherd. Otherwise, people made their own entertainment. Children played whip and top, tipcat, fishing willowrod, hopscotch, marbles, and there were lantern slides and silent films.'

CONCERTS WERE POPULAR

'Most entertainment at Wichenford was home produced in the early 1920s, and at social gatherings there would be singing, games and dancing. The most popular dance then was the Lancers, when the girls would be swung off their feet. Concerts were also popular and there was a local glee club. My father had a good baritone voice and a man from a neighbouring village had a concertina with which to accompany his comic songs. My father also had a "magic lantern" with comic slides that were very sought after.'

A RADIO IN THE BATH

'My father and his friend were enthusiasts, experimenting and building their own radio sets after 2LO started in 1922. They put their sets into a zinc bath to amplify the sound, and our homework went west. We were all so thrilled when we heard the first broadcasts.'

'In 1927 one of the family made his own radio with a kit using valves, wires and an accumulator. The valves and wiring were fixed to a piece of board and an aluminium sheet had the controls attached to it. This was built in a few days and was a great novelty. The aerial was an extension on the clothes line in the garden! We had this radio for several years; it was a Philco and it could be tuned to Radio Luxembourg which gave the Australian cricket scores. Radio sets sometimes had several sets of earphones which could be used.

When football matches were broadcast on the radio the commentator would explain where the ball was by saying which square it was in. This related to a grid published in the *Radio Times* with squares marked one to eight. With this it was easy to follow the movement of the ball.'

FROM SPORTS TO WHIST

'There was a very successful football team in Lower Moor which won several cups. Cricket was played on the same field with teas served in the village hall. In the mid 1930s two tennis courts were laid out, but were abandoned at the outbreak of the Second World War. Generally, entertainment was provided by local people.'

'The village social club was held in the old stables opposite Hanley Castle post office. The local fishing club had its own stretch of the river Severn. Whist drives were held in the schools.

The early crystal set radios were replaced by battery run ones, using a "dry" battery and an accumulator. Later these had to be recharged and were collected once a week by the "wireless man". Television could not be afforded by many in the early days, though I well remember friends gathering to watch the Coronation in 1953 at a neighbour's house.

The church organist was the local butcher, who also ran a dance band. When he was called up during the war, a young man from a neighbouring village kept his band going for him.'

'Ashton under Hill had a village cricket team and played other villages around Bredon Hill; it is still going today. The church and chapel had a choir and orchestra; the Colton family played the viola, cello and piano accordion, which helped with the singing. The first people in the village to have a television were very popular and as children we were invited to go and watch some of the early programmes on this very small screen.'

'There was plenty of entertainment for everyone in Blakedown. From the 1920s there was a small orchestra, a choral society, a country dance group, a youth club, Scouts, snooker, bowls, cricket, tennis and football clubs, and a flourishing Women's Institute and a group affiliated to the Royal & Ancient Order of Buffaloes which met in the pub.

Each year a garden fête was held to raise money for the maintenance of the churches. It was held in the grounds of one of the bigger houses such as Harborough Hall, Springbook, Churchill House of The Reddings, and was very much a village affair.'

'Bicycles were a much used form of transport, taking their riders for short trips from Droitwich to Hanbury woods, for example, or into Worcester to the cinema. Sometimes they went further afield on a day's outing to Stratford on Avon or Broadway. Young men often replaced their bicycles by motorbikes later on.

Target shooting was a popular hobby. In Droitwich at the working men's club, teams practised with their air rifles and then took part in competitions against other local teams. These usually took place at public houses such as the Crab Mill and the Britannia in Bromsgrove and the Hare and Hounds at Lickey End.'

'My husband was a farm bailiff and shepherd at Lower Tedney Farm. Around 1960 he would help to organise a sheepdog trial which became very popular; this trial was held in a field at Poswick Lodge.

The sheep were driven from Lower Tedney to Poswick Lodge and back again at night. Both sheepdogs and men were very tired at the end of the day.

Before the 1960s film shows were put on in the ex-servicemen's hut at Whitbourne, which were greatly appreciated by all. The entrance fee was two shillings. We used to cycle over from Knightwick to attend these evenings. The local show and fête was held in the field opposite the school (now a housing estate). Also held in the ex-servicemen's hut were dances, whist drives etc. We also used to cycle over from Knightwick to attend the country dances and square dancing lessons which were all very enjoyable.'

SWIMMING IN PARK'S PUDDLE

'The evening of the first Monday in May was looked forward to with eagerness and trepidation; this was the day that Worcester Swimming Club opened the season at Park's Puddle.

Changing was a work of art – strictly girls and ladies to the left, boys and gentlemen to the right. Each concrete changing cubicle opened onto the poolside, the door merely a strategically placed modesty panel. Swimmers of average height were adequately screened but taller ladies needed to act with caution!

The not so brave dipped in their toes and tested the water but more seasoned and braver souls just took the plunge and hoped for breath. A pool attendant stood armed with a long pole, ready to deliver a sharp prod in the ribs if the cold took away one's breath.

The highlight of the evening was the steaming mug of Bovril which helped restore life to our fingers. However, despite the lack of heating, a great deal of pleasure and a high standard of swimming were both achieved in the pool we called Park's Puddle.'

SOCIAL LIFE LOOKED UP

'On the social side, the men went to the Red Hart at Kington for their treat of the much renowned ham and egg supper and a pint or two of ale or cider. The ladies stayed at home sewing and looking after the children. Then in 1937 a new village hall was built in Dormston, the previous one being in Kington, on land donated by a former landlady of the Red Hart.

Once completed the ladies of the villages started a WI and soon members were coming from all the surrounding villages. During haymaking the meetings were held in the afternoons to enable the ladies to return to the hay fields in the evening to carry on raking the hay. With the onset of war, in the summers of the early 1940s,

Opening the village hall for Kington and Dormston in June 1937.

during the fruit season they met regularly, armed with jam kettles and wooden spoons and made jam, under supervision, on borrowed oil stoves and occasionally hired a canning machine and canned fruit. During the winter months they met in various members' houses for sewing and knitting parties and made clothes out of cast off garments, particularly coats, dresses and trousers for children of poorer families and soldiers' families. They also knitted socks, gloves and balaclavas for the troops.

Social life was now looking up in the villages with the new hall. Whist drives and dances were being held regularly, and became much easier to organise when in 1948 electricity arrived and mains water followed in the early 1950s.'

HONEYBOURNE MEMORIES

'Like most villages, Honeybourne had a football team and a cricket team. Early memories are of the cricket team travelling to neighbouring villages by horse-drawn dray. Whist drives were a very popular form of entertainment. There were cribbage contests, dances and cinema shows in the village hall. There was a thriving WI and the plays put on by the Institute are still remembered. The church and chapel both organised annual outings – the church to Barry Island and the chapel to Pittville Park in Cheltenham. A form of entertainment possibly unique to Honeybourne was a family stroll on a Sunday afternoon to have something to eat or drink in the refreshment room at the station!

Throughout the 1950s Honeybourne had a very popular and successful table tennis club which met twice a week in the village hall, and there was an annual competition for the Honeybourne Invitation Challenge Cup. One year the club entered a national competition and were drawn in the preliminary round against RAF Innsworth. It was only after they had been comprehensively beaten that they discovered that the RAF team were due to represent England at Wembley the following week.

One unusual memory of entertainment is of a small circus which visited Honeybourne during the war. They brought with them an "unridable donkey" and challenged anyone who felt like having a go to prove otherwise. A number of Canadian servicemen, fortified by perhaps more than just a little drink, tried to ride the animal bareback. None were successful, however, and so the donkey kept his title.'

THEATRE AND CINEMA

'Every small town had a theatre and Kidderminster folk were very proud of their "Opera House". It was a gem of Victorian baroque architecture, complete with red plush interior and gilded light fittings. It had a resident orchestra and regular performances by touring and repertory companies. Many eminent actors and singers of the time trod the boards of the "Opera", as it was called by the locals. During the Second World War the theatre was closed and used for the storage of perishable food (so we were told). It was restored to its former glory – red plush and all – quite soon after the war and renamed The Playhouse. It had a very successful revival until it was demolished for road widening.

Cinemas sprang up like mushrooms during the 1920s and 1930s and even the smaller towns such as Bromsgrove, Bewdley and Stourport had their "picture house" with programme changes at least once a week and a different programme on Sundays. The performances at larger cinemas were usually continuous, from 1 pm to 10.30 pm so one could see the whole programme round two or three times for the price of one – or have a nice cosy sleep on a cold day!

Practically every small town in my area of Worcestershire had its choral, amateur operatic and dramatic societies and a brass band, so one didn't need to go far for entertainment and activity. Gradually, in the 1920s, the crackle of the cat's whisker wireless was increasingly heard – the family huddled, with their earphones, over the crystal and valve sets and no one dared to utter a word. In the late 1930s television was just coming in, but the war delayed mass production and it wasn't until the Coronation in 1953 that sales took off.'

FROM SILENTS TO TALKIES

'The memory of films in Catshill goes back to silent movies run by Mr Bowers and shown in the old school house, which is now part of the dairy in Stourbridge Road. Apparently the afternoon charge was a penny and the evening shows were threepence.

The village hall was built in 1893, organised and presumably funded by the Quakers of Barnt Green. The object was to provide an alternative venue for the men rather than the pub. It was a temperance hall. During the First World War meals were supplied to the public for a halfpenny. The Band of Hope was based there, and the village football team, the George Wagstaff Team, used it as their headquarters.

One of its earliest uses was for domestic science classes from the primary school (Stourbridge Road) and "washday" was taught at a row of tin baths all along the hall. During the Second World War it was used as a factory turning brass components for aircraft.

After the war, slowly but surely entertainment crept back into everyone's lives. Theatre shows, excursions and the cinema, all had their heyday. Not to be outshone Catshill followed suit, with its own cinema. A truly one man/one woman show affectionately called the "Blood Tub", Archie Holloway's cinema was originally a converted pig pen opposite the village hall. It had a corrugated iron roof and when it rained heavily it was deafening, almost drowning out the sound of the film, so everyone cheered. Throughout the film your legs itched, then when the lights went up at half time you discovered it was grass growing up between the floorboards. When he could afford it, eventually Archie moved across the road into the village hall. He cleaned and decorated the place and when it needed curtains and tie-backs, he painted them on the walls each side of existing blacked-out windows. If it needed soft drapes and pelmets, he painted those as well, all done in heavy gloss paint.

Archie operated the projection box and did the maintenance. He also made amazing ice lollies, each of which was always hollow. These were naturally dubbed "Archie Holloway's hollow lollies".

Mrs Bruton, who worked for Archie, did the other half of the jobs. First, as you entered she took your money, then nipped around the back of the kiosk to the entrance proper, where she took and ripped your ticket in half, then shone her torch showing you to your seats. The front seats were benches on boxes and these were known as the "bobs", then graded towards the back were the rejects from the Plaza and the Regal, these were Archie's best seats.

At half time Mrs Bruton would take the orders for cups of tea which were passed along the row, then next the fish and chip orders were taken and purchased from the wooden hut which was Jarvis' chip shop just round the corner in Woodrow Lane. These too were passed along the row to the regulars. By now, the place had an interesting aroma!

The advent of television sadly saw the demise of Holloway's Catshill cinema, but in spite of its shortcomings, the Blood Tub was a happy place, and during its time the cinema raised a lot of money for the North West Ward Association.

Catshill's churches and chapels each had their own clubs and sports teams, as did the pubs and working men's club. In the past Catshill had its own racecourse (the Horsecourse) which is now partly a council housing estate. During the war and the "Dig for Victory" campaign the field became allotments. The village also had its own cricket team based in Crown Meadow at the back of the Crown Inn – this too is now a housing estate.

At the top of Gibb Lane there was a Co-op hall which was sold in the 1960s when the Co-op shop closed. This was used for private hire and for Co-op sponsored activities – including the Glee Singers and a children's drama club. The Glee Singers were a mixed voice choir and when it folded, several members joined the Male Voice Choir which is also now defunct. The Annual Music Festival still flourishes and attracts competitors from all over the country.

The youth of the village had an over 18s youth club called the Chadstone Club which met in a wooden building in the middle school grounds, whilst those from 14 years nine months met in what is now the middle school. In the 1950s classes were held in various subjects – craft and recreational – and the school sports facilities were also used.'

A PRECIOUS TIME

'It all began in 1950, when a few WI members decided to put on a play for the Christmas party. *The Bonny Earl of Moray* was chosen, and proved popular, despite its many weaknesses. The acting bug was born!

Outrageous Fortune by Cherry Vooght followed, and exhilarated by its warm reception, it was decided to enter the Bromsgrove Drama Festival. Some of the cast demurred at first. "We really aren't good

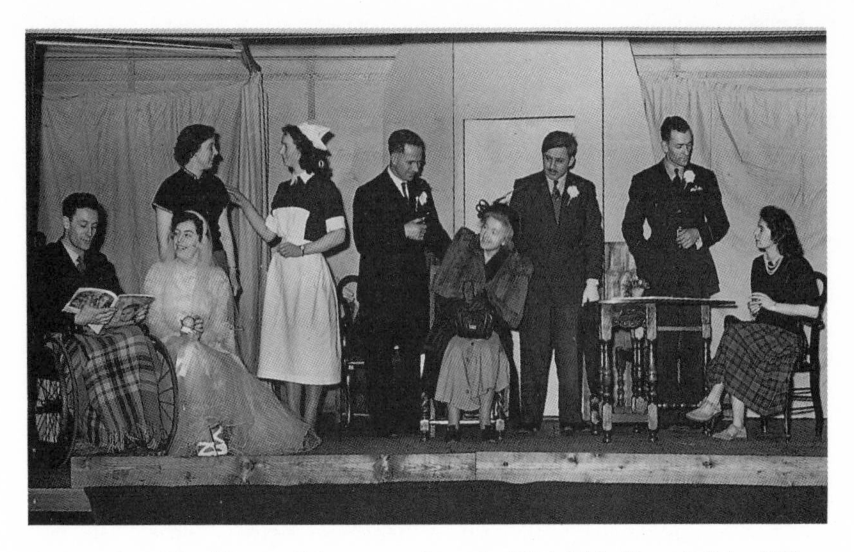

A scene from The Happy Prisoner *performed at Fairfield village hall in 1951.*

enough!" But the producer won them over, and they rehearsed and rehearsed. The great night arrived! Everyone was in a state of jitters, including the prompter, a somewhat nervous, reluctant husband. Stoically, they performed in front of the reputable adjudicator, Stanley Hildebrandt. And it came off – it really came off! Mr Hildebrandt praised the production and awarded them the Runners Up Cup. It was specially sweet success, because Fairfield had competed against well known, experienced players. The group became wildly enthusiastic, and presented the play at Droitwich Winter Gardens, and at the Kidderminster Playhouse, and what a thrill it was to act in a real theatre. Other plays followed, with success at Henley in Arden Drama Festival.

In the meantime, the producer became impatient to put on a three-act play with a mixed cast. So the Fairfield Drama Group came into existence. *The Happy Prisoner* by Monica Dickens was chosen, and despite its rather rickety set, still remains a favourite.

The local baker kindly let the group use his bakehouse for rehearsals, and very warm and cosy it was on a cold January night. He also lent them his bread van, so that they could take their plays to other villages and enter festivals. Those days bubbled over with fun and joy.

There were plenty of hair-raising incidents, too! For instance, one funny moment occurred in *Reluctant Heroes*. The wings had been extended with trestle tables, so as to make more space for entries. The Sergeant, a heavily-built man, was awaiting his entrance. Unfortunately, his weight proved too much. The trestle table collapsed, and the prompter, perched on the edge of the table, was catapulted into the audience, accompanied by a mighty bang. On stage, two soldiers undauntingly continued with the script. By a remarkable coincidence the line spoken by one soldier was, "What was that?" His fellow actor should have replied, "I think it was a sheep." But possessing a strong sense of humour he replied, "I think it was a mouse." His companion, determined at all costs to keep to the script said, "Well, then, what about catching it for breakfast?" The audience rocked with laughter, and it was some time before their hilarity ceased, and the players were able to continue with the play.

One bitter night, a stalwart actress, returning home from a production, broke down in her car, and had no choice but to leave the car, costumes and props and trudge three miles home in the snow. And true to the spirit of the group she took it all in her stride.

The carefree camaraderie, with its many rich, endearing memories of the 1950s, was a precious time, never quite recaptured during later years.'

ROYAL OCCASIONS

All over Worcestershire, towns and villages celebrated royal jubilees and coronations with enthusiasm.

JUBILEE AT BROADWAY

'On George V's Silver Jubilee in 1935 all the larger gardens in Broadway were thrown open to visitors, free of charge. There were games and races in the recreation ground, where the children were given commemorative mugs. It was a general holiday and everybody thoroughly enjoyed themselves.'

'I remember climbing all the way up the footpath through the fields to the top of Broadway Hill to see the bonfire which had been lit to celebrate the Jubilee in 1935. They had fireworks as well and there was great excitement as we watched a chain of bonfires being lit all around on the hills – Dovers Hill, Malvern, Meon Hill and as far away as the Welsh Mountains. I was so tired that my father had to carry me on his back all the way down that steep footpath.

Whenever there was a royal occasion to be celebrated at Broadway, there were sports, races and other activities in the recreation ground and the field next to it, called Broad Close. In the evening I remember a team of runners carrying torches up the path to the Tower and lighting the beacon fire at the top.'

CORONATION 1937

'My father was a sergeant in the Worcestershire Regiment and we lived in married quarters at Norton Barracks. On Coronation Day 1937 lots of games were organised for the children and food was laid on in the gymnasium. I wore a white blouse, a blue pinafore dress over it with red lacing down the front – most of us were dressed in patriotic colours. The band played on the square, and cricket and football matches took place. It was a very happy day.'

TRIMPLEY ROYAL DAYS

'Like other villages throughout the country, Trimpley took part in the celebration of royal events. I can well remember going with Trimpley school to Park Attwood, a large house in the northern part of the parish, for the Silver Jubilee celebration of King George V and Queen Mary on 6th May 1935, for sports on the terrace, followed by a special tea in the ballroom. This, to a small child, was a marvellous occasion, to be sealed in the memory by the gift of a commemorative mug bearing the portraits of the King and Queen in a medallion surrounded by the flags of the Empire and with the royal motto and emblems of the United Kingdom. Above was a crown signifying their royal majesties.

By the time of the Coronation of George VI and Queen Elizabeth on 12th May 1937, I had moved to a junior school in Kidderminster. We had sports and tea in Brinton's Park and again received a commemorative mug, presented by the Mayor of Kidderminster, Mr E.G. Eddy. The children of Trimpley celebrated by planting a copper beech tree on the village green. I well remember listening to the wireless and trying to conjure up in my mind's eye the beauty of the ceremony in Westminster Abbey. Some weeks later I was taken to the cinema to see the wonderful splendour and majesty of this historic occasion.

To commemorate the Coronation of Queen Elizabeth II the

Villagers at Crowle celebrating the coronation of Queen Elizabeth II in June 1953.

children of Trimpley school marked the occasion by planting some oak trees in the form of a letter E on the village green and a stone was erected bearing an inscription. Again all the children had a commemorative mug and a party.

By this time I was teaching in a slum area in Birmingham where the children had street parties and received a commemorative mug, but the significance of the occasion was lessened for me personally. That is, until I heard the broadcast on the wireless and, more especially, when I went to the cinema and saw the actual happenings take place before my eyes. Then it was that I realised its significance and could enter into the spirit of such spectacular splendour in that wonderful setting of Westminster Abbey.'

CELEBRATIONS THROUGHOUT THE YEAR

Each year brought its round of celebrations, fairs and holidays. In the days when leisure was a rare treat, such breaks in routine were eagerly anticipated. Some have now passed into history, such as Empire Day on 24th May, when every schoolchild could look forward to a half day's holiday.

EMPIRE DAY

'At St Peter's school, Bromsgrove, we celebrated Empire Day in style. When I was nine (my birthday was on 24th May) I was given a major role in the proceedings. One of the boys and myself played an elderly couple who were supposed to be watching a parade. I wore a dress belonging to one of my teenage sisters (pink cotton sprinkled with white daisies) which reached to the ground on me, and a sun-bonnet, and carried a parasol. My partner had borrowed his dad's jacket and an older brother's long trousers, and wore a cap and smoked a pipe, empty of course.

Various classmates represented the countries of the Empire and as they paraded before us they spoke a short rhyme describing the country they in particular represented, listed its products and industries, and as they did so held up the items, such as sugar, cocoa, tea, coffee, etc.

I particularly remember a friend of mine represented Jamaica. We had had the morning off and were on our way to school in the early afternoon, a walk of about a mile and a half. Parents were invited to watch the pageant. As a group of us children walked to school to get ready I can clearly remember Tom dressed in a loose shirt and a very large straw hat which he had managed to borrow from someone, practising his verse continually as we walked along. One of the items involved a bunch of bananas and these were sadly much the worse for wear by the time we got to school.'

'All children had a holiday from school on Empire Day, and it was quite usual for children to be gathered together to salute the Union flag, as we did at Chaddesley Corbett.'

'Overbury school produced a May Queen and a concert on May Day, from the 1930s, and later in the month was Empire Day. After we had all been to a morning church service we had the rest of the day off. Ascension Day, too, was a day off for us after church service.

In May and October villagers would attend Stow Fair, for purchasing ponies and saddlery requirements. In the summer there was Pershore Fair, and in October the Mop Fairs at Tewkesbury, Evesham and Stratford on Avon. These were always very special occasions, and for the Stratford Mop there were special trains to Broom Junction.

In the early 1930s we held a special Egg Day for the Cheltenham group of hospitals, when all the villagers donated eggs.'

'The village hall at Chaddesley Corbett was a brick building with a corrugated iron extension and was heated by a log and coal fire in a large fireplace. Water was boiled in a corner boiler, fired by logs or coal, for making the tea and for the washing up. Dances to the music of Rolando Rhythmics cost sixpence, tea and biscuits threepence. Needless to say, to get to the dance it was either Shanks's pony or bicycle.

A highlight of village life was the annual fête with its Carthorse Derby, Tossing the Sheaf, guessing the weight of the live pig and the tug of war for the prize of a barrel of beer. The Punch and Judy man and a host of sideshows were always enjoyed. The flower, vegetable and produce show took place at another time of the year.

There was the Annual Farmers' Show of cattle, sheep and pigs with the Young Farmers assisting the judges, thereby enabling them to gain experience. Competition must have been keen for "The Best Farm", firstly of up to 200 acres and secondly over 200 acres. The circus came once a year for two evening performances in a large tent in what is called the Doctor's Meadow; music for the acts was by gramophone!

The hunt would gather by the church lychgate and would enjoy a stirrup cup from the Talbot Inn opposite. The schoolchildren would come to see the meet and enjoy the excitement before the hunt moved off up Fold Farm Lane towards Chaddesley Woods.'

'In 1929 a Miss Gwen Lally produced a pageant at Tewkesbury Abbey (and also at Eastnor and Ledbury later). The ladies of Eckington Women's Institute helped to make the many costumes, as all our village was involved – children and villagers were members of the cast. My father made some special metal buckles for the

Cavaliers' shoes, while Mother knitted "chain mail" in a sort of string, which was silver-painted to represent the Crusaders.'

'My father recalled the ginny horses and roundabouts up at the top of Bredon Hill in his youth, as well as cheese rolling and other sports.'

BROADWAY WAKE AND BRASS BAND

'I would save up my pennies to go to Broadway Wake, which was always held on Whit Wednesday and Thursday on Broadway Green and the Lower Green below the Swan Inn. There were ginny horses, the cake walk, the dodgems, the Noah's Ark, swinging boats, coconut shies and lots of stalls selling home-made rock, nougat and mouthwatering brandy snaps. The proprietors of these amusements were Curtis's in the early days, then later R. Edwards & Sons from Swindon and then, following them, Mr Billy Kimberley, the local showman from Evesham. During the war they were not allowed to hold the Wake on the village green and so my father allowed them to come into his field. I remember thinking it wasn't fair that I still had to pay for my rides, but not to worry, I got a bit of it back afterwards from the pennies dropped in the grass!

I can remember seeing the Snowshill Mummers doing their play on the village green, which was very interesting to watch as I knew

Broadway Brass Band in 1923 – many towns and villages enjoyed the music of local bands between the wars.

some of them quite well and one was a relative. This must have been well over 50 years ago.

For the Broadway school sports day and tea party, we walked in crocodile fashion from the school to a field in Wells Lane, close to Bibsworth Farm, where the sports were held, and then we went into the large barn for our tea. Here the floor had been covered over with clean straw and we sat down to mugs of tea, sandwiches, currant buns and bread pudding.

While still at Broadway school in the 1930s, we always attended a service at the war memorial on 11th November, all walking down the village street with our teachers. The church choir and the vicar led the procession, and in the early days also the Broadway brass band of which my grandfather was bandmaster. The service was at eleven o'clock and the hooter at Gordon Russell's furniture workshops was sounded. Everything literally came to a halt, even cars (what few there were in those days), and the whole village went completely silent for two minutes.

The brass band played for village fêtes, weddings and lots of other festive occasions. Sadly, when my grandfather got too old they were disbanded in the late 1930s and the band was never reformed. My grandfather used to take them round the village at Christmas playing carols, mostly to the "posh" houses at the top of the village, where lived Madame de Navarro (Mary Andersen, the actress) and Lady Maud Bowes-Lyon. I have in my possession a little notebook in which Grandad kept an account of how much money each house had given them – from a shilling upwards but nothing much more than five shillings, even from the "toffs".'

THE HOP AND CHEESE FAIR

'I was born in 1905 and I can remember as a child being taken to the Hop and Cheese Fair held anually on 19th September in Worcester.

Packets of hops were sold in the Worcester Hopmarket and farmers brought their cheeses for sale. Stalls were set up in both Angel Place and Angel Street on which were displayed goodies to delight the eyes of children who were eager to buy a "fairing".

The sweet stall had kali suckers, gobstoppers, liquorice laces and scented cachous. There were toys galore: ticklers, trumpets, rattles and drums, the noisier the better. Dolls of all sizes were for sale, from cut-out paper ones to the lovely jointed dolls.

The brandy snap stall was well patronised and the hand-operated roundabout did very good business.

In the evening, kerosene flares cast a bright but flickering light on the noisy, happy, jostling crowd who had gathered to join in the annual delight of Fair Day.'

DROITWICH SPA

FESTIVAL PROGRAMME

TUESDAY—*May 1st.*
CROWNING OF THE FESTIVAL QUEEN by His Worship the Mayor at the Winter Gardens at 6-30 p.m.

SUNDAY—*May 6th.*
UNITED RELIGIOUS SERVICE in the Brine Baths Park at 3 p.m. (In St. Andrew's Church if wet.) Conducted by the Reverend Russell Shearer, Chairman of the Birmingham District of the Methodist Church, accompanied by the Salvation Army under the direction of Senior Captain J. Bramwell Dunkley.

WHIT. MONDAY—*May 14th.*
MOTOR CYCLE SCRAMBLE RACE at Egg Hill Farm, Hampton Lovatt, under the auspices of the South Birmingham Motor Club.

THURSDAY—*May 17th.*
Church of England Society (Waifs & Strays) MAY FAYRE in the Winter Gardens. Opening ceremony by the Countess Beauchamp at 3 p.m.

SUNDAY—*May 27th.*
"MAYOR'S SUNDAY" Divine Service at St. Andrew's Church at 11 a.m. attended by His Worship the Mayor, Aldermen and Councillors.

TUESDAY—*May 29th.*
LIGHT ORCHESTRAL CONCERT by the Banbury Light Orchestra in the Winter Gardens at 8 p.m.

THURSDAY—*June 14th.*
ST. PETER'S and ST. NICHOLAS CHURCH FETE at St. Peter's Vicarage at 3 p.m.

SATURDAY—*June 23rd.*
"Toc H" GARDEN PARTY, Worcestershire Brine Baths Hotel Gardens at 3 p.m.

THURSDAY—*July 5th.*
ST. ANDREW'S CHURCH FETE, at St. Andrew's Rectory.

THURSDAY—*July 19th.*
OPENING OF A NEW BOROUGH PARK at Covercroft by Sir Frederick Minter, K.C.V.O., at 7 p.m. This Park occupies the site of the old Salt Works which were demolished in 1922 and has been laid out as the Borough's contribution to the Festival.

SATURDAY—*July 21st.*
CHILDREN'S DAY at Brine Baths Park at 2 p.m.

SATURDAY—*July 28th.*
SHOPPING WEEK COMMENCES. Special window displays and competitions.

CARNIVAL DAY. Grand Procession of Decorated Vehicles, Fancy Costumes, etc. Fun Fair, Fire Fighting Display.

SATURDAY—*August 4th.*
TOURNAMENT organized by the Droitwich Spa Bowling Club in the Brine Baths Park.

SATURDAY—*August 4th.*
METHODIST CHURCH ANNUAL GARDEN PARTY and Fete in the Church Grounds, Witton.

SATURDAY—*August 4th.*
HAMPTON LOVETT GARDEN FETE in the Hampton Lovett Parish Hall, at 2-30 p.m.

BANK HOLIDAY MONDAY—*August 6th.*
DROITWICH SPA & DISTRICT HORTICULTURAL SOCIETY'S ANNUAL SHOW at St. Andrew's Meadow at 2 p.m.

TUESDAY—*August 7th.*
DROITWICH HORSE SHOW AND GYMKHANA organised by the Droitwich Horse Show Society in Westwood Park.

CRICKET MATCH. Droitwich Cricket Club *v.* A Malvern XI at King George V. Playing Field at 3 p.m.

THURSDAY—*August 9th.*
DARTS MATCH organized by the Droitwich Darts League in the Winter Gardens at 7 p.m.

FRIDAY—*August 10th.*
GRAND FESTIVAL FLANNEL DANCE at the Winter Gardens, 9 p.m. to 1 a.m.

SATURDAY—*September 8th.*
OPENING of the new BOROUGH BOWLING GREEN in Vines Park by H. B. Everton, Esq., at 3 p.m.

TUESDAY—*September 11th.*
DROITWICH SPA AND DISTRICT HORTICULTURAL SOCIETY'S OUTDOOR CHRYSANTHEMUM SHOW at 6-30 p.m.

THURSDAY—*September 20th.*
PRESENTATION of the FREEDOM of the BOROUGH OF DROITWICH by the Mayor and Corporation to Alderman Dr. E. Shirley Jones.

THURSDAY—*September 20th.*
Evening performance of MERRIE ENGLAND in the Salters Cinema by the Malvern Amateur Operatic and Orchestral Society.

SATURDAY—*September 22nd.*
M.G. CAR CLUB ALL ENGLAND RALLY at the Chateau Impney.

FRIDAY—*October 5th.*
Conclusion of Festival—MAYOR'S BALL.

For further details together with any deletions, additions or alterations to the above programme, see current advertisements. Any information concerning the above programme to be addressed to the General Secretary, Festival of Britain, Droitwich Spa.

This page has been donated by INGALL, PARSONS, CLIVE & Co. LTD., whose Droitwich Spa Factory at Berry Hill, is the latest addition to the INGALL manufacturing "family" at Upton-on-Severn, Harrow, Aston and Birmingham; with Regional Depots in London, Glasgow, Manchester, Leeds, Liverpool, New Zealand, Australia, South Africa, Malta, etc.
Head Office: BRADFORD STREET, BIRMINGHAM 12.

Droitwich Spa was a popular leisure venue, and put on a full range of events during Festival of Britain year, 1951.

BANK HOLIDAYS

'There was always a rowing regatta on the river Severn at Worcester on August Bank Holidays, and barrow boys sold fruit and sweets along the river bank. Sometimes a gymkhana would be held at the Raven Meadow, opposite the Raven public house on the A38 at Claines.

August Bank Holiday (then at the beginning of August) was also a big occasion in the cricket enthusiasts' world as Worcestershire always played Essex during that weekend. In Droitwich a sports day was held on the Old Acre near the railway station. Droitwich and District Motorcycle and Car Club took part and there were special obstacle courses and things like plank jumping for the motorcyclists, and motorcycle football. Tug of war competitions were another popular draw.

Some families went away on holiday, going as far as Blackpool by train from Droitwich. Seaside holidays were much looked forward to. The journey was always part of the fun and people played cards or other games to pass the time while they were on the train.

Day trips were very popular in the 1920s and 1930s. Sometimes public houses or local clubs would arrange a day out. One gentleman remembers a day out to Blackpool. The group left Droitwich at about 2.30 am, travelling by train, and arrived in Blackpool by about 6 am for breakfast. They enjoyed a good long day by the sea and at the fair. You could get plenty of rides for sixpence in those days but it cost one shilling to go on the Big Dipper. The party left Blackpool late in the evening to return home.'

THE SEASON IN HABBERLEY VALLEY

'Habberley Valley, our local beauty spot, has been loved by many generations of Kidderminster people and others from farther afield, as a favourite venue for picnics and other leisurely pursuits. For over a hundred years the inhabitants of the various cottages welcomed visitors by providing thousands of cups of tea and teas throughout the season.

After considerable preparation, the season commenced on Mothering Sunday when it was customary for families to walk to the valley for their traditional breakfast of ham and eggs.

Easter Sunday was particularly busy because the people came to breakfast and stayed throughout the day so requiring additional refreshments. The visitors thoroughly enjoyed the fresh air and tranquil rural setting by walking, climbing Peckett's Rock and Jacob's Ladder, playing games and generally having a happy time.

Perhaps the largest influx of visitors came on Whit Monday, for, besides family groups, there were many hundreds of Sunday school children and their teachers who came, mainly by lorry, for a pleasant afternoon of sports and tea parties. This followed the annual Whit Monday Sunday school Procession of Witness, organised by the Sunday School Union, which represented the nonconformist churches, although Anglicans took part as well.

After assembling in the cattle market, the colourful procession moved along the streets lined with parents and friends. Most Sunday school children walked behind their banners with the younger children riding on decorated floats. The procession ended in front of the town hall, where a service was held. This procession, together with the visit to Habberley Valley or other venues was the highlight of the year for Kidderminster children!

For several years, Habberley Valley was the setting for open air services, conducted by Canon Jolly and Dr D'Arcy Chapman with the music provided by St James' church choir conducted by Mr George Howell and the Salvation Army Band. Visitors were appreciative of these services which seemed most appropriate for worshipping God – in the open air surrounded by so much beauty.

Throughout the summer months, Sunday school parties from the Black Country area in particular thronged to the valley for their annual outings. Shrieks of joy announced the arrival of excited children as they scrambled down "the rock" (the old entrance into the valley near to what is now Valley Close) and raced into the valley. The first attraction was always the fair belonging to the Jennings family. This fair occupied the centre of the valley and consisted of roundabouts, swings and other traditional fairground attractions as well as a stall selling home-made ice cream. There was also a shop belonging to the Osborne family which sold sweets, toys and souvenirs, to be eagerly purchased by the children for their parents and friends. Tea, sports and general exploration amid the rocks, trees, heather and bracken made a wonderful day for these happy child visitors!'

CHRISTMAS AT OMBERSLEY COURT

'At Ombersley Court a few weeks before Christmas the puddings were made. All the staff stirred the mixture and made a wish. The great hall is very large – I was told it would hold 200 people. The floor is in black and white stonework, and there are two log fireplaces in this hall where very long logs were burnt in winter. It was lit by a chandelier of five paraffin oil lamps. I was a housemaid at the Court in the early part of the century.

On Christmas Eve the vicar and choirboys from the village church came to sing carols. The staff collected in the gallery above to hear them. The vicar always gave an address afterwards. I remember one Christmas Eve as he was speaking he had to stop for breath for a moment. The parrot, whom everybody had forgotten, was in a cage nearby and suddenly shouted, "Go on!" The choirboys were very much amused. They were always given hot drinks, cakes and oranges.

Christmas Day was a wonderfully happy day there. We had a grand Christmas dinner; it was the first time I had tasted brandy butter on Christmas pudding. In the evening we could invite any friends we liked to have in for party games or card playing. At midnight the youngest of the staff were sent to bed. It was always the end of a very happy day. Lady Sandys was always very kind to me, she gave us all Christmas presents.'

CHRISTMAS AT BENTLEY

'At Christmas in the 1930s the whole school went to a party at Bentley Manor. When we arrived Mrs Ellis would give us the call of welcome on the Old Squire's hunting horn. There was a large Christmas tree in one room. Rev Gillingham did magic tricks and, when I was older, there were film shows in the billiards room. We had games; musical bumps was the best. Then we lined up and paraded past a large picture of Mrs Cheap (the late Squire). Each of us had to stop and salute. When we came out, Father Christmas (Miss Patsy) in an old hunting jacket would hand us a bundle, a big tied-up red hanky. Inside were all sorts of sweets and cakes, an orange, even a quarter pound tin of cocoa. Dad had the hanky, he always had one in his braces at harvest time to mop his face with.

December 21st was the Old Squire's birthday. Mrs Ellis held a dance in remembrance of her mother on that day. There was dancing to Redditch Enterprise Band and songs and poems. The Squire's birthday cake would be wheeled in at eleven o'clock, when it was cut. Cards were sold in aid of the district nurses or St Mary's church. Christmas morning, Mrs Ellis delivered Christmas shortcake to the tenants in the pony and trap with Miss Patsy.

If you worked for Bentley estate you had a joint of beef for Christmas. We did well as we had three people working for the estate. Also at Christmas the Windsor Blanket charity was doled out. We were entited to have one, so I cycled to Tardebigge church for it. I collected other people's too.'

THE SQUIRE

'At Christmas the squire's wife at Heightington gave two oranges and a box of sweets to every child in all the schools on the estate. The only other gift received was some biscuits tied to a bough of mistletoe. Families never had a tree.'

'Each Christmas the local landowner at Wichenford gave three "red riding hood" cloaks for the girls at the local school and three warm overcoats for the boys. The cloaks looked delightful bobbing along the road.'

MEMORABLE DAYS

'Christmas parties were always memorable occasions at Park Attwood, when we schoolchildren from Trimpley were invited for a party by Mr Thomas Charles, who purchased the estate in 1912. There were magic lantern shows and conjurors, and a specially delicious tea followed by crackers and party games. It ended with Father Christmas distributing wonderful presents. I still have my doll's tea service of cups, saucers, plates, sugar basin and milk jug, made of Crown Ducal china. After singing carols round the large, decorated tree, we were given a big bag containing nuts, sweets and fruit to take home. A truly happy time was had by all. After Mr Charles' death in 1938 the estate was split up and sold.'

The school Christmas party at Wichenford in 1939.

HOLLY AND MISTLETOE

'Mistletoe grows best on old apple trees. This may explain why the country's largest holly and mistletoe market is held each year in Tenbury Wells, "The Town in the Orchard".

For as far back as anyone can remember, on the four Tuesdays from mid November to mid December, the market area becomes a sea of greenery. The colours range from the lime-green of the mistletoe, through the differing shades of the variegated holly leaves to the familiar dark green. Contrasts are provided by the dark red and pale white of the berries. Good quality Christmas trees, under ten feet in height, are piled up behind them also waiting to be sold.

Traditionally gathered by gypsies, the greenery is sold in hundred-weight bundles, the buyers coming from far and wide. Buyers at the earliest markets tend to be institutions, such as hotels, decorating for Christmas parties. The holly and mistletoe sold at the later markets tends to finish up on market stalls.

Each Christmas, houses in many counties will be decorated with greenery that has passed through the market in the little town on the river Teme, where Worcestershire, Herefordshire and Shropshire meet.'

Index

List of Contributing Institutes

Contributions have been received from the following Worcestershire Women's Institutes:

Abberley, Alvechurch, Areley Kings, Barbourne, Barnards Green, Barnt Green, Belbroughton, Bentley Pauncefoot, Beoley, Blakedown, Broadwas on Teme, Broadway, Brockencote, Callow End, Catshill, Chaddesley Corbett, Childswickham, Claines, Cleeve Prior, Clent, Clifton upon Teme, Cofton Hackett, Cookley, Crowle, Cutnall Green, Drakes Broughton, Drakes Cross, Droitwich, Earls Croome, Eckington, Evesham, Fairfield, Far Forest, Finstall, Franche, Frankley, Great Comberton, Habberley, Hadzor & Oddingley, Hagley Afternoon, Hagley Evening, Hallow, Hanley Castle, Harvington, Heightington, Hill & Moor, Himbleton, Honeybourne, Ipsley, Kempsey Afternoon, Kempsey Evening, Kingfisher, Kington with Dormston, Kinver Village, Knighton on Teme, Leigh and Bransford, Link Top, Little Comberton, Littleworth & District, Lower Broadheath, Malvern, Malvern Link, Naunton Beauchamp, Norton & Lenchwick, Offenham, Ombersley & Doverdale, Pebworth & District, Pedmore, Powyke, Queenhill & District, Rock, Romsley & Hunnington, Rubery, Rushwick in Bedwardine, St Andrews, St Gabriels, Salwarpe, Sandhills Green, Stoke Prior, Stone, Storridge, Stourton, Tenbury Wells, The Littletons, The Shelsleys, Tibberton, Trimpley & District, Upton upon Severn, Webheath, Welland, West Malvern, Whitbourne, Whittington, Wichenford, Wickhamford, Witton, Wolverley, Wribbenhall, Wychbold, Wychbury.